LOST ARLINGTON COUNTY

LOST ARLINGTON COUNTY

CHARLIE CLARK

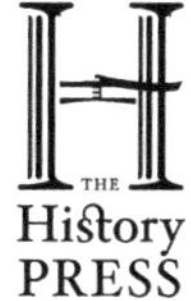

Published by The History Press
Charleston, SC
www.historypress.com

Front cover: From 1895 to 1917, the renamed Arlington Brewing Co. operated from a red-brick gothic tower on Rosslyn Circle. *Courtesy of the Center for Local History, Arlington Public Library.*
Back cover: A street-level view from the putt-putt mini golf course of Parkington, the indoor shopping mall that was central to Arlington in the 1950s and 1960s. *Courtesy of Lloyd Wolf.*

First published 2021

Manufactured in the United States

ISBN 9781467150644

Library of Congress Control Number: 2021941022

Charlie Clark is Arlington's favorite historian. His written word is every bit as captivating as when he speaks in public. His accounts of Arlington's past puts you back in the moment as if it were just yesterday. Whether you are a native Arlingtonian, new to the area or just interested in history, Clark's writing style brings Arlington's past to life as he takes you on a memorable journey you won't regret.

—Patrick Hope, delegate representing Arlington in the Virginia General Assembly since 2010

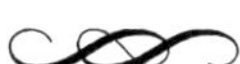

Charlie Clark has proven once again that he is the dean of Arlington's popular historians and a true raconteur. His loving presentations of Arlington's past and those who formed our county continue to amuse, delight and educate one and all.

—Frank O'Leary, former Arlington County treasurer

CONTENTS

PREFACE

Glittering memories of the old hometown? Sometimes they clash with a shifting present. Only twenty-six square miles make up Arlington, Virginia—famous as the nation's smallest self-governing county. But it has provided the backdrop for my own now-spent youth. Hence, I claim the right to freeze the place in time and arrest its development, right? Believe that, and I'll sell you Chain Bridge.

I do claim a role in recording the sweet and sour changes that the march of time inflicts. In Arlington, they're unfolding at an accelerated pace that begs for action to ensure that the county's shared history is not lost.

Since its early days three centuries ago, as the farmers' section of Alexandria County, Arlington emerged in the twentieth century as the hippest suburb (joking) of the nation's capital. Global notice came after the creation and expansion of Arlington National Cemetery, along with Fort Myer (the site of the first airplane casualty on September 17, 1908) and the Pentagon. Add in some modern marquee-name employers—PBS, WETA, Nestlé, the Foreign Service Institute and, with perhaps the highest impact, Amazon's HQ2—and we have a new local world.

All those modern prizes were built around a rich backstory, the basics of which I boil down to five handy eras:

1801 Under an act of Congress, our patch became Alexandria County, District of Columbia, part of the new federal capital.

1847 Alexandria County "retroceded" from its half-century status as part of Washington, D.C.

1861–65 Arlington Heights, as a key strategic site for defense of the capital during the Civil War, and its area became host to two dozen forts.

1871 A post–Civil War state law allowed residents of the city of Alexandria to separate their policy prerogatives from those of rural Alexandria County.

1920 The Virginia General Assembly, after receiving complaints about confusion from a brand-new county civic association, approved an Alexandria delegate's bill to change the name of the once-rural part of the county (now with its own courts and schools) to "Arlington."

Why Arlington? The alternatives that were considered included Pocahontas, Alcova (shorthand for Alexandria County, Virginia) and George Washington County. The winner, already the name of a county administrative jurisdiction, derived from Arlington House, built between 1802 and 1818 in the vision of George Washington Parke Custis. That home (now on the grounds of Arlington National Cemetery) looked out on the Georgetown and Alexandria Turnpike, the Potomac River and the growing city of Washington, D.C., across that river.

Arlington was also the name of a Custis family plantation on the Eastern Shore of Virginia. The fact that confederate hero Robert E. Lee married Custis's daughter and called Arlington House home for decades probably also figured in the county's choice in 1920, a time when Lee's star was rising.

Both world wars spawned growth in Arlington, particularly in the 1940s and 1950s. The county's modern-day population explosion included only one dip (in the 1970s), according to census data:

Multiplying Arlingtonians

1920: 16,040
1930: 26,615
1940: 57,040

1950: 135,449
1960: 163,401
1970: 174,284
1980: 152,599
1990: 170,786
2000: 189,453
2010: 207,627
2020: 228,400

As souls proliferated, so grew the county government (which set a national standard in 1932 by adopting the nation's first county manager system). In just the last decade, the county budget rose more than 50 percent, from $946.8 million in the 2010 fiscal year to $1.4 billion in the 2021 fiscal year.

Where do you put all those people? Where do they shop, go to school, recreate? Whose priorities prevail? How has Arlington dealt with the national problem of race relations?

Growth in Arlington has accelerated the conflict over preservation. Clearly, one Arlingtonian's progress can be another's loss of heritage. The nostalgist's desire to protect landmarks inevitably forces engagement

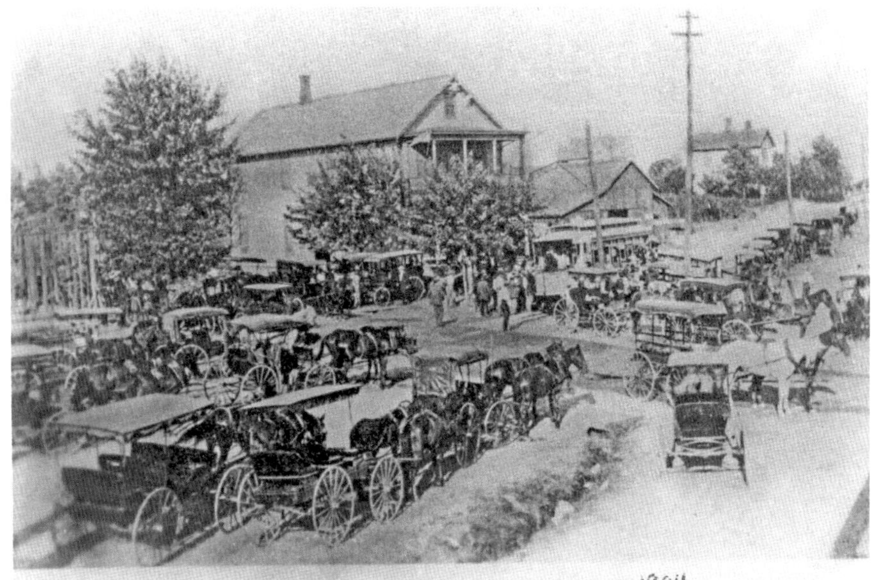

Rail and automobile traffic converge at the East Falls Church Station around 1900. *Courtesy of Eleanor Lee Templeman,* Arlington Heritage.

in policy: land-use planning, by-right property ownership, free-market boosterism. To investors in commercial property, beloved old brand names are seldom a high priority. Consider the employers who left us: USAirways, *USAToday*, the Newseum, the U.S. Patent Office, the U.S. Fish and Wildlife Service and the National Science Foundation.

In the residential arena, a homebuilder expanding a business through a rash of teardowns might replace postwar ramblers worth $600,000 with modern Craftsman-style homes worth $2 million. It's all about land value and sellers' nest eggs. Such changes are both thrilling and heartbreaking, as they threaten properties' longtime legacy.

I understand that the politicians face issues involving public health, education, income disparities, transportation, stormwater drainage and safety to balance against preserving history. But might improving our understanding of history increase sensitivity among those who make policy? The future of preservation in Arlington is endangered at best, and prospects for arresting growth are almost nil.

Lost Arlington County reflects an effort not to resolve the conflicts but to remind our community of its shared heritage. It strives to preserve "things that used to be here but are gone" in the realm of ideas if not on the ground.

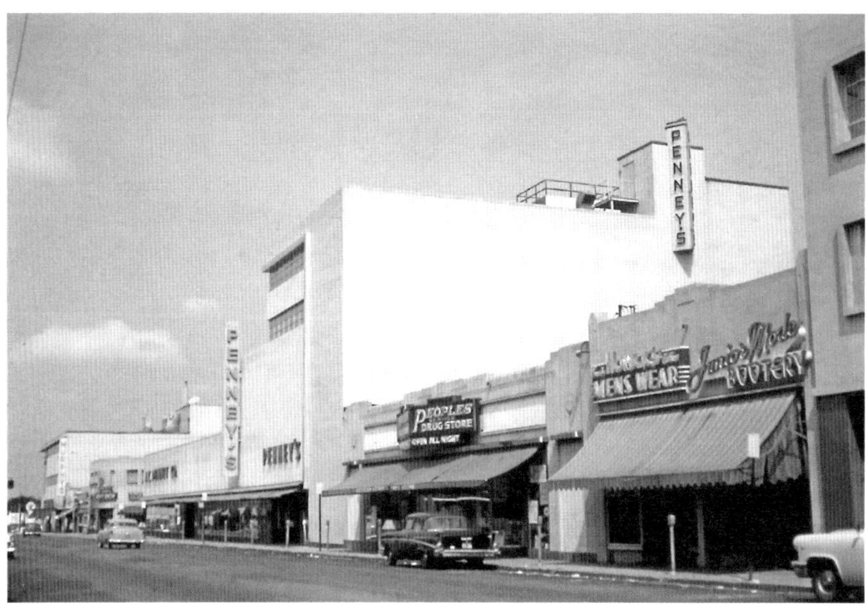

Clarendon in the 1950s and 1960s hosted a JCPenney and Peoples Drug. *A Clarendon business community photograph, courtesy of John Cameron Peck.*

Cultural turmoil has also accelerated, as dramatized in the recent spate of schools, parks and streets being renamed. But those debates at least force some history into the discussion. I also have insisted that readers are entitled to a little fun with the old shared memory bank. So, there's material on lost lifestyles, some personal to myself and some that are emblematic of the generation that came of age during Arlington's postwar boomtime. One example: among the most popular games played by users of the Facebook site "I Grew Up in Arlington, VA," is one in which they recall their childhood telephone numbers with prefixes (mine was Jackson 7-3360). Not all that was lost was pleasant. The vestiges of segregation, for instance, are covered in detail.

Perhaps most importantly, the book's profiles should help modern readers "find" some lost notable people, the doctors, business folks, athletes and civic activists who gave and still give Arlington character.

Many of the photographs in this book are being published for the first time. Much of the text is based on my weekly "Our Man in Arlington" columns in the *Falls Church News-Press.* But new material has been added to balance the portrait.

I dedicate the result to those who helped record and preserve Arlington's rich history and to those who help ease the preservation conflicts that continue to this day.

Charlie Clark
July 2021

1
ALONG THE ANCIENT POTOMAC

THE NATIVE AMERICAN PRESENCE

Every American community can—and should—honor the Native American peoples who inhabited the land long before we moderns. Arlington's territory is one of the richer in terms of evidence, with surviving vestiges of Native settlements dating back thirteen thousand years. The first recorded details were supplied by Captain John Smith during his 1608 voyage up the Potomac River. Some ten sites have been discovered within our borders, most on the banks of the river. Digs farther inland have produced artifacts near North Glebe and Military Roads, the southern end of Four Mile Run and along the border with Falls Church on what once was the Isaac Crossman farm. That's according to C.B. Rose Jr.'s *The Indians of Arlington*, which she published in 1957 to mark the 350th anniversary of Virginia's Jamestown settlement.

Their more prominent site was one that Smith—viewing the exotic peoples onshore from the safety of his canoe—called "Nameroughquena" (opposite today's Roosevelt Island). Those people were known as the Necostins, likely part of the larger Piscataway Nation in Maryland.

Surrounding the Necostin community of perhaps three hundred (of whom eighty were able-bodied men, to quote Smith) was a settlement of people called Nacotchtank (near today's Anacostia). In the 1940s, a work site near the mouth of Marcey Creek inserted Arlington into the annals of archaeology as a site of early Native American civilization. Major Carl

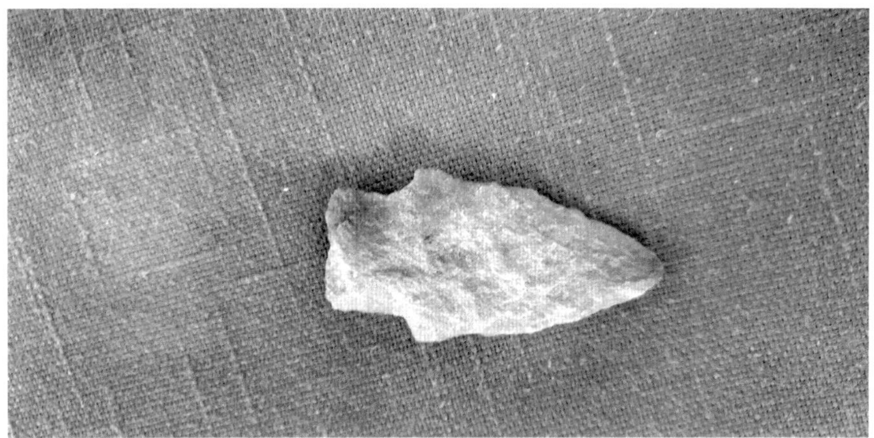

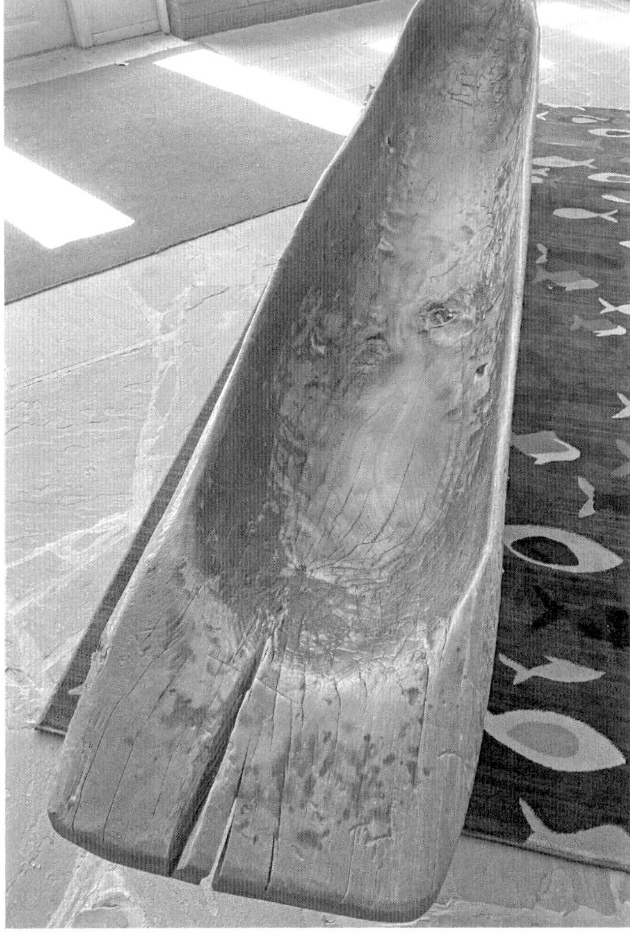

Arrowhead found by archaeologists near Marcey Creek in the 1940s. Arlington Historical Society; dugout canoe made using both modern and ancient-like tools by staff at Gulf Branch Nature Center. *Author's image.*

Manson dug up cord-marked pottery fragments that went on display at the Smithsonian Institution (and they are still there in the anthropology department of the National Museum of Natural History). "The Marcey Creek site was a small village, occupied by a sedentary people for sufficient time to enable the soil to increase in thickness as much as 23 inches," Manson wrote in 1948 in Cambridge University Press's journal *American Antiquity*. "The depth of the culture-bearing layers, the crudeness of the stone artifacts, the absence of organic material, and the complete absence of pipes indicates a greater antiquity for this site than for any other thus far excavated in the Potomac Valley."

Today, Arlingtonians can view locally unearthed arrowheads from the Woodland period (three thousand years ago) at the Gulf Branch Nature Center, one of only two Northern Virginia sites included on the Virginia Indian Heritage Trail. The Gulf Branch staff re-created an accurate dugout canoe. Built with modern power tools rather than the clamshells probably used by the natives, it famously sunk on its first outing. But onlookers can get the idea.

The Arlington Historical Museum (at the old Hume School) displays pottery shards found near the Potomac, plus various tools found elsewhere in Arlington. A stone axe was uncovered near the sixteenth hole of the Army-Navy Country Club. Also exhibited is a souvenir of Arlington's contribution to the 1957 statewide fair celebrating Jamestown, a scale model of a Potomac-side Native village. That occasion clearly raised awareness of the Native peoples' heritage among Arlington's largely European-descended populace.

BOUNDARY STONES

In Arlington, we're lucky to be home to ten of "the oldest federal monuments."

Those forty oft-overlooked boundary stones were laid beginning in 1791 to mark borders of the spanking-new District of Columbia.

Arlington is also lucky to be home to a self-taught expert on the artifacts—civil engineer and ace tour guide Stephen Powers. For more than a decade, Powers has led an annual drive-around to visit all forty of the labeled stones in Virginia and Maryland.

Personally, I have visited Arlington's ten in their steel cages, as well as the four in Alexandria—but not without a hesitancy to trespass on homeowners' private property (where many of the stones sit without clear markings).

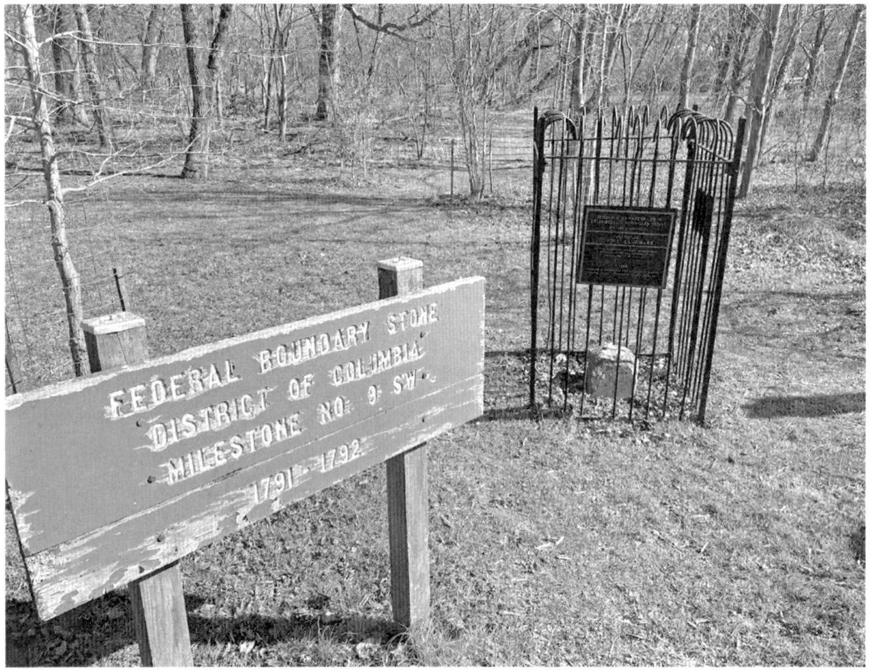

Boundary stone at Benjamin Banneker Park. *Author's image.*

And certainly, I traveled without the fine-grained knowledge that Powers acquired through the years about the soft sandstone objects quarried from Aquia Creek in Stafford County. Many of them, after two centuries, have faded both in legibility and memory.

Before he became a chair of the Nation's Capital Boundary Stones Committee, Powers was a father at Arlington Traditional School (ATS). His kids were assigned to come up with "a fun fact about Arlington," he told this author in February 2019. In 2000, he had already taken his toddlers to see the outdoor art "Party Animals" in the district. They created a photograph album of 348 pandas and other statues. So, it came naturally to take ATS kids to all forty boundary stones. He drew maps and sketches, noting the ones that were hard to find or heavily damaged.

Powers joined up with the Daughters of the American Revolution (DAR), the American Society of Civil Engineers, D.C. land surveyors and history groups long involved in boundary-stone-ology.

The creation story: after President George Washington, Secretary of State Thomas Jefferson and city designer Pierre L'Enfant finalized the new nation's capital, the ten-square-mile boundaries were first surveyed in February 1791 by scientist (and Black role model) Benjamin Banneker. Each stone, a mile apart, would mark a clearing twenty feet on each side of the border.

But Banneker was only personally present for the installation of the first southern stone, at Jones Point in Alexandria. (That didn't stop Arlington from naming a park for him in East Falls Church.) The rest were plotted by his boss, Major Andrew Ellicott, whose name graces a stone on Arizona Avenue at our Falls Church Border.

The tale of who is legally responsible for the monuments gets technical. "The federal government gave up the rights to the stones in Virginia, which are actually owned by the property owners," Powers said. The twenty-six in Maryland, a lawyer's study determined, are owned by the District's Department of Transportation.

Responsibility for the restoration of the stones—many marred by the elements—has been delegated to scout troops and other volunteers (Powers himself has helped repaint or replace fences on twenty-two).

Of the original forty, thirty-six are in place today, plus three replicas and a plaque substituting for one in Silver Spring, Maryland. One stone at Upton Hill disappeared but was found in the late 1990s in the basement of the Arlington Courthouse.

Some stones have been moved to make way for roads (if Arlington had built the Columbia Pike Streetcar—a proposal rejected in 2014—the stone at South Jefferson Street would have required shifting).

But that has happened before, Powers said. Most property owners, he assured me, "are proud of their stones but prefer that visitors knock before entering."

VESTIGES OF ABINGDON PLANTATION

Most of the hurrying passengers at Reagan National Airport are oblivious to what lies behind short-term Lot B, the southward exit, which leads to the beautiful park with reconstructed ruins of Abingdon Plantation.

The house, built around 1746 and once Arlington's oldest home, commanded a spectacular view of the Potomac River.

It saw eleven generations cross its threshold before it burned in 1930. Those VIPs included several presidents, plus an array of historic characters this author decided, on a sunny Sunday, to reassemble in his mind's eye.

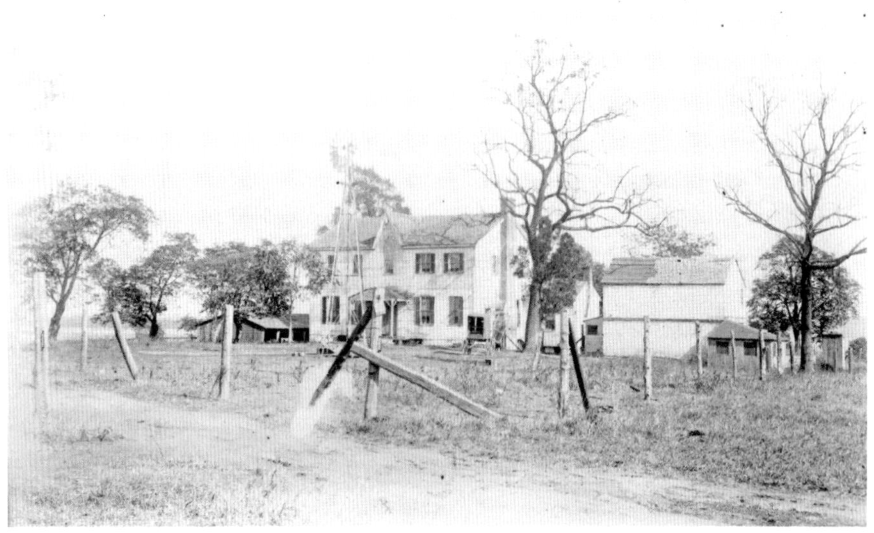

The original house at Abingdon Plantation burned in 1930. *Courtesy of the Columbia Historical Society.*

Abingdon was constructed by Gerard Alexander (1712–1761), whose great-grandfather Captain John Alexander is the namesake for the city of Alexandria.

Gerard's sons, during the Revolutionary War, sold the house to Jacky Custis, the stepson of the commander of the Continental army, George Washington. (Washington thought Jacky was naive and warned it was a rip-off.) Jacky and his wife, Eleanor, begat Nelly Custis (whose birth there merits a plaque at modern Abingdon arranged by the airport authority).

Eleanor, in 1781, gave birth across the river, in Prince George's County, to our county's primo citizen, George Washington Parke Custis. (He would go on to inherit Alexander land for the building of Arlington House.) Those Washingtons and Custises were steady visitors to Abingdon in the latter part of the eighteenth century—George and Martha Washington favored a bedroom on the northeast corner.

After the widowed Eleanor remarried, she and her husband, Federal City commissioner David Stuart, occupied Abingdon before it reverted to the Alexanders in a lawsuit.

Then came the principal nineteenth-century owners, the Hunter family. "We lived on a splendid estate of 650 acres lying on the Potomac, between Alexandria and Washington," reminisced Alexander Hunter in his 1904

Civil War memoir *Johnny Reb and Billy Yank*. The mansion's "beams and rafters are of solid oak, two feet in diameter, and strong enough, as was proven, to bear the weight of two centuries."

Hunter's uncle was a U.S. marshal and received Presidents Jackson, Tyler and Polk at Abingdon. His household included twenty-two enslaved persons, according to an 1850 inventory uncovered by Arlington attorney George Dodge. Aged between two and seventy years, those workers bore names such as Daniel, Dinah, Hannah and Bushrod. Listed along with livestock, the enslaved were valued at $5,035. After his fellow Confederates lost the war and the enslaved were freed, Hunter became a federal land clerk and noted author.

In the early twentieth century, Abingdon was sold to a brickmaking company, which leased it to farmers. Those Arlingtonians included Vivian Thomas Ford (born there in 1912), profiled as "Abingdon's last surviving resident" by Sherman Pratt in the *Arlington Historical Magazine*. "We often had beautiful, warm and sunny spring days at Abingdon with numerous blooms from fruit and other trees," Ford recalled. "The area was mostly quiet and peaceful, except for occasional trains," which crossed the Potomac railroad bridge.

On that fateful day, March 5, 1930, Ford was a student at Hume School on Arlington Ridge Road. She and her classmates suddenly heard fire engines with motors grinding and bells clanging. Someone in her class shouted, "Look! There's a fire down below, near the river!" Vivian told the magazine she rushed to the window and saw columns of smoke a mile away. She ran over to watch the flames engulf her childhood home of historic Abingdon. Ford died in 2014 and was buried at Columbia Gardens.

MINOR'S HOUSE ON A HILL

The highest point in Arlington County is Minor's Hill. An easy stroll up from a park where Williamsburg Boulevard meets North Sycamore Street, those heights were used during the Civil War by both sides as a lookout. The hill is named for the family of George Minor Sr. (1753–1808). With his wife, Ann Adams Minor (1752–1786), Minor built onto a house there in the 1770s that would endure for more than 250 years.

The home is technically in Fairfax, in the Franklin Park section of McLean (whose neighborhood history provides some of the research this essay), but

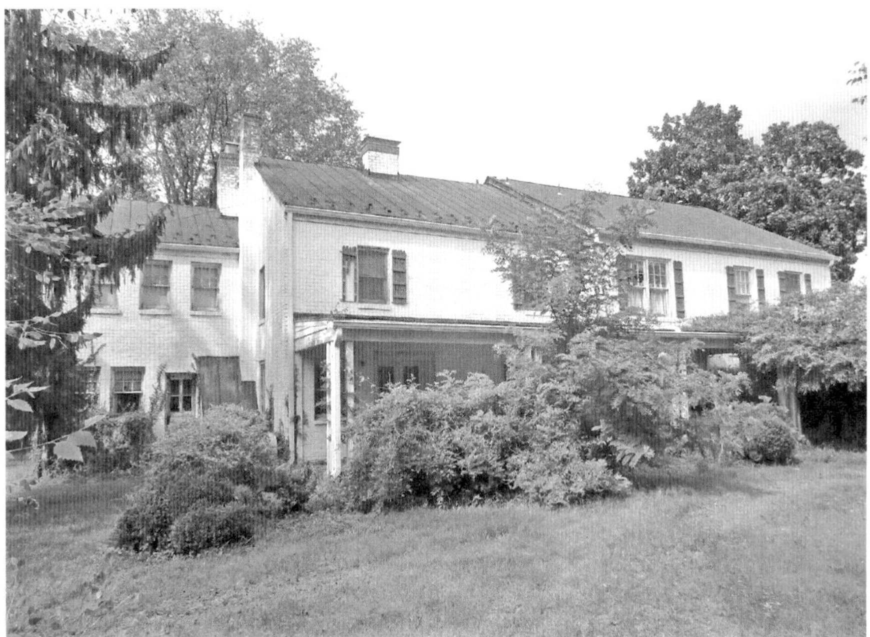

The George Minor house was demolished in 2016. *Courtesy of Tom Dickinson.*

it contributed to the Arlington saga with its dramatic role during the War of 1812.

When the British invaded Washington, D.C., in August 1814, a fleeing President James Madison was forced, for security purposes, to travel separately from his wife, Dolley. She came over Chain Bridge, while he took a ferry through what is Roosevelt Island today. (Also being moved during the crisis were the original copies of the nation's founding documents, saved from the British pyro threat by an alert clerk at the State Department, who stored them temporarily near Chain Bridge.) The Madisons originally planned to meet in Frederick, Maryland, but a storm created confusion. Their probable routes on August 24–26, as traced in modern times by the White House Historical Association, showed that while Dolley made her way to Falls Church, the president was tracked "within a mile" of Wren's Tavern, near Minor's Hill. He spent an evening at the Minor home. Dolley passed a night with her friend at Rokeby (a farm in today's McLean) and then spent two nights with the Minors. They finally rendezvoused at Salona (a home still standing in McLean off of Dolley Madison Boulevard).

The Minor home (George Minor Jr., as a militiaman, had been summoned by Madison to help defend the capital), would figure later in the

Civil War. General George McCellan visited there with troops in January 1862. Minor's Hill had become a sniper's nest for Confederate troops, but then it became an observatory for two thousand Union troops. The home, added onto, stood until 2016, when it was demolished to make room for three modern homes. Family members who had grown up in the historic Minor house were there to watch the wrecking ball, some bemoaning the lack of a plan by Fairfax County for a historic marker. Neighbor Mike Ryan, a descendant of the Crimmins family who farmed Minor's Hill after the Civil War, displayed an 1899 photograph of his ancestors at a nearby home that was under construction.

Wally Sansone, the president of the Franklin Area Citizens Association, told this author, "Many of us are sad to see this historic property developed." But builders and the county say the demolition plan will "meet all applicable zoning laws and regulations"—letter of the law and all that.

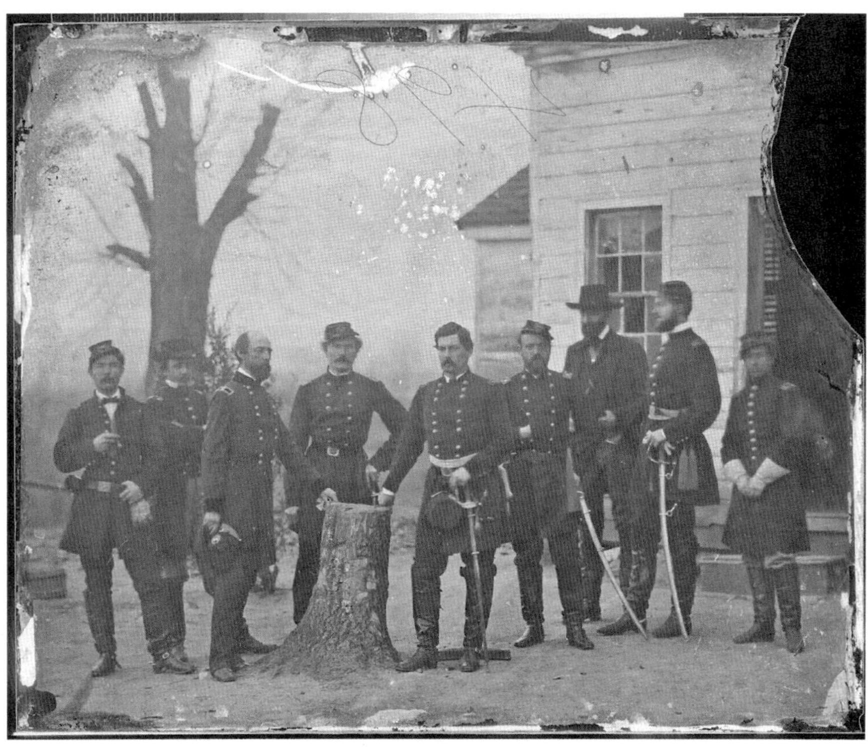

Union general George McClellan at the home's porch. *Courtesy of the National Archives.*

Inside Analostan-Mason-Roosevelt Island

Just over the footbridge over the George Washington Memorial Parkway, behind those dense deciduous trees, lies the interior of Roosevelt Island.

Centuries before the construction of that bully memorial to our twenty-sixth president was begun in the 1930s, the eighty-eight-acre island once known as Analostan was glimpsed by Captain John Smith and inhabited by Native Americans.

But this same turf that is within spitting distance of the nation's capital also plays an intriguing role in Arlington history. This author heard the details in June 2017, when a National Park Service cultural resources specialist presented to the Arlington Historical Society at Central Library.

Bradley Krueger laid out the travails of John Mason (son of the Gunston Hall owner who conceived the Bill of Rights), who built a summer mansion there beginning in 1806.

Mason owned a sizable plot of land, Kreuger said, stretching from modern Arlington Cemetery to Chain Bridge and west up to Lee Highway. (That would include the mid-nineteenth-century home Dawson Terrace and a mill on Spout Run.)

A banker, Mason had a main residence in Georgetown and enjoyed the ferry service to the island that was begun decades earlier. But one day, a fire broke out at the in-progress home. The event was recorded in a letter from President Thomas Jefferson: "One wing was burnt down and the middle nearly so. They saved their furniture. Suspicions arising that it was done by one of his house servants who wished the family to go back to Georgetown, he was arrested, and on his way to prison with the constable, he jumped out of the boat and drowned himself. I understand the family will continue through the summer in the remaining wing."

By 1807, the island had a causeway, Kreuger said, and that bridge and ferry were likely used in 1814 by President Madison when he was fleeing from the British to Falls Church and McLean.

Mason planted gardens and orchards. He owned nine enslaved workers (according to his 1856 will). He competed in sheep shearing against neighbor George Washington Parke Custis, who was building Arlington House around the same time. Both enjoyed views of Georgetown and may have used the same British architect, George Hadfield.

Keeping the island's south side private and the north side public, Mason's British gardener achieved in creating what one period travel guide writer called "the most enchanting spot I've ever beheld." According to Gunston

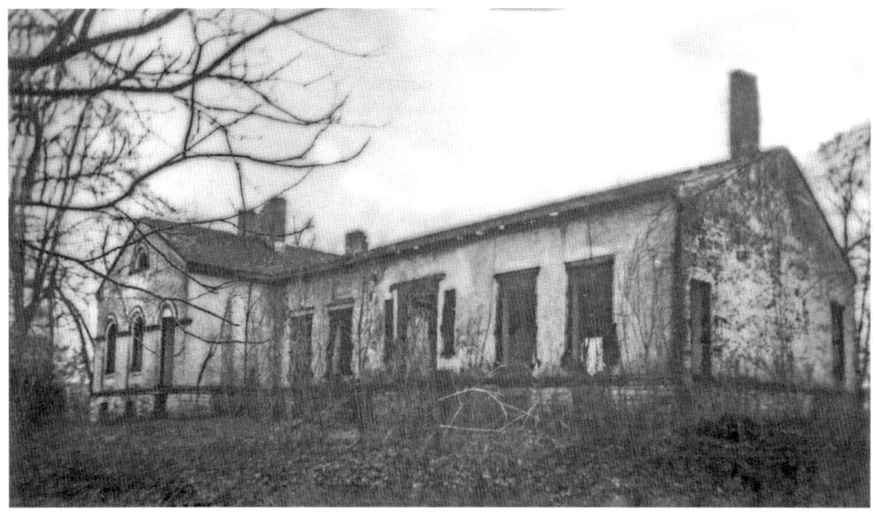

Mason's house on today's Roosevelt Island. *Courtesy of the Center for Local History, Arlington Public Library.*

Hall curators, Mason Island hosted James Monroe and Louis Phillipe, Duc d'Orleans, later the king of France.

But in 1833, Mason had fallen on hard times and had to sell. The public reason: mosquitos. He departed to Fairfax to raise sheep. Mason's Island was bought by the Carter family and then by Washington, D.C. postmaster William Bradley, who created a retreat there, where the wealthy enjoyed dancing, feasts and jousting.

During the Civil War, "colored" Union troops drilled there, secluded from local White people, Krueger said. Troops would also train there during the Spanish American War and World War II. In the 1880s, the island became the Columbia Athletic Club (a photograph of the house survives from 1890).

In 1913, the Washington Gas Light Co. bought the island. The Ballston Boy Scouts camped there.

In 1931, it was sold to the Roosevelt Memorial Association. The Civilian Conservation Corps was brought in to restore the island's rare plants, and archaeologists excavated the Mason home ruins.

The statue of Roosevelt there wasn't completed until 1967. It is the area's largest statue, hidden from all but island visitors.

The High View at Chain Bridge

In two-plus centuries, no fewer than eight structures have spanned the Potomac at the site residents now call Chain Bridge. That flood-prone strategic crossing that has been located below Little Falls since it was planned during George Washington's administration has been the scene of layers of important history—both local and national.

Today, narrow roads and heavy traffic make the area difficult to access. But using a hiking trail from North Randolph Street (or the half-dozen parking places favored by fishermen and hikers), you can read the 2011 historical panel describing action during the War of 1812. As British invaders approached the White House after burning the U.S. Capitol in August 1814, an alert clerk named Stephen Pleasanton secured the original copies of the Declaration of Independence, some texts of laws, journals of the Continental Congress and some letters of George Washington and fled in a horse-drawn cart. He temporarily stored them in linen sacks in a Lee family gristmill near the bridge on Pimmit Run before they were moved to Leesburg.

By the beginning of the Civil War, Chain Bridge (the name came from an 1808 suspension bridge there) was guarded regularly by Union troops at the entrance and at nearby Fort Marcy to prevent Confederate incursions into Washington, D.C.

As emancipation approached, Black Americans freed from slavery bought lots and formed a community along nearby Pimmit Run called the "Bottom." Their tale was detailed through maps and memoirs by Jessica Kaplan in the 2018 *Arlington Historical Magazine*. The steep valley in the wooded area "remained their home through challenging times: war, Reconstruction, Jim Crow, segregation and suburbanization," she writes. The construction of the George Washington Memorial Parkway (leading to its opening in 1932) dismantled the community, which, by the 1950s, was defunct.

Shift to the Victorian era, and atop the highest hill, directly overlooking Chain Bridge, entrepreneurs at Potomac Electric Light Company, in the early 1890s, built a ten-room luxury hotel. "High-View-on-the-Potomac, 3½ Miles from the City at the head of tidewater," read an illustrated promotional lithograph. "Verandahs 200 feet above the water. Road lighted by Electricity. Breakfast, Dinner and Supper Parties. Geo. H. Lawrence, late of The Arlington and Hotel Arno."

The High View was reputed to attract classy clientele—at least at first. It went through a succession of owners and managers, detailed again by Kaplan in the 2019 *Arlington Historical Magazine.* The end of the nineteenth

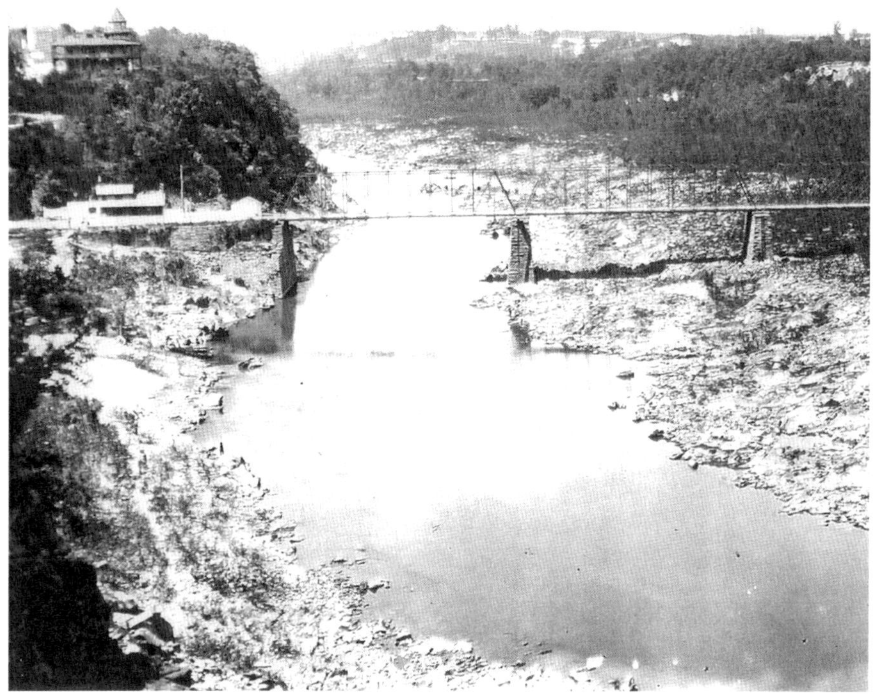

The High View Hotel, visible above Chain Bridge in the early twentieth century. *Courtesy of the estate of Joya Cox.*

century brought commonwealth's attorney Crandal Mackey's crackdown on Alexandria County's gambling, prostitution and illegal drinking. Though concentrated in Rosslyn and Jackson City, his raids eventually became associated with the High View. Reports of crimes and corrupt management lead to court battles, as well as one attempted murder of a manager in a knife attack. As the *Evening Star* editorialized, "Every disreputable resort from Chain Bridge to Alexandria can be closed instantly and by exercise of ordinary vigilance be kept closed until the weary gamblers and other law-breakers shall cease to struggle for local existence."

By 1912, the High View had been abandoned and burned down—but not until a tavern by Chain Bridge at the ground level had opened called "Woody's Store." It became an attraction to "notorious characters," according to Carole Herrick's 2012 history of Chain Bridge, *Ambitious Failure.* Ironically, it was run by the Mackey family, who owned land nearby.

The steep promontory over Chain Bridge continued to attract buyers. President Woodrow Wilson, according to historian Eleanor Lee Templeman, considered it for a new home, and a pre-presidential Franklin Roosevelt favored it for oyster roasts.

Flash forward to 1924. William Doak, a railway union leader who was the labor secretary in President Herbert Hoover's cabinet, bought the hill. His wife, the former Emma Marie Cricher, designed their terra-cotta-roofed white dreamhouse around the spectacular view of the Potomac (featured in the July 1945 *National Geographic*). They named their home "Notre Nid" (French for "our nest"), according to historian Eleanor Lee Templeman. The Doaks did memorable entertaining.

Today, Notre Nid continues to overlook the river. The Lou Cox family bought the 2.7-acre property in 1956. Rich in wildlife and flowers, it was renamed Highpoint. Joya Cox inherited it from her mother in 1993, and it became the setting for classical piano concerts. In 2000, she donated funds for an easement to the Potomac Conservancy to protect the fragile cliffs from overdevelopment. That easement was renewed in 2020, when, after Joya Cox's death, the home was bought for $5.5 million by a neighbor who owns several homes on the high cliffs above historic Chain Bridge. Though many on that palisade like the "cachet" of calling themselves residents of McLean, Highpoint, for purposes of mail delivery, voting and emergency response, is a part of Arlington.

FUN AT ARLINGTON SPRING

Two centuries before the sparklers of our modern Fourth of July celebrations, there was a different marking of the patriotic day that helped put Arlington on the map.

George Washington Parke Custis (1781–1857), the conceiver of Arlington House whose onetime plantation is now Arlington National Cemetery, threw a heck of an Independence Day party annually for three decades during the first half of the nineteenth century.

The location for his come-one-come-all affairs was a Potomac riverbank site called Arlington Spring. Its precise location, I'm told by Matt Penrod, a retired park ranger who worked at Arlington House for twenty-eight years, was near Boundary Channel, close to the Pentagon's North parking lot.

"Come over to the shades of Arlington, where peace and pleasurable breezes, good air, good water, and a tolerably good fellow will make you welcome," Custis wrote to a friend, as recounted in Murray Nelligan's

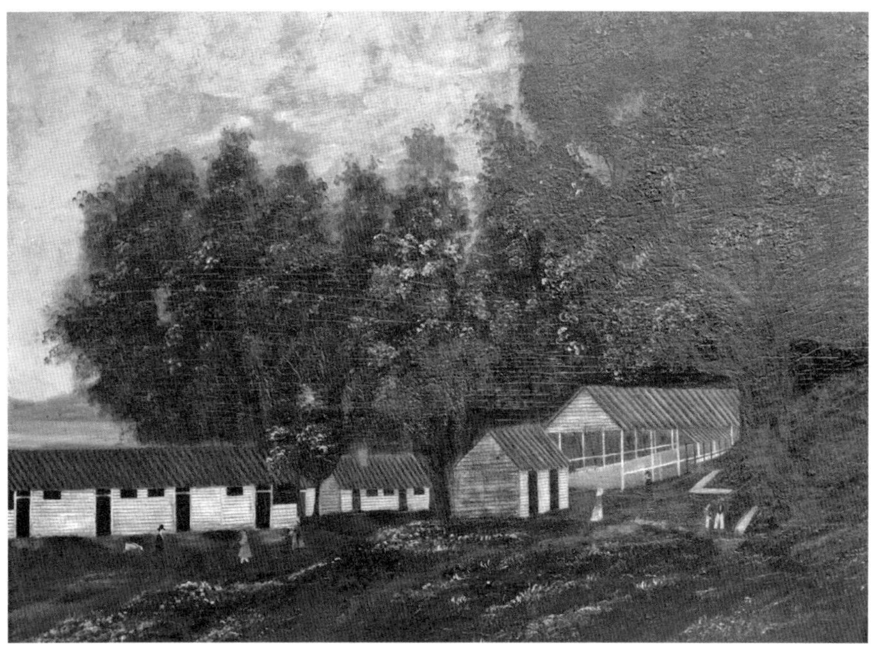

For decades, George Washington Parke Custis hosted Potomac-side picnics at Arlington Spring. *Courtesy of the George Washington Memorial Parkway.*

1953 National Park Service book, *Arlington House: The Story of the Lee Mansion Historical Monument*.

Back in the day, the parties at Arlington Spring unfolded alongside the cabins of the enslaved workers, an icehouse and farm managers' quarters that was erected by Custis after he inherited this family land when he came of age.

The spring, which "gushed between the rocks" near a huge old Arlington Oak, was the site of what newspapers called "natural beauty" that attracted visitors from across the region. It was sketched for *Harper's* magazine by journalist and Custis archivist Benson Lossing.

As a host, Custis first used the site in 1805 for sheep shearing exhibitions for hundreds of gentlemen farmers whom he hoped to impress with a new Arlington sheep breed. By 1825, the super patriot, who knew every U.S. president during his lifetime, would celebrate July 4 by pitching the actual battlefield tents used by General George Washington during the Revolutionary War. Custis's personal guests—patriotic societies, Sunday school classes, military companies—would hear him expound the values of freedom and liberty.

For years, Custis allowed the militia called the Washington Guards to drill at Arlington Spring, served them dinner and awarded their best marksman a silver cup. One Fourth of July, he presented a silk flag to the Potomac Dragoons regiment.

After Custis entered his dotage, in the 1850s, his son-in-law Robert E. Lee made improvements to the spring site, leasing it to a concessionaire. Events there then included a German music festival, a picnic to benefit an asylum and even a jousting tournament.

"Everyone speaks in praise of the good order in which the beautiful spring and surroundings are now kept," a newspaper reported. After Custis died in 1857, Lee let the public know that they were still welcome. Some two thousand showed up on the banks of the Potomac for July 4, 1859. Lager flowed. The *National Intelligencer* newspaper's comment: "There were no rowdies."

The Ambitious Alexandria Canal

As part of the District of Columbia (initially)—and always a stone's throw across the Potomac from the capital city—Arlington, early on, was a prime target for urban developers.

In 1830, two years after construction began on the 184-mile-long Chesapeake and Ohio Canal, which connected Western Maryland to Georgetown, Congress sought to extend it. The Alexandria Canal would allow boats to traverse the Potomac via the 1,000-foot-long engineering breakthrough called the Aqueduct Bridge, which linked Georgetown to what would become the Rosslyn section of today's Arlington. The mule-powered barges would then travel by canal seven miles to Alexandria City, where four locks would lower them to loading docks on the river for long-distance transport, saving shippers much in labor costs.

At the Alexandria Canal groundbreaking on July 3, 1831, a crowd assembled in Old Town Alexandria for a procession, an artillery salute and a ceremony at the town hall. The speaker: George Washington Parke Custis. The chairman of the newly formed, congressionally chartered Alexandria Canal Company presented a spade to Mayor John Roberts.

But with no federal appropriation, the planners had to raise private capital. The company went to court to fight the citizens of Georgetown over cost sharing and rights to use the Potomac. The Corporation of

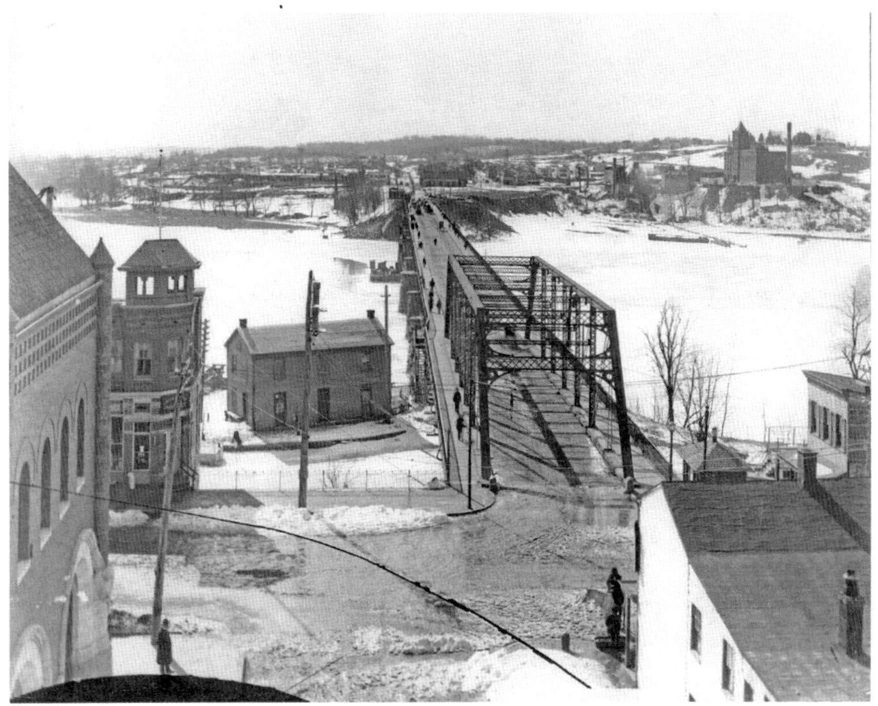

Originally, the Aqueduct Bridge carried barges across the Potomac. *Courtesy of the Center for Local History, Arlington Public Library.*

Georgetown, in turn, sued the canal company, claiming that the Aqueduct Bridge was within the corporate limits of Georgetown. The plaintiffs argued that the Potomac was a public highway and that persons working near the river, as guaranteed under the 1785 navigation compact between Virginia and Maryland, were free to use the river but were being blocked by the new canal's construction, as summarized in recent years on the legal website Justia. The canal company rebutted, citing its authority from Congress under its 1830 charter. A circuit court dismissed the Georgetowners' case, and in 1838, the U.S. Supreme Court affirmed.

During construction (a ditch forty-five feet wide at the surface), Custis petitioned Congress, in 1836, to be compensated for alleged damages to his riverside fishing grounds by the dredging machine used by the Corporation of Georgetown. In 1839, he negotiated with the Alexandria Canal Company to give it right-of-way through his land. He also offered a foundry as a setting for manufacturing on his land and hired out his Irish laborers for the construction.

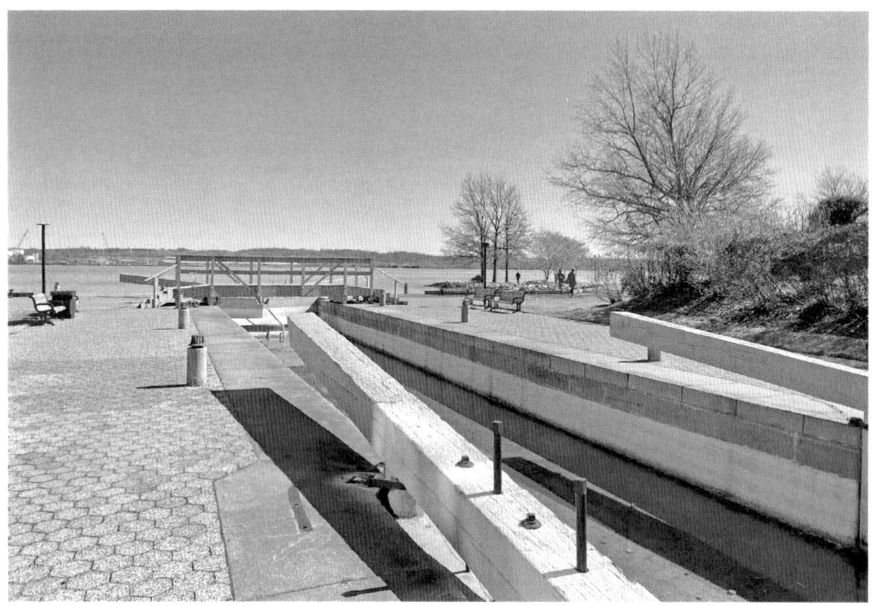

A re-created Potomac-side lock for the Alexandria Canal. *Author's image.*

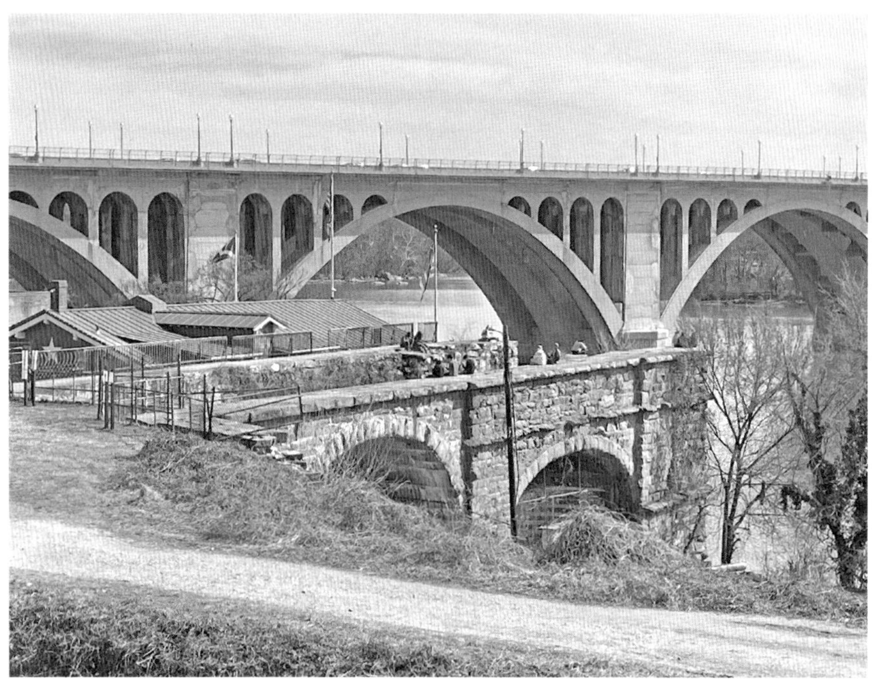

A vestige of the Aqueduct Bridge remains in Georgetown. *Author's image.*

The canal was completed in 1843. (It roughly followed today's Metro blue line and South Eads Street in Crystal City.) Canal shipping, though interrupted by the Civil War, continued in and out of Alexandria until 1886, by which time, railroads had rendered it obsolete.

In modern times, remnants of the Aqueduct Bridge are visible from both the Virginia and Georgetown sides of the Potomac. Abandoned with the completion of Key Bridge in 1920, its superstructure was taken down in 1933 by Franklin Roosevelt's Civil Works Administration. In 1962, the U.S. Army Corps of Engineers, according to research by the Arlington Library's Center for Local History, removed the tops of seven of the old bridge's remaining eight stone piers.

GRIMY JACKSON CITY

In the early 1830s, with Andrew Jackson in the White House, a plot of Arlington land near the Long Bridge known as the "Mason Tract" attracted the attention of some New York merchants and speculators. To boost their planned suburban city of private homes and shops, they named the five-hundred-acre tract Jackson City—the kind of commercial endorsement that most modern presidents would shun. The "city" was to be placed at the confluence of the river and the Columbia Turnpike, with nearby "Roaches Run" (as we call it today) as a handy port.

In the fall of 1835, the entrepreneurs wrote flattering letters to the president, likening him to George Washington. "It has appeared to us also as peculiarly proper that the second man of the Union should have his name placed by the side of that of the first," they enthused. Jackson was willing to lend his name and attend a cornerstone laying that was set for January 8, 1836 (the anniversary of the Battle of New Orleans). Foul weather caused it to be postponed for three days. Then, with wind whipping and a crowd of seven thousand in attendance, Jackson and his cabinet members appeared.

The foundation's box "was deposited and the slab let down," read a news account cited by historian Eleanor Lee Templeman. "The general gave it three knocks with a small gilt hammer, the Masons gave nine claps with the hands, the artillery thundered in the air, and 'Humbug City' unlike Rome, was built in a day!"

There followed a speech by George Washington Parke Custis, who saw the "city's" potential for economic development. And he welcomed his

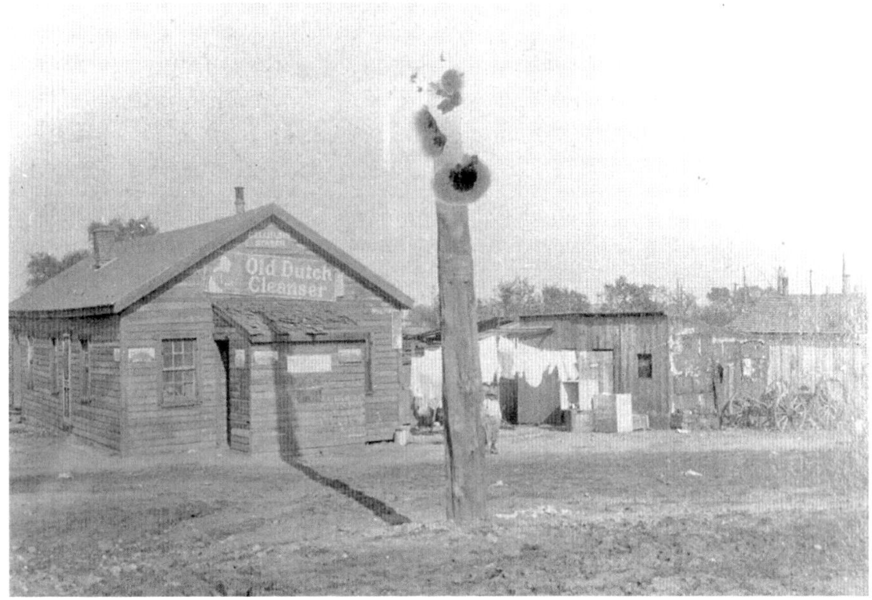

Jackson City on the Potomac attracted crime. *Courtesy of the Center for Local History, Arlington Public Library.*

"northern brethren," who were bringing their "wealth, their industry, their spirit of enterprise."

But a decade later, Jackson City was only a ghost town of a single home. Local Black residents were using the cornerstone to pound their hominy. After the Civil War (during which the U.S Army used the city to protect the Long Bridge Potomac crossing), Jackson City deteriorated into a high-crime row of saloons and gambling dens.

Those Civil War Forts

Arlington's role in the War Between the States was, at once, major and minor. It was large because Arlington Heights, the high bluff on which Arlington House was built, became a key asset in the Federal defense of Washington. And it was incidental in the sense that no Bull Run–caliber battle was fought here.

Yet, a skim of the county's history highlights (and more recent scholarship) suggests that Arlington, during that conflict, wasn't as quiet as reputed.

Six weeks after the war broke out in Fort Sumter, South Carolina, the State of Virginia, on May 23, 1861, held a referendum on whether to secede from the Union. Heavily rural Arlington (with a population of 1,400), which was more dependent on markets in the District of Columbia than those in Richmond, was the only district in the state to vote no. President Lincoln then flooded Northern Virginia with troops, and Arlington became the site of one of the region's earliest wartime actions. On June 1, 1861, Union soldiers dispatched from Michigan and New York were in Virginia, guarding the train tracks at Columbia Pike that were laid as part of the Alexandria, Loudoun and Hampshire Railroad. That was also the site of the flour mill that was built in 1836 by George Washington Parke Custis (across from what is now the Arlington Mill Community Center at South Dinwiddie Street). At 11:00 p.m., the troops were fired on by Virginia militia, as detailed on the historical marker the county installed in 2019. One Union soldier was killed and another wounded, and one Virginian was wounded. The Southern militia was driven off, but the need for studier defenses of Washington, D.C., became clear. Troops would use that same Columbia Pike for their two-day march to the July 21 Battle of Bull Run.

To counter the threat of Confederates crossing the Potomac, Union planners proceeded to erect a ring of sixty-four forts around the capital city, where a whopping ten thousand men were stationed. Arlington was, "in some respects, the largest military base in the world," as Marymount University professor Mark Benbow noted in *Arlington Magazine* in 2013.

Some twenty-three of the earthen and wood-planked structures (the count depends on definitions) were placed in modern-day Arlington. Many trees were felled to build them hastily, denuding the land and depriving Southern attackers of hiding places.

To protect three crossings (Chain Bridge, the Aqueduct Bridge and the Long Bridge), forts providing "the proper defense of Washington" were planned by Major General John Cross Barnard. They were dubbed "the Arlington Lines," as detailed in the 1988 volume *Mr. Lincoln's Forts: A Guide to the Civil War Defenses of Washington*, by B. Franklin Cooling and Walton H. Owen.

Were they effective? None of the three Potomac bridges were traversed by the enemy, though farther north, Lee's troops crossed the Potomac for what became the Battle of Antietam and the Battle of Gettysburg. And Confederate colonel Jubal Early famously crossed to attack Washington, D.C.'s Fort Stevens in 1864. But inside Arlington, the troops mostly trained and passed idle hours, though their forts hosted breakthroughs in

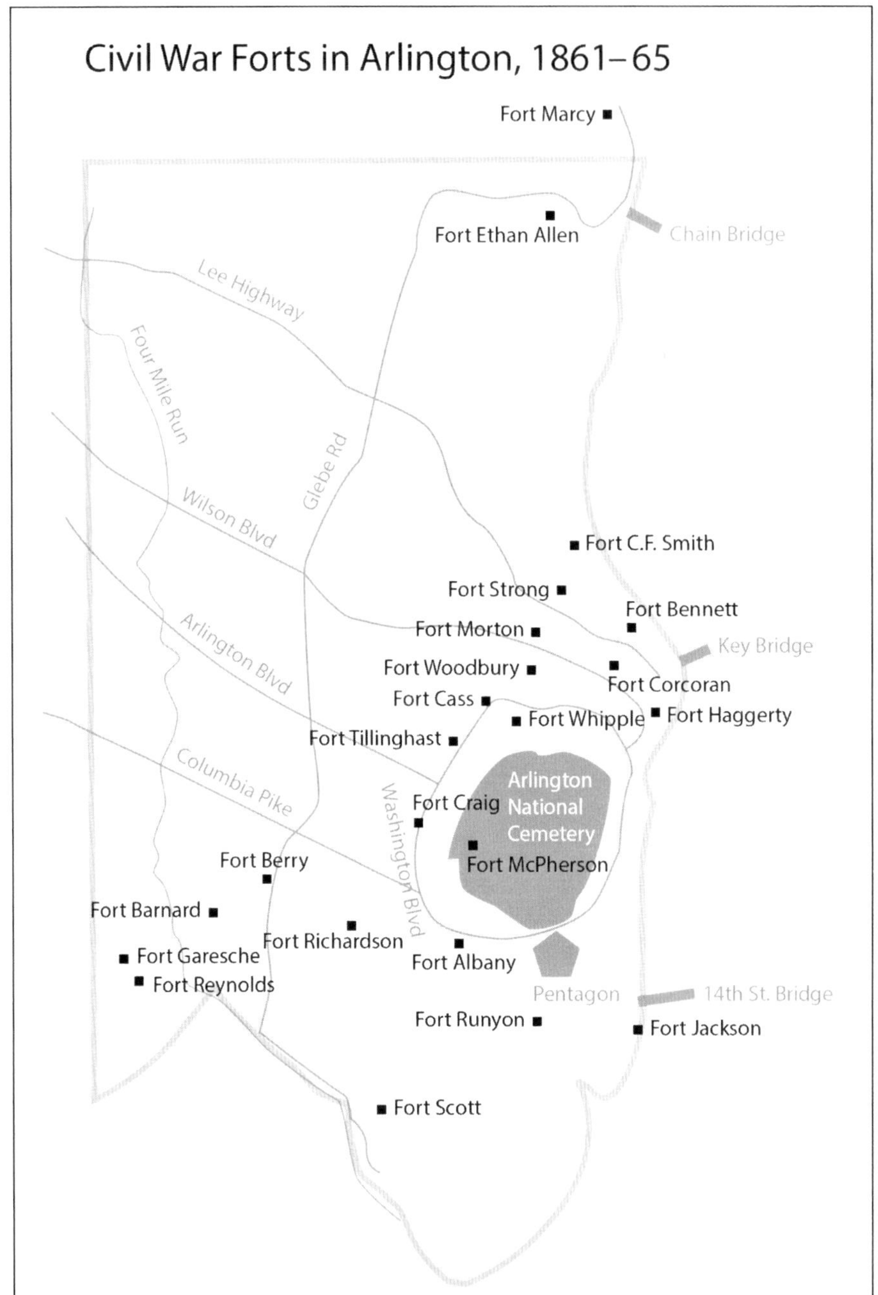

Map by Mariner Media.

the telegraph and intelligence via hot air balloon. Today, the best place in Arlington to experience the troops' lives and the roles they played is the park at Fort C.F. Smith, near Spout Run, which the county acquired in 1994. The outdoor signage at Fort Ethan Allen, near Chain Bridge, was erected in March 2014.

Now, move over to today's Wilson Boulevard. Following the surprise Confederate victory at Bull Run (called Manassas by Confederates) in July 1861, Rebel troops, that August, assembled for a brief clash at Munson's Hill (near Seven Corners on today's Route 7). The emboldened Southerners, among twenty thousand in the region commanded by P.G.T. Beauregard, J.E.B. Stuart and James Longstreet, stole skillfully into Arlington's Upton Hill to gain an outpost with a view of the Washington skyline.

But by September, the Rebel forces had withdrawn, allowing General George McClellan to march up Upton Hill (now a recreation park near a hill where Yankees discovered the Rebels' fake "Quaker cannon"). Thousands of Union troops camped in tents on the lawn of the Febrey home that stood until 2021 at the corner of Wilson Boulevard and North McKinley Road. It also served as a soldier's hospital. McClellan, at Bailey's Crossroads, then held what became a record-setting grand review of troops to prove the strength of the Army of the Potomac.

That same summer and fall, Union troops were also stationed at Hall's Hill (at today's Lee Highway and George Mason Drive) following the Confederate shelling of the plantation home of Bazil Hall. According to regimental letters that described the campsite, the Union troops exploited slaveowner Hall's crops, livestock and trees. In letters published for the first time in 2001, Hall's Hill, in the winter of 1861–62 was described in the *Arlington Historical Magazine* as "a round top, sloping in all directions from the flagstaff, which was planted in front of the centre of the line…with three Sibley tents on each side of the company streets for the men, with two wall-tents for the company officers…[and] a line of cook-houses.…An ample parade-ground for company and battalion drills was afforded.…A fine stream of water ran along the base of the hill, affording water for cooking and bathing.…Part of Hall's farm consisted of woodland, which furnished fuel for the camp."

Modern scholarship has revealed that Arlington was not spared fatal action, as had been believed. Avocational historian Peter Vaselopulos, in February 2020, gave a talk to Encore Learning enthusiasts titled "Arlington's Little War." He described an August 27, 1861 skirmish near modern-day Ballston. A key unit stationed there was the Union's New York Twenty-

Third Volunteer Regiment (whose uniform Vaselopulos wore during his talk), based at the railroad hub of Elmira. Arlington, for them, became the scene of exhausting training, both for calvary and infantry. The soldiers came "through Rosslyn and spent the first night near Clarendon," Vaselopulos said. Others camped near Carlin Springs and, later, what is now Bluemont Park.

The "Skirmish Near Balls Cross Roads" was reported in detail by the *New York Times* and in soldiers' diaries. Union cavalry were sent into thick woods to seek stragglers from Bull Run. The four hundred Union troops confronting six hundred Confederates had orders to make contact but not to try to win, Vaselopulos said. For two hours, beginning at 2:00 p.m., the two sides engaged in small arms fire. The Rebels (about where Ashlawn School is now) held their ground. In the end, the Southerners could claim they won the skirmish, despite eleven dead versus only "several" Union deaths.

Last but, of course, hardly least, one of the main dramas of the Civil War took place at Arlington House when army colonel Robert E. Lee, the former superintendent of West Point whose wife inherited the Arlington property in 1857, faced his agonizing decision: whether to accept the Federal government's offer to command Union troops or to fight for his family homeland, the South.

"General Lee, of the Confederate army, a son-in-law of Mr. Custis, and in that way connected to the Washington family, recently occupied Arlington House," wrote a special correspondent for New York's *Commercial Advertiser* on June 26, 1861, from nearby Fort Corcoran. Lee "has repeatedly threatened to retake it; a step he is slow to attempt, for prudential reasons," the reporter warned. "When again he rests at Arlington, it will be as a loyal and repentant citizen of the United States, if his life be spared at all."

THE NOT-FORGOTTEN FREEDMAN'S VILLAGE

Of the multiple uses that were carved out of Custis's former Arlington House property, the project most central to American racial history was Freedman's Village. Maps show its borders being located about a half mile from Arlington House, stretching roughly from today's Fort Myer to the Pentagon. The planned community became necessary after the Emancipation Proclamation in January 1863 prompted the arrival of hundreds of newly freed Black people and war refugees who were ghettoized

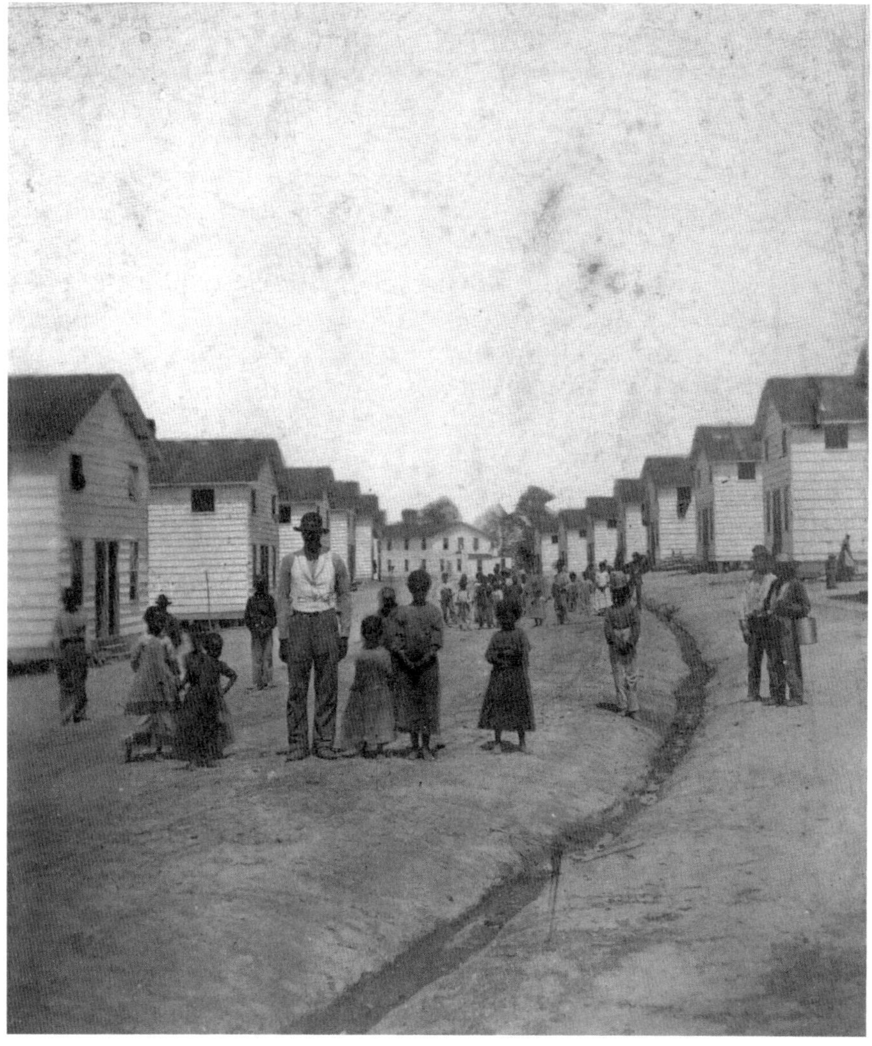

Freedman's Village housed freed Black people on Arlington House land from 1863 to 1900. *Courtesy of the Oshkosh Public Museum.*

in Northern Virginia and crowded "contraband" camps in downtown Washington, D.C. The Virginia estate, formerly owned by Robert E. Lee's family, was confiscated by the government and appeared to be a perfect site for the settlement of these people to abolition-minded Lieutenant Colonel Elias Greene, chief quartermaster of the Department of Washington, and Danforth B. Nichols of the American Missionary Association. Greene envisioned that the newly freed would gain the "salutary effects of good pure country air and a return to their former healthy avocations as field hands under much happier auspices than heretofore, which must prove beneficial to them and will tend to prevent the increase of disease now present among them."

Freedman's Village endured from 1863 to 1900. It contained one hundred whitewashed houses in neat rows, each holding two families, that could be rented for three dollars a month. Nearby was a school, a hospital, an old people's home and a laundry. After serving an initial population of one hundred, the village accommodated eight hundred newly emancipated Black people who were seeking training for roles achieving economic self-sufficiency such as blacksmiths and carpenters. Many of the Black people who were formerly enslaved at Arlington House resided there, as did the abolitionist Sojourner Truth.

The federal authorities operating the Freedman's Village Bureau and working with Mount Zion and Mount Olive Churches, however, always intended the community to be temporary. They clashed with residents, who began resisting payments of rents and dues for village upkeep. The U.S. Army made some noise about closing the project down as early as 1868, as did the superintendent of the cemetery a bit later. And local taxpayers in Alexandria County bemoaned the expenses, the crime and the health hazards in the community that attracted many of what today we know as the homeless. The Arlington Board of Supervisors, as historian C.B. Rose recounts, in 1875, asked the commonwealth's attorney to petition Congress for "support and maintenance for the paupers and indigent persons who infest the Arlington estate in this county." Politically, the Black enclave was not exactly welcomed. The *Alexandria Gazette*, as Arlington author Sherman Pratt noted, in 1887, editorialized (perhaps exaggerating):

> *The presence of negroes on the reservation has had a curious effect on the politics of Alexandria County. Numbering between 300 to 400, they have virtually controlled the county, electing, until very recently, their county clerk, commonwealth's attorney, overseer of the poor and Board of Supervisors.... It has been frequently argued that those people, being squatters on a government reservation, had no right to vote as citizens of Virginia, but this question has never been brought to a direct issue.*

Residents of Freedman's Village saw it differently. Many wished to stay on the property. They appointed John Syphax, whose mother had been among those enslaved by Custis, to approach the secretary of war for redress. In

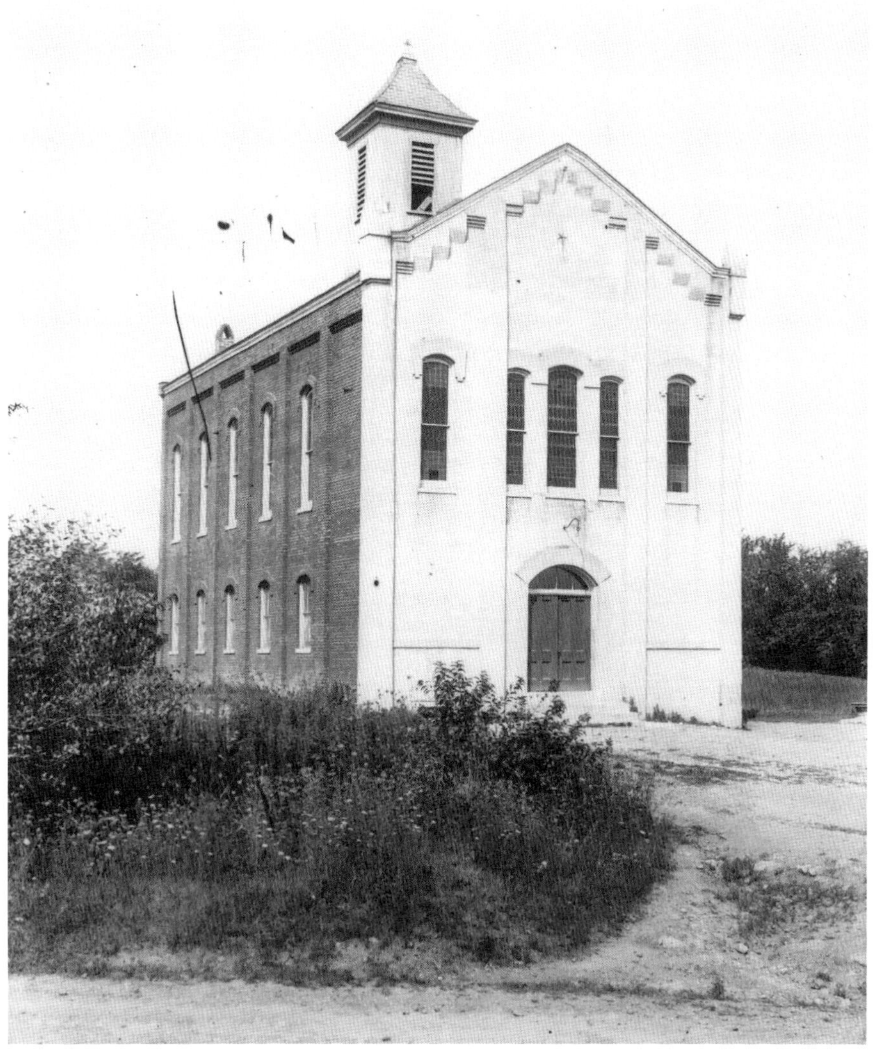

The early twentieth-century Mount Zion Baptist Church, founded by African Americans, was on today's South Arlington Ridge Road. *Courtesy of the Columbia Historical Society.*

1888, he requested that the residents who had made improvements to homes on the property be compensated $350 for the increased property value, as the National Park Service explains. "Twenty-four years' residence at Arlington, with all the elements involved in this case, inspire the hope that full and ample justice will be done even to the weakest members of this great republic," Syphax wrote. In the end, the federal government compensated the residents for the appraised value of $75,000 their collective back taxes. The village was shuttered in 1900.

Flash forward to September 10, 2015. How Arlington has changed. Thanks largely to campaigning by Black educator Talmadge Williams (who didn't live to see the finale), the name of Freedmans Village was attached to the refurbished automobile bridge at Washington Boulevard and Columbia Pike. Virginia governor Terry McAuliffe arrived to dedicate the bronze medallions that honor the community of former and fugitive enslaved people. Arlington Black Heritage Museum president Craig Syphax spoke, as did Arlington Historical Society president John Richardson and county board members.

In the attention-to-detail department, county preservation staff explained their recommendation that Freedmans Village be spelled without the usual apostrophe, to keep with nineteenth-century practice.

John Barcroft's Mill

Our minds on baseball, few of us who've suited up to play on the diamonds at Barcroft Park gave much thought to the facility's namesake. Now, later in life, this author can compensate.

The broader Barcroft neighborhood (with its school) owes its name to Dr. John Woolverton Barcroft (1817–95), a physician and technological innovator whose legacy is in the fields of energy and water supply Arlington shares with Fairfax County.

Thanks to good neighborhood histories (and descendants' memoirs), we learn that Barcroft, born in Kingwood, New Jersey, graduated from Lafayette College in Pennsylvania before earning his medical degree at Philadelphia's Jefferson Medical College (now Thomas Jefferson University). He married Lucinda Bray in 1844.

Restless in his New Jersey medical practice, Barcroft came to the Arlington area in 1849—right before the railroad came through—to join his father in Fairfax. In the area that is now Holmes Run at Columbia Pike, he constructed a home and a mill while continuing to practice medicine.

That joint career lasted until the Civil War. The Union army, in retreat after its second shellacking at Bull Run in 1862, ransacked his mill. That sent Barcroft, a man "of strong Union sentiments," back to his New Jersey and Pennsylvania havens until the smoke cleared.

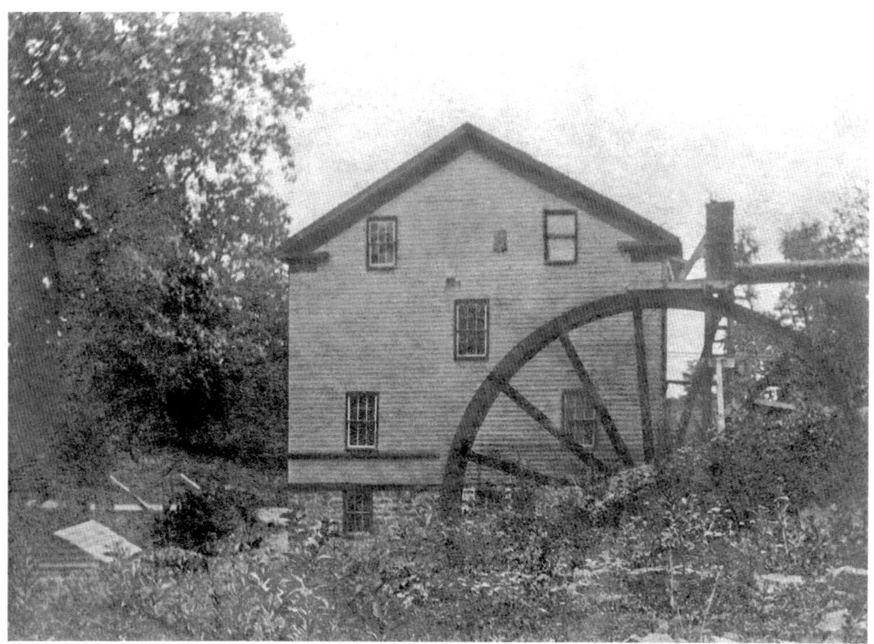

Barcroft Mill at Columbia Pike and South Columbus Street. *Courtesy of the Center for Local History, Arlington Public Library.*

After the surrender at Appomattox Court House, Barcroft returned to what is now Arlington and took over the land along Four Mile Run (near the Pike and South Columbus Street), where George Washington Parke Custis built a wood and stone mill back in 1836. (It was the site of a Civil War skirmish you can read about on a sign near today's Arlington Mill Community Center.) Barcroft built a home nearby with a view of the district's skyline.

Using Custis's foundations and his own quarry, Barcroft in 1880 built his flour mill and millrace on that site, said to be powered by the largest mill wheel (at thirty-six feet tall) on the East Coast. He rented it to professional millers, and it was used for both grains and as a sawmill, reflecting Barcroft's interest in carpentry. The nearby rail lines aided in the transport of products.

Before the mill burned down in the 1920s (and the site became an ice plant), it served for decades as a stimulus to the commuter neighborhood's commercial development, stretching well into Bailey's Crossroads.

In the twentieth century, Fairfaxians gave Barcroft's name to Lake Barcroft after it was created in 1915 by the construction of the dam that provided the water supply for the city of Alexandria.

Lake Barcroft, today, is a thriving suburban subdivision, and the lake is a favorite of recreators.

Barcroft died in Northern Virginia in 1895. But he and his wife were buried in York County, Pennsylvania, according to the Barcroft School and Civic League's account by descendant Sjana Barcroft-Hundt.

His name lives on, the civic association says, as a frequent write-in on the ballots during local elections.

Arlington's Barcroft Shopping Center on Columbia Pike was so named in 1949.

The ballpark, built as Arlington Little League got going in the early 1950s, was known in that decade as Four Mile Run Park. As it emerged as an institution enjoyed by Arlingtonians countywide, the ballfield was renamed for the proud neighborhood that honors the multitalented Dr. Barcroft.

CARLIN SPRINGS PAVILION

With Americans rebuilding in the post–Civil War period, there came a yearning for distractions. Entrepreneurs in Arlington spotted their opportunity. The railroad line that was laid in the late 1850s by the Alexandria, Loudoun and Hampshire Railway (used to move troops during the war) chose for a key station Carlin Springs in the woods (near today's S. Kensington Street). J.E.E. Carlin, the grandson of the neighborhood's namesake, William Carlin, had inherited the springs. His vision, as announced in the *Evening Star* on June 12, 1867, was for it to become a "delightful summer resort, within seven miles of Alexandria." By 1872, working from his downtown office on 12th Street, Carlin had opened the Carlin Springs Pavilion, featuring (south of the tracks) a dance pavilion, an ice cream parlor, a swimming hole and a bar (north of the tracks) that could host 250 guests (although it was respectfully closed on Sundays). A notice in the *Evening Star* on July 11 of that year promoted a "Grand Steamboat and Railroad Excursion" to Carlin Springs, leaving by the Dunbarton Street Sunday School in Georgetown. The fares: adults, one dollar; children, fifty cents. The following year brought the announcement that a "festival fair and picnic will be held at Carlin's Springs in aid of a Catholic church, to be erected at Falls Church, Fairfax County, Va.," according to the paid announcement in the *Star* from June 14, 1873.

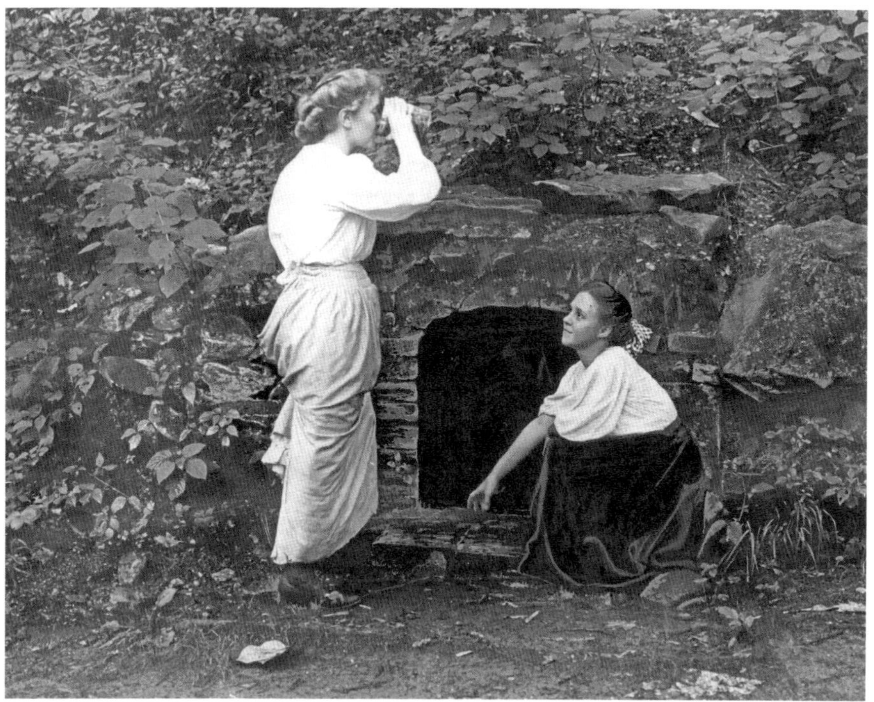

Glencarlyn residents, in the 1960s, pose at the original Carlin Springs. *Courtesy of the Center for Local History, Arlington Public Library.*

A greased pig race that was planned during the festivities was canceled for the oddest of reasons. As reported by the *Alexandria Gazette* on August 20, 1873: a "roasted" pig, described as "fleet of foot" and "thin as a rail," was brought to town and delivered to the managers. "But being a high-spirited animal," that pig "deliberately beat his brains out against the bars that contained him and thus deprived the owners of their gain and the contestants of their prize."

The Carlin Springs Pavilion flourished for two decades, with family picnics staged annually by the Odd Fellows of Potomac Lodge, as the *Star* reported on July 2, 1889. The rumored gold deposits there never panned out, as noted in the Glencarlyn neighborhood history. The pavilions closed in 1893, when the area became residential.

2
TWENTIETH-CENTURY BOOMTOWN

The Railroads' Heyday

The railroads were the internet of nineteenth-century America, and Arlington's special place in the environs of the nation's capital gave it a decent share of the traffic. Traces of those iron horses are visitable in the twenty-first century.

The tale involving a dense family tree of owner-investors began in 1848, with the organization of the Orange & Alexandria Railroad. As the City of Alexandria says proudly on its website, the city emerged as a major hub, linking cargo shippers in the north to central Virginia towns. The Alexandria, Loudoun & Hampshire line expanded in the 1850s (though it never fulfilled its initial plan to access rural coal in what today is West Virginia). Disruption and commandeering during the Civil War brought a new array of rail companies, as detailed in the history *Washington & Old Dominion Railroad Revisited*, by David A. Guillaudeu and Paul E. McCray. By 1900, the Southern Railway had taken over the tracks through Arlington to allow the shipping of wheat and dairy products from farms and to carry vacationers to the town of Bluemont at the base of the Blue Ridge Mountains.

Enter *Washington Post* owner John McLean and U.S. senator Stephen Elkins, who assembled what became the Washington & Old Dominion Railroad (W&OD). They began in 1901 by purchasing the embryonic Great Falls and Old Dominion Railroad. By 1906, their firm had laid tracks for leisure seekers to ride from the District of Columbia through Arlington and out for a picnic overlooking Great Falls. It was a lot of fun for recreators and commuters, though segregation laws caused anguish and occasional clashes between White people and "colored" passengers. A W&OD employee timetable from 1939 specified that "conductors shall set apart and designate in each car certain seats to be occupied by white passengers and rear seats to be occupied by colored passengers and shall not discriminate between the races as to the quality or convenience."

Most importantly to average Arlingtonians, the rail companies branched out into the electric trolley business. In 1896, the Washington, Arlington & Falls Church Railway began running trolleys from Rosslyn to Falls Church (the present routes of Fairfax Drive and Interstate 66). A car barn, railyard, workshop, general substation and general office were, beginning in 1910, housed at what was called the Lacey Car Barn. A historical marker and photographic panels describing it can be seen near Fairfax Drive and North Glebe Road.

By 1907, that line linked downtown Washington, D.C., to Ballston, Vienna and the town of Fairfax, says the county's marker. By 1924, the larger Washington–Virginia Railway had sixty-four trolley stops in Arlington alone on four branches. Lines crossed the Potomac on the old Aqueduct

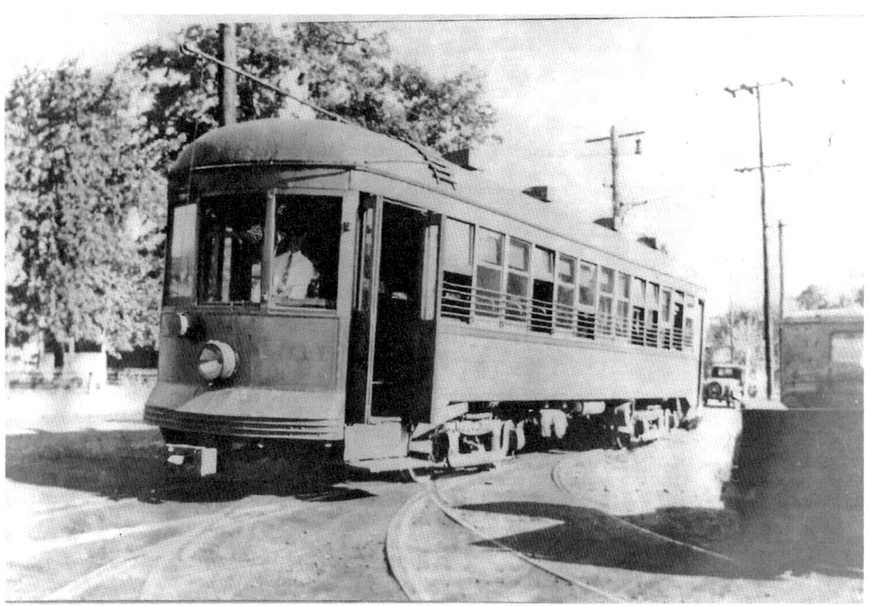

Early twentieth-century rail equipment at Lacey Car Barn. *Courtesy of the Arlington Historical Society.*

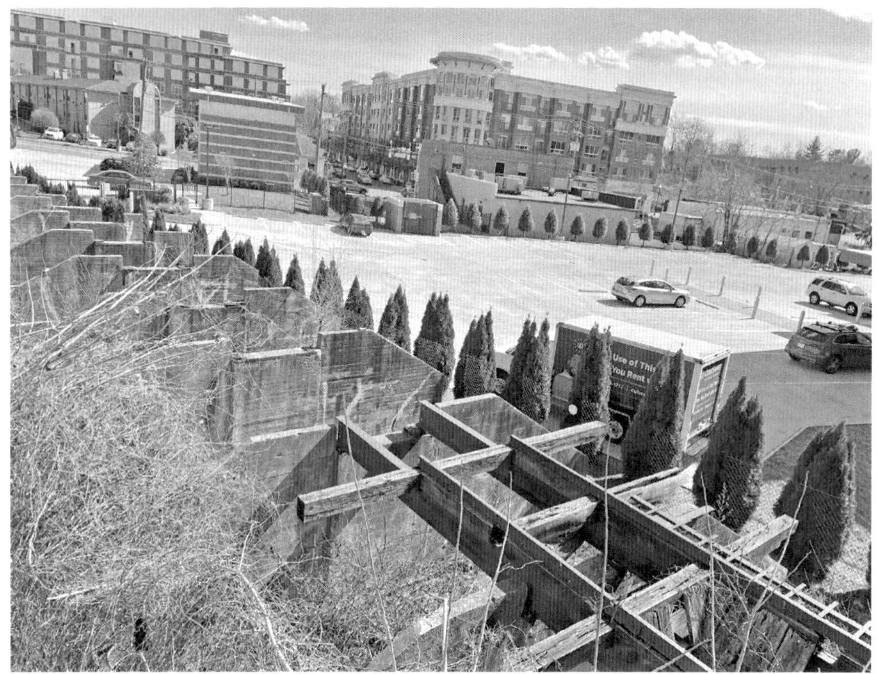

Coal trestle at East Falls Church Station. *Author's image.*

Bridge (now dry) and on another branch on what became one of the spans of the 14th Street Bridge, taking passengers through "Arlington Junction" in what became Crystal City and all the way out to Mount Vernon.

The trolley railway to Fairfax City ceased operations in 1939, but the W&OD passenger service lasted until 1951. After the Chesapeake and Ohio Railway purchased the W&OD in 1956, freight shipping continued until 1968, as described in Herbert H. Harwood Jr.'s 2000 book, *Rails to the Blue Ridge*, which he wrote for the Northern Virginia Regional Park Authority.

As the nationwide "rails to trails" movement got going in the 1970s, the park authority (now NOVA Parks) joined with what was then the Virginia Electric Power Company (now Dominion Energy) to convert the tracks to much-beloved bicycle and hiking trails, with power lines routed overhead.

Along the trail at Bluemont Park (named for the rail junction and station there), an actual Southern Railways caboose is preserved and is available for weekend tours. Farther west, where the trail crosses Lee Highway at the Arlington–Falls Church border (beside the W&OD Bridge, completed in 2021) lies a more specialized vestige of the W&OD Railroad. Benjamin Elliott's Coal Trestle was built in 1926 by the Elliott family of coal shippers as a concrete receptacle for unloading coal from train cars. The vital energy source was distributed to residences and businesses by the Robert Shreve Fuel Co.

Arlington Experimental Farm

As early as 1853, the idea of a government-sponsored experimental farm along the Potomac was proposed by the area's most conspicuous landowner, George Washington Parke Custis. But after his death in 1857, and after a disruptive event called the Civil War, four decades lapsed before Congress and the U.S. Agriculture Department made it happen.

This section of Custis's former property was still under the control of the War Department in the 1880s, its soil neglected and removed for an expanding Arlington National Cemetery. According to a USDA pamphlet from 1928, Agriculture Secretary Jeremiah Rusk eyed three hundred acres that had the potential to become a cutting-edge outdoor research laboratory that would seek innovations in plant and crop breeding, selection, disease and transportation. The land—near a turnpike and river for easy shipping—was controlled by the War Department, which, as it turned out, was simultaneously eager to disband the nearby community of Freedman's Village, though it hoped to use the land for the cemetery.

Action was delayed, however, as interim steps were taken slowly. It took the arrival of the McKinley administration in 1897 to break the logjam. The House Military Affairs Committee, however, was concerned about the property's bleak appearance, as cited in a 1966 article in the *Arlington Historical Magazine* by Wayne Rasmussen and Vivian Wiser: "At present, the premises in question have the appearance of an abandoned estate, with neither buildings nor improvements thereon. The surface is much gullied and cut up from rains and the flow of water in the small creek and rivulets which cross the same and empty into the Potomac River."

So began the Experimental Farm in 1901, an ambitious effort to redirect aging and flooding drainage ditches. Trees and prickly underbrush had to be chopped to open up fresh soil. With the aid of manure from the army cavalry stables at close-by Fort Myer, the USDA planners in the Bureau of Animal Husbandry, Bureau of Plant Industry, Bureau of Chemistry

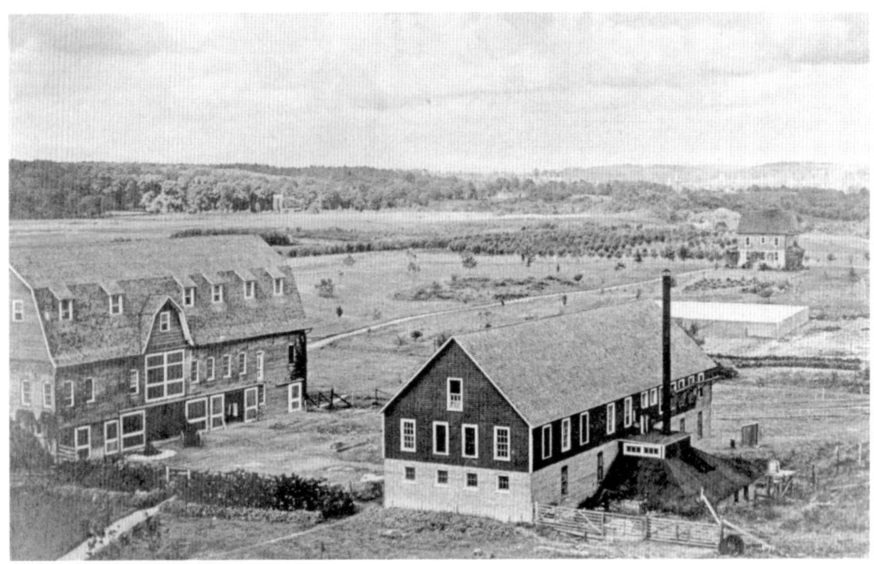

USDA's Arlington Experimental Farm. *Courtesy of the Center for Local History, Arlington Public Library.*

and Soils and the Forest Service planted cowpeas, rye, buckwheat, hemp, potatoes, tomatoes, nuts, mushrooms and crimson clover. They steered clear of livestock.

During three years of construction, barns, greenhouses and sixteen storage warehouses sprang up. They would house bulbs for Easter lilies, hyacinths, daffodils, tulips and bulbous irises. There was an apple orchard and plots for medicinal crops. There was a grapevine, experiments in the canning of juices and jellies and plots devoted to lawn grass—even experimental turf for putting greens for golf courses. Soil microbiologists began testing disinfectants to combat threats faced by America's farmers, such as smuts, rusts, blights, viruses and root rots that damaged wheat, oats and barley. The labs tried out strategies for fertilizers, mold prevention, the use of daylight, crop rotation, soil fertility and food coloring—as well as efficiencies in road building to ease farmers' transport challenges.

Americans who were serving overseas began sending home more exotic plant life, such as soybeans, as noted by Nan and Ross Netherton in their *Arlington County in Virginia: A Pictorial History*.

The taxpayer-funded experiments rolled on until the 1930s. By then, the National Park Service and the War Department wanted the land. Also, the National Capital Park and Planning Commission pushed through the

George Washington Memorial Parkway nearby, not to mention demands for the land for the coming National Airport and the War Department's anticipated construction of the Pentagon. The USDA agreed to move much of the experiments to Beltsville, Maryland, and Congress acted on November 29, 1940, to transfer the farmers' advocates to return the land to the War Department. Congress directed the removal of all Agriculture Department activities from the Arlington tract and its retransfer to the War Department. That was achieved by the beginning of 1942, two months after the Pearl Harbor attack. Much of the Experimental Farm's land, during World War II, was used for the rapid construction of dormitories called "Arlington Farms." The dormitories housed a share of the influx of new government workers, including many of the "code girls" who were working to hack enemy intelligence messages down the road at Arlington Hall (page 172).

Notorious Racetracks

Gambling in Virginia in the late nineteenth century was ostensibly illegal. But the Jones family in the Arlington of the 1890s used a loophole in the state's new anti-gambling law that allowed gambling at recreational and farm-related enterprises. They built a racetrack at Jackson City on what was called Alexander's Island (near what is, today, the Pentagon Lagoon). Another racetrack sprang up nearby in Alexandria's Del Ray neighborhood.

Alexandria County sheriffs took notice of the gambling. As laid out in detail by Arlington writer George Axiotis in his 2020 booklet, *Shoutout at Jackson City*, the dangerous neighborhood known as "Hell's Bottom" by the 1890s drew raids by newly elected sheriff William Palmer and his deputies. They targeted a criminal element that was protected by local politicians. One night in February 1896, a posse expanded by eight local Black men hit up a gambling saloon and drew gunfire. One died, and four were wounded.

That set the stage for tougher and more famous raids in 1904 by commonwealth's attorney Crandal Mackey. He had been elected on a cleanup platform and backing from a Good Citizens League. The prosecutor said that gamblers in the poolrooms—who paid off some local authorities—were betting illegally on horses at the nearby St. Asaph's Racetrack (and horseracing elsewhere via telegraph). They were generating profits as high as $150,000 annually.

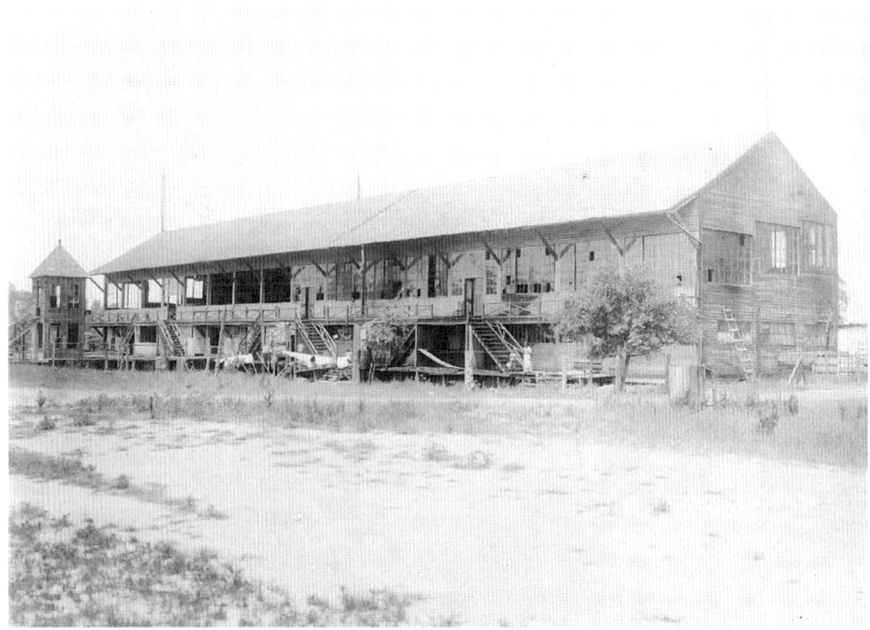

St. Asaph's Racetrack in nearby Del-Ray. *Courtesy of the Center for Local History, Arlington Public Library.*

Mackey's posse, on May 4, arrived by train from Pennsylvania Avenue downtown. At the time, there was no official stop at the iffy Jackson City, as noted by historian C.B. Rose, but Mackey persuaded a conductor after the posse dumped paper bags in the aisle and distributed sledgehammers, axes and guns. "The passengers in the train were terrified. They thought it was a holdup," Rose wrote. Exiting at the Virginia side of the Long (railroad) Bridge, the posse broke up the tables, chairs and jukeboxes of the illegal saloons. The popular Mackey would apply the same tactics in cleaning up vice in the gambling halls and brothels of the Rosslyn neighborhood.

By the 1920s, the half-mile horse race track on Alexander Island had shifted to the automobile age. It attracted "thrill-seekers and daredevils," as the Center for Local History staff phrased it in a write-up. At one five-mile race in open-top cars, the winner covered the route in six minutes and seven seconds. That meant they had a top speed of fifty miles per hour.

But soon, aviation became the neighborhood priority. Today's Reagan National Airport is not the first or second but the third airport in the area to be named for a U.S. president. In 1925, as the Center for Local History notes, the top executive of the Philadelphia-based Rapid Transit Co.,

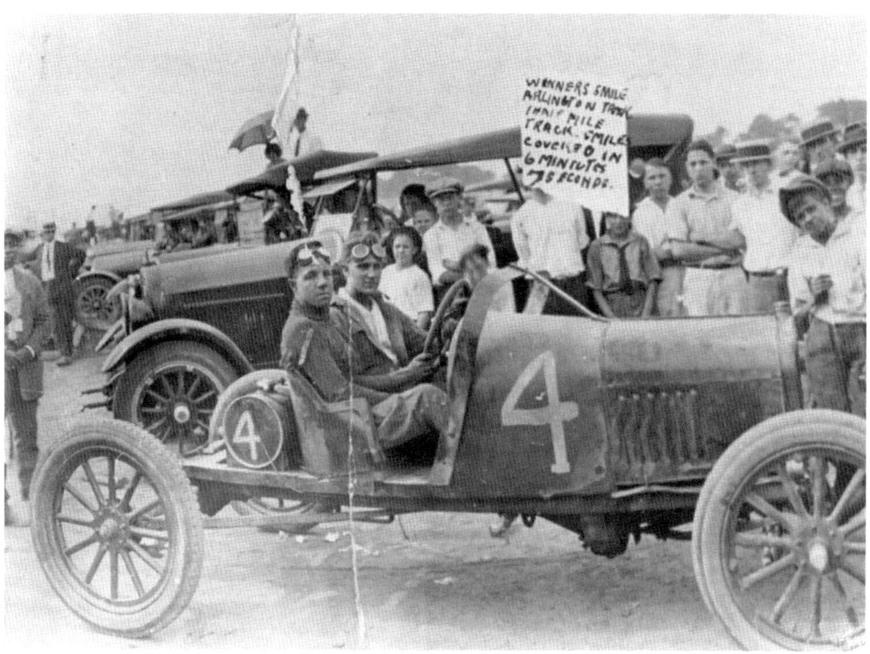

Speed contestant at the Arlington Racetrack, near Jackson City. *Courtesy of the Center for Local History, Arlington Public Library.*

Thomas Mitten, had the idea of direct daily air service from Philadelphia to the nation's capital. Hence, a single runway and hanger for three tri-motor Fokker mail, freight and passenger carriers were carved out as an airfield (again, near the modern Pentagon). It was christened Hoover Field in honor of then–commerce secretary (and postwar international aid hero) Herbert Hoover. On July 16, 1926—two years before his run for the presidency—Hoover attended the ceremony with dignitaries.

Hoover Field, however, proved to be too small for safe flying. Poor visibility caused by smoke from a trash-burning landfill was cited as the cause of accidents. And in 1927, a patch of land alongside the runway was outfitted as "Washington Airport," merging six years later as "Washington-Hoover Airport." As the storm clouds that would lead to World War II gathered, the federal government judged that the nation's capital needed a superior airport. So, the Hoover field was replaced by Washington National Airport, which President Franklin Roosevelt dedicated in 1941.

FUN AT LUNA PARK

Arlington's bid to be a regional playground played on after the dawn of the twentieth century. A vacuum in the entertainment market was created after commonwealth's attorney Mackey's cleanup. Pittsburgh entrepreneur Frederick Ingersoll spent $350,000 to build, near the rail line and Four Mile Run at the Arlington–Alexandria border (the edge of today's Crystal City), what promoters called "unquestionably the grandest and most complete amusement and recreative place between the great ocean resorts."

When it opened in May 1906, Luna Park was forty acres of tackiness with space for three thousand picnickers, restaurants, a circus arena and a ballroom in varying Gothic, Moorish and Japanese themes. At night, attendees were thrilled to behold fifty-one thousand electric lights. A 350-foot-tall inclined chute spilled riders into an 80-foot-deep lagoon.

The press enthused: it was like "a silver city set with diamonds," said the *Washington Post.* Guests were entertained by Liberati's sixty-piece band and by the Bessie Valdare All-Girl English Bicycle Team, as reported in a 2012 narrative by Jim McClellan and Shirley Raybuck in the *Northern Virginia Review.* Their article "The Pachyderm Panic of 1906" is the most detailed account of an oft-told tale that has brightened books on Arlington since the 1950s.

To liven the offerings at Luna Park, impresarios brought, by boxcar, four live elephants from Coney Island, New York. The much-hyped act, Barlow's Elephants, arrived in August 1906 as a procession of the animals debarked from a Potomac barge. Dubbed Queenie, Annie, Jennie and Tommy, the elephants were trained to perform tricks, such as playing barber and shaving a man. But on that first night, a violent storm hit Alexandria County, which frightened the pachyderms that were chained together inside their hippodrome. They began kicking equipment (destroying an ice cream vendor's cash register). To the screams of onlooking women and men, three made their escape. "Across country, over ditches, fences, cornfields and right through barns, the trio lumbered at a speed which challenged the best the horses could do," the *Washington Post* wrote.

Owner Peter Barlow assembled a posse to give chase. But after a fruitless day, he offered a reward and soon called in reinforcements from the crew of Wild West entertainer Pawnee Bill, who happened to be in the area. The beasts ended up in the Arlington and Fairfax areas of Bailey's Crossroads, Burke, Lincolnia and as far south as Clifton. Farmers were furious at their trampled fences. In Glencarlyn, a Miss Backus on South Fifth Street was playing along a stream but dashed home, terrified of the strange noises

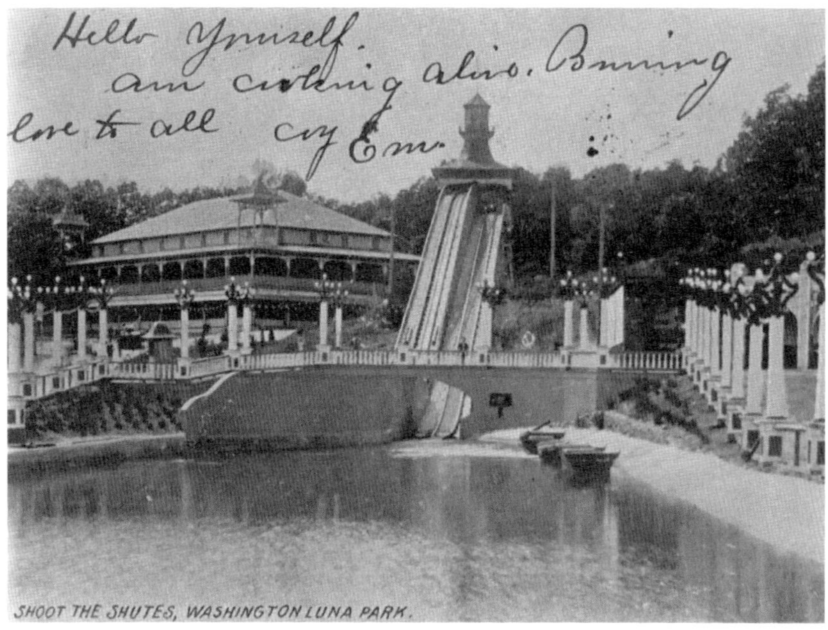

Luna Park at the Arlington–Alexandria border. *Courtesy of the Center for Local History, Arlington Public Library.*

rising from the woods. One eleven-year-old boy in Alexandria, as recalled in the 1980s by his daughter, the late bookseller Irene Rouse, was driven by the shrieking noise to hide under his back porch, thinking he was being punished for a bad deed. He was awakened by the sound of "a great pounding of hoofs and the bellowing of tropical animals," Rouse wrote. "Looking out from under the porch at the huge stomping feet, he was terrified and felt instant remorse for his earlier wrongdoing."

After eight days, the marauding performers were finally caught—only Barlow himself could calm them down—and loaded onto a train at Burke Station on the Alexandria Leesburg rail line.

Luna Park flourished for a time, but it did not fare well after World War I broke out. On April 19, 1925, a fire destroyed the roller coaster and damaged other features. That ended the enterprise, and the lot devolved into a stagnant breeding ground. It became Arlington's sewage treatment plant.

The exotic memory of Luna Park continues to reverberate among Arlingtonians. Preservation Arlington activist Eric Dobson, in 2021, worked with the county land records staff to produce a precise plat of the amusement park site, which, he assures the author, was "not completely along Four Mile Run and covers only a portion what is now the treatment plant."

RADIO ARLINGTON

The advantage of proximity to the nation's capital lent Arlington the chance to host "firsts" in the history of radio. In 1913, at the intersection of Columbia Pike and South Courthouse Road, the Department of the Navy erected three steel transmission towers. Two were 450 feet high, and one, at 600 feet, became the world's tallest at the time. Locals romanticized them as the "three sisters" (not to be confused with the Native American appellation for a group of Arlington-area rocks in the Potomac).

This military installation (marking the shift from the word "wireless" to "radio") went down in the annals as the "founding station of the radio broadcasting industry," in the phrase of Arlington historian Eleanor Lee Templeman. But that historian differed from competitor C.B. Rose Jr. on how the next record was set. Templeman says the first long-distance telephone-radio conversation was transmitted by these towers in 1915, when navy secretary Josephus Daniels spoke to the crew of the USS *Nebraska* off the Virginia Capes. But Rose hands that feat to the navy and American Telephone & Telegraph president Theodore Vale, who spoke from New York through the Arlington towers to sailors at the naval station out in Mare Island, California. Soon, electronic chats with Pearl Harbor and the Eiffel Tower were achieved.

Radio Arlington played a dramatic role during World War I, as a recent Arlington Historical Society write-up noted. On April 6, 1917, Congress, early in the day, finalized a joint resolution declaring the United States' entry into the European war that President Wilson long promised to keep the nation out of. Wilson was expected to sign the resolution at 1:00 p.m. So, fifteen minutes beforehand, the navy directed all systems to clear their wires and prepare to receive a signal that war approached. As soon as the president applied his signature, a navy commander at the White House used hand signals to an aide next door at what is now called Eisenhower Executive Office Building. The navy team then alerted the Arlington Radio station, and the first U.S. declaration of war sent by radio was instantly broadcasted to U.S. ships at sea.

In 1922, two smaller towers were added to Arlington Radio, as detailed by the Center for Local History in a 2019 blogpost. Federal authorities had initially outfitted the tower transmitter with a one-hundred-kilowatt Fessenden rotary-spark but then switched to superior thirty-five-watt Poulsen arc transmitters and the newfangled vacuum tubes.

The Arlington Radio towers became a beloved sight on the Arlington landscape, appearing on tourist postcards.

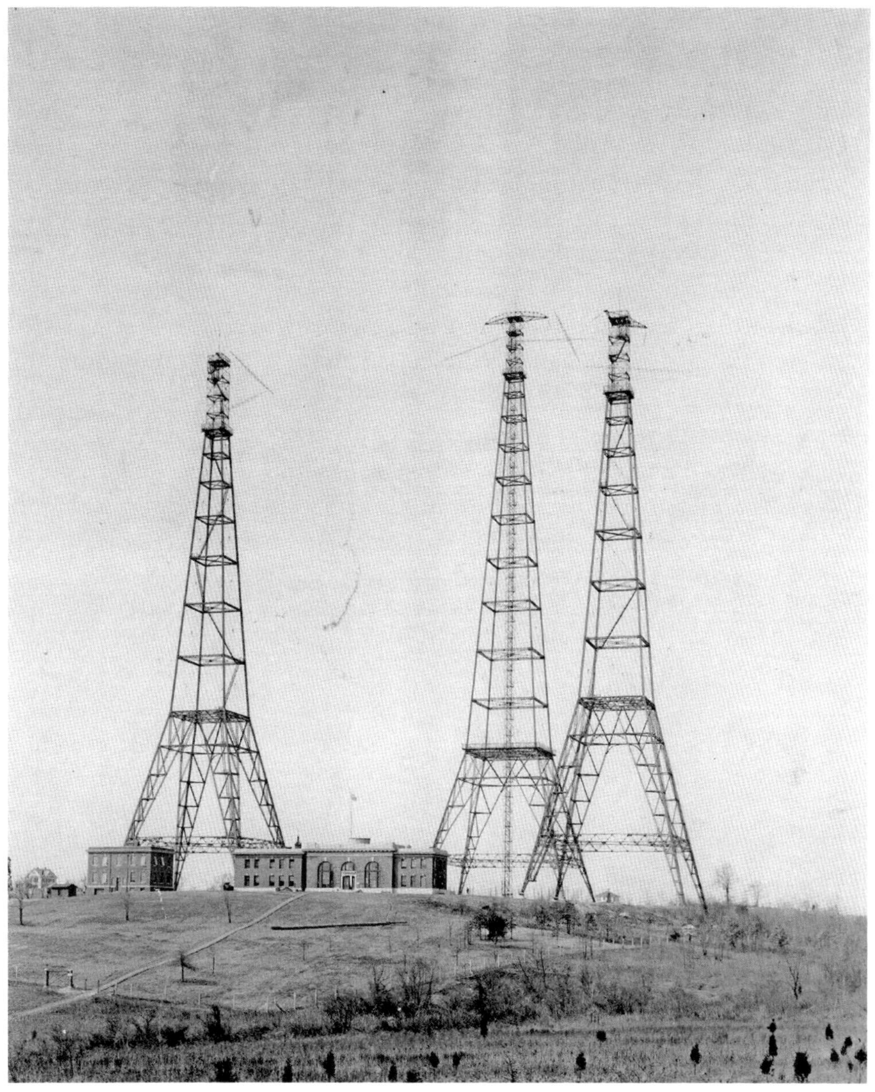

Broadcast towers that stood near today's South Courthouse Road. *Courtesy of the Center for Local History, Arlington Public Library.*

But by the dawn of World War II, the tall facility had become a threat to aviation at the nearby airports. Over the objections of army general George S. Patton, President Franklin Roosevelt, a navy man, agreed the land was needed for other purposes. The steel "three sisters" were dismantled by a contractor, and the transmission function was moved to Annapolis, Maryland.

Arlington Beach

Back when the Potomac was swimmable, recreators in the newly renamed county flocked to Arlington Beach. Roughly around the present site of the Pentagon, north of today's 14th Street Bridge, entrepreneurs at the Arlington Beach Amusement Co., on May 30, 1923, opened what today might be considered a theme park. Aside from a dip on the river, visitors of all ages during the postwar boom of the Roaring Twenties could enjoy a dance pavilion, a merry-go-round and a Ferris wheel there. There were modern bathhouses and plentiful parking, as noted in a 2008 blogpost from the Center for Local History.

In a 2017 oral history for the center, longtime Arlingtonian Ruth Jones recalled good times at Arlington Beach as a fourteen-year-old in 1927. The games offered included "throwing darts to win a bunny or whatever they had. And eating places, hot dog stands. And the dance pavilion was wonderful. It was a big, round pavilion, good music, big band music in those days." Jones recalled that some fisherman actually lived in shacks near the

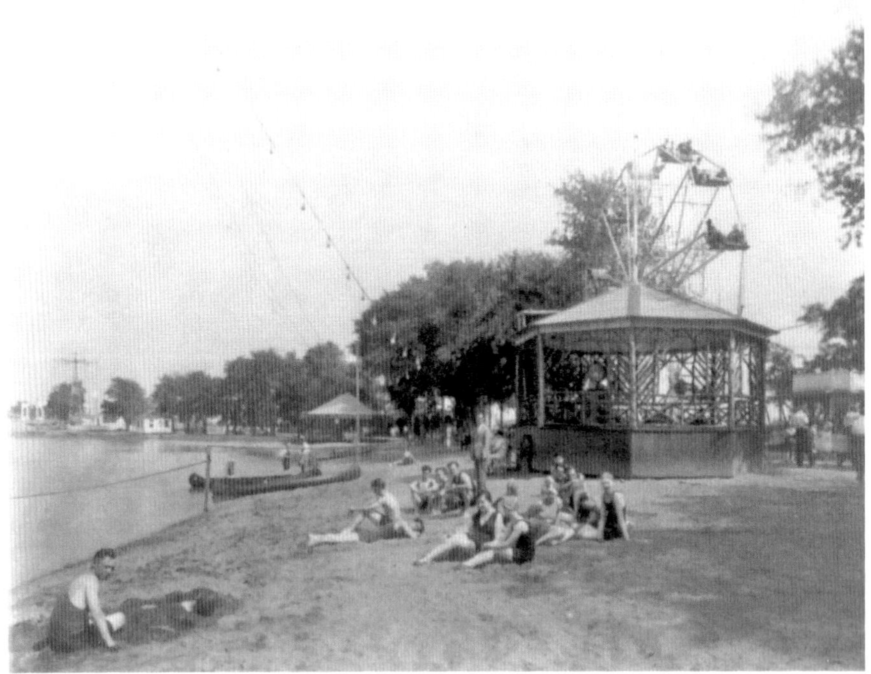

Potomac-side fun at Arlington Beach. *Courtesy of the Library of Congress.*

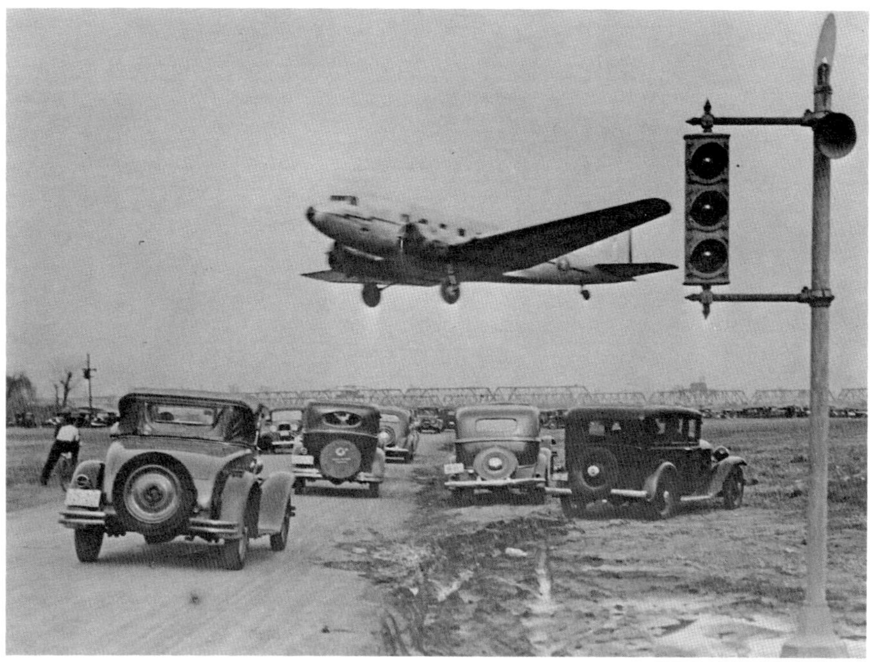

Landing at Hoover Airport, predecessor of Reagan National. *Courtesy of the Center for Local History, Arlington Public Library.*

beach in a riverside area that in the 1920s "was all woods, weeds." During Prohibition, Arlingtonians in Jones's family went there to pick elderberries and wild grapes to make illicit wine.

Fun times at Arlington Beach lasted until 1929, when the Washington Airport Corporation bought the land to create safer landing space (following numerous accidents) for what would become Hoover Airport.

REAL ESTATE ROYALTY

Who was the early-on queen of Arlington real estate?

Ruby Lee Minar (1883–1952), whose name still inspires awe in homebuilders, was tops in the 1920s among the visionary investors from across the Potomac who created the Arlington suburb.

"The most successful woman in realty development in the country," as she was dubbed by a 1929 business journal, worked alongside Arlington luminaries Frank Lyon and Admiral Presley Rixey to create prize subdivisions.

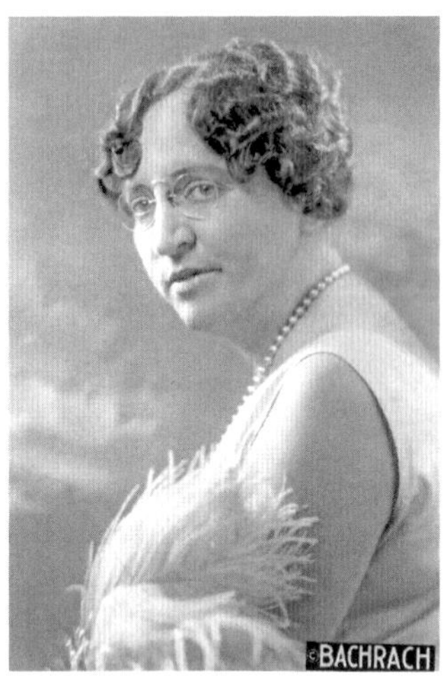

Real estate pioneer Ruby Minar. *Courtesy of Terry Showman.*

Born in Montana to a Baptist minister, Ruby earned degrees from Kalamazoo College and the University of Chicago before becoming a speech teacher and women's suffrage activist. Her marriage to journalist John Minar brought her to Washington, D.C.

World War I left the couple with a meager $200 in liberty bonds. Minar invested it in home lots in Chevy Chase, Maryland, and soon set up a downtown office on New York Avenue Northwest. Noting the new Key Bridge and improvements to Lee Highway, she got the idea of buying a four-hundred-acre set of tracts between Washington Golf and Country Club and Lee Highway. She christened the enclave Lee Heights, and she advertised its proximity to tennis courts at the country club and boating and fishing opportunities on the Potomac.

Minar insisted on having views of the river and the monuments from "where dust and smoke from the city and passing trains would not reach it," she said. Lee Heights was four hundred feet higher than downtown's Pennsylvania Avenue. The automobile is responsible for the lure of suburbia, she said. "When a man can live in a healthful and beautiful suburban community and still get to his office in town within 15 or 20 minutes, he naturally picks the suburbs." A motorcar would deliver a commuter to, say, the Treasury Department in twenty minutes, or a motorbus would do it in twenty-five. Sales prospects improved when cars became enclosed, and suddenly, house-hunters were more willing to venture over to the booming suburb, even when it was raining or blustery, Minar observed.

Those 130 large-scale homes in Lee Heights were soon worth $3 million altogether, according to news reports from back in day when they put individual purchaser's names and occupations in news stories. "Washington is becoming a great world capital," Minar told the *Washington Post*, "and Lee Heights is, today, an integral part of the metropolitan area of Washington."

In 1921, she continued to earn press attention. "Ruby Lee Minar Sells Land at Lyon Park worth $225,000," read the headline in the *Washington Herald*. The deal was followed by a reception with Frank Lyon at the still-standing Lyon Park Hall. Like many fledgling Arlington neighborhoods of the era, the neighbors agreed to form a civic association.

In 1922, Minar opened a new office in Cherrydale. Its six-man staff handled sales in Maywood, Thrifton, Dominion Heights, Park Lane and Livingstone Heights. Salesmen who made their quota by the twenty-second day of the month received Thanksgiving turkeys that were displayed live in the New York Avenue office as an incentive.

By 1923, Minar's tout went further. "Indications are," she told the *Washington Post*, "that next year will be the biggest building year that Arlington County has ever had….Construction in the county began to mount shortly after the armistice and is now going on at a rate many times that of any period in its history." After those upscale subdivisions, Minar built more modest homes in Brandon Village (near Ballston) to take advantage of three Arlington highways and two electric rail lines. "How would you like to live at the top of the monument?" her promotions asked.

Minar lost much of her wealth in the Great Depression, according to current-day builder Scot Harlan, who quoted his ninety-three-year-old father, who observed Minar's projects. But by the 1930s, she was ensconced in a mansion near Lorcom Lane at Military Road, said current builder Terry Showman, a fan of hers. That was the land bought in 1907 by Joseph Taser Johnson, the prominent surgeon who named his farm Lorcom for the combined names of his sons, Loren and Bascom.

Minar hosted neighborhood parties, often with a group called the Lorcom Marching and Chowder Society. One night, a fire broke out at the mansion, according to Cherrydale memoirist Dean Phillips. A confused Minar had to be rescued in her nightgown as the bucket brigade and Cherrydale volunteer firemen went back for her boarders.

In 1942, she moved to Miami Springs, Florida. Builder Harlan performed the demolition of her home in 2004 to make space for a row of modern brick Georgian-style houses; Arlington Historical Society volunteers came by to go through some of the artifacts. Minar, for decades, had been active in the women's service club Soroptimist International. She became the federation's first president in 1928, and the group named an award for her. In August 1952, she was on the Swedish ship *Stockholm*, accompanied by her daughter Patricia Lee Minar, to go to the Soroptimists International meeting in Copenhagen. Ruby Lee died of a heart ailment off the coast of Denmark. She was sixty-eight.

LONG-LOST NEWSPAPERS

In Arlington, we're fortunate to maintain an array of choices when it comes to news sources, from the *Sun-Gazette* to the *Connection* newspapers, to the online ARLNow and distribution to parts of Arlington of the *Falls Church News-Press.*

Most Arlingtonians also depend on broader coverage in the *Washington Post*, the *Washington Times* and the *Examiner*.

The aforementioned all have ancestors and erstwhile competitors, many of which molded this author's career.

The oldest (and still operating) newspaper that circulated on Arlington streets is the *Alexandria Gazette*. It dates back to 1834 as a successor to several papers dating to 1800, according to a Library of Congress reference. It began as a voice of the Whig Party but gradually adopted the Southern Democratic Party view. (Today, more than a century after Arlington County separated from Alexandria City, it is published by the *Connection Newspapers* as the *Gazette-Packet.*)

Also published in Arlington in the 1830s until the Civil War was a paper edited by Charles Upton, an Ohioan whose home was on the Wilson Boulevard hill still bearing his name.

The *Evening Star* appeared downtown in 1852 and, renamed the *Washington Star*, lasted until 1981, when its final parent (this author's then-employer) *Time* Incorporated shuttered it. (Today *Time* is confronting its own digital-age survival challenges.)

The *Post* (where this author did two stints on staff) arrived in 1877 as a "four-page organ of the Democratic Party," the Britannica says. It was joined in the twentieth century by the original *Washington Times*, the *Times-Herald* and *Washington Daily News*.

In Alexandria County, following the 1846 retrocession and the Civil War, a slew of newspapers appeared; among the most prominent in the 1870s was the *Daily State Journal.*

The *Monitor* was a crusading Arlington paper. In the early twentieth century, it was owned and edited by attorney Frank Lyon, the builder of Lyon Village, Lyon Park and Missionhurst. He used it to pressure for the closure of violence-prone saloons in Rosslyn and Jackson City.

An *Arlington Chronicle* was published from 1941 to 1951, or perhaps longer, according to the stewards of the microfilm collection at Central Library's Center for Local History.

In 1946, the city's first Black-owned newspaper, the *Virginia Arrow*, was launched in Halls Hill under the editorship of Naomi Thompson-Richards, according to a neighborhood history.

Add to that the *Arlington Daily*, of which this author owns a yellowing copy. The front page from January 5, 1950—packed with national news—reports that an addition to Westover's Walter Reed Elementary School was postponed and that the county was fighting the private Arnold Bus Lines over a fare increase.

The *Arlington News*, which the author recalls from the 1970s, was cited in a 1976 Congressional record for its coverage of alcoholism.

The early 1970s also brought a chain of newspapers with zoned editions that included Arlington called the *Globe Newspapers*. An editor there gave this author his first shot at town council coverage. That period also brought the *Arlington Journal*, part of a round-the-Beltway chain (where the author first launched a column) that was eventually subsumed by the *Examiner*.

But perhaps the steadiest hometown newspaper in Arlington was the *Sun-Gazette*, née the *Northern Virginia Sun*.

The paper's inaugural issue on December 12, 1935, which this author viewed on microfilm, was a far cry from today's expressly local and conservative-leaning chain-owned *Sun-Gazette*. The original was a high-

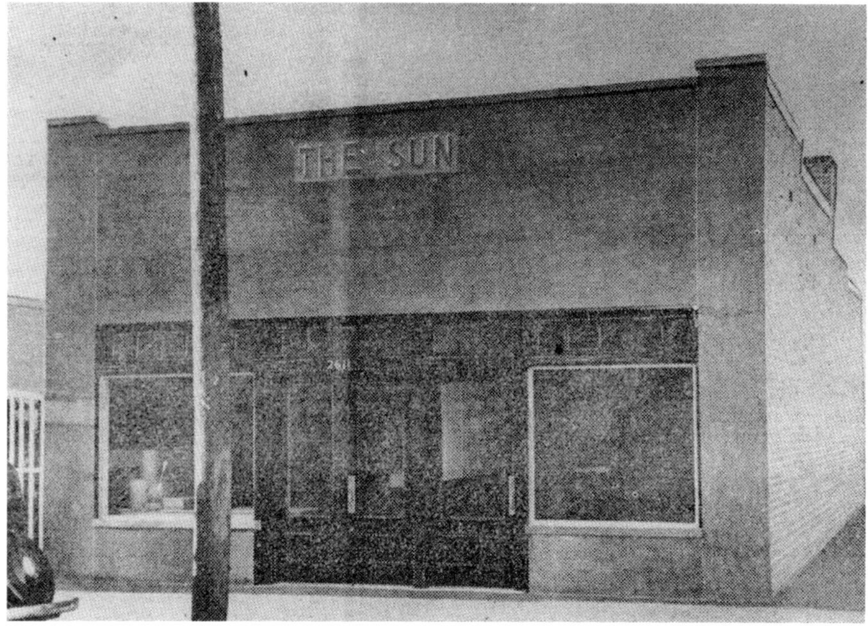

One of the several Clarendon offices for the *Sun*. *Courtesy of the Center for Local History, Arlington Public Library.*

brow, region-wide compilation that included global UPI dispatches and a commitment to racial progress.

"I enjoy the weekly column from the first editor, which ran from the start of the paper to about 1951," *Sun-Gazette* editor Scott McCaffrey, the author's friendly competitor who has written on *Sun* history, told him in 2018. "It really was the 'blog' of its day—filled with interesting and a sometimes-irreverent take on facts and foibles of the growing community. It's my hope that, someday, the columns could be edited into book form, because they are a tremendous asset for someone who would want to chronicle the community's evolution."

When Street Names Were Reshuffled

If you harbor gripes that Arlington's county government gets too ambitious, consider an episode from the 1930s.

In what probably ranks as the most disruptive Arlington project ever, the county's entire street grid was renamed. The modern system of (mostly) logical groups of streets by numbers and syllables was an engineering and citizen consultation feat that foreshadowed what locals call the "Arlington Way."

The tale was told in a 1959 *Arlington Historical Magazine* by C.L. Kinnier, who directed Arlington's Engineering Department when the streets were renamed.

Authority came after 1932, when Arlington switched to the county manager system and the board appointed Roy Braden to the new job. Braden's recommendation for a new street system diagnosed a status quo that inflicted multiple hassles.

Duplication was an issue; too many "improperly named" streets were labeled Washington, Lee, Arlington or Fairfax. Some residents had to add their subdivision (Radnor Heights, Country Club Hills) to their address to receive mail or deliveries. Rural folks had to use "Alexandria RFD." The old streets were a hodgepodge of "tree names" followed by streets named for friends or family, both local and historical, Braden noted.

The problems were traced to understaffing and the county's growth from 16,040 persons in 1920 to 26,615 in 1930.

The board farmed the job out to the Engineering Department after naming a committee on March 1, 1932, chaired by Monroe Sockett. It heard pleas from the Arlington Civic Federation and the Chamber of Commerce, which pointed out that reforms were vital if Arlington was to get a central

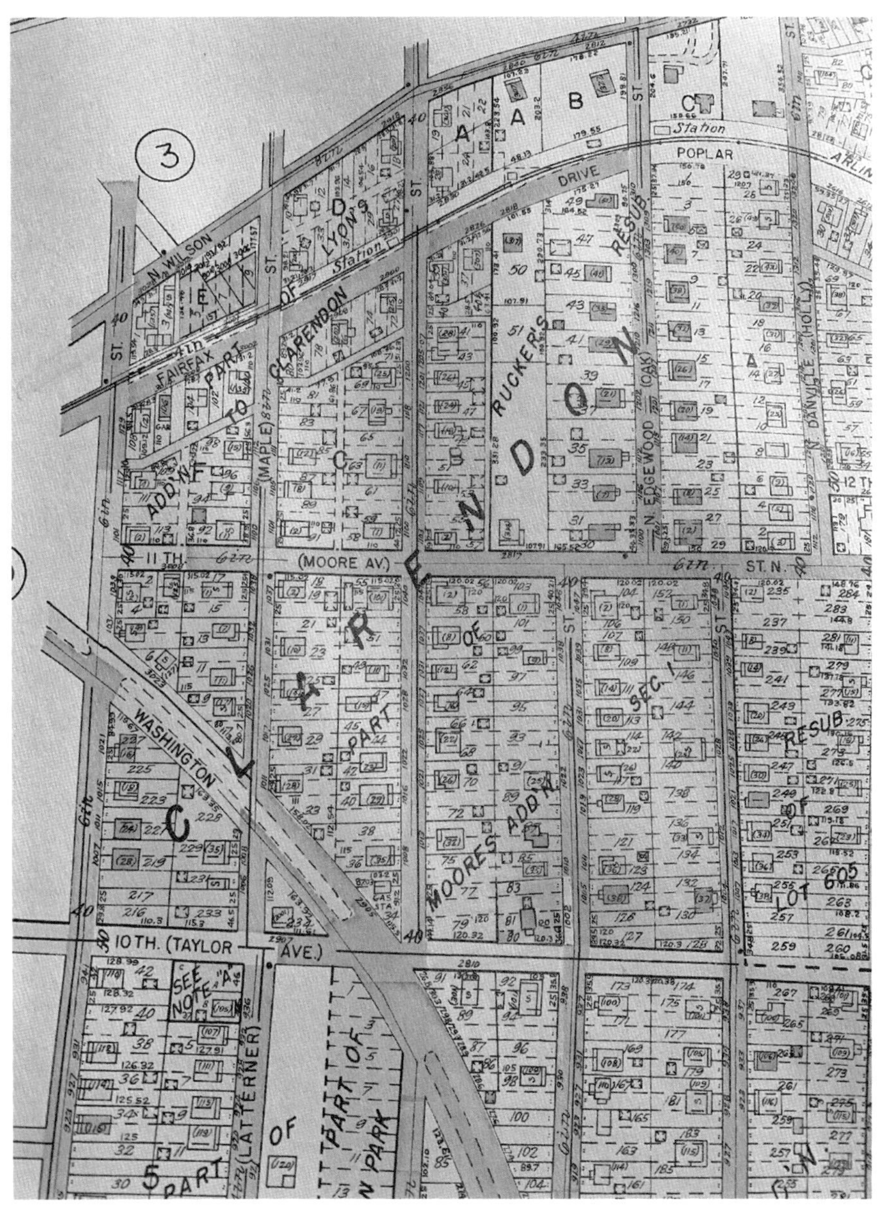

Arlington's old streets mapped by the Franklin Survey Company. *Courtesy of the Center for Local History, Arlington Public Library.*

post office. The committee also sought advice from the American Municipal League, the County Managers Association and engineering firms.

Kibitzers suggested new street names, even whole schemes. Some wanted a continuation of District of Columbia streets. "Each thought it better to change the name of the other man's street rather than his," Kinnier wrote.

The planners hung a giant map in their workroom. They had to divide the county into northern and southern sections (rejecting a proposal for quadrants). They considered what today is Washington Boulevard as the divider. (At the time, that road had sections called Memorial Drive, Garrison Road and Brown Avenue.) Instead, they chose Lee Boulevard (now Arlington Boulevard).

The list of must-keep old names included traditional Virginia standbys and state roads—Lee Highway, Old Dominion Drive and Jefferson Davis Highway (that lasted until 2019; Lee Highway will be renamed Langston Boulevard after 2021).

Rules required that streets at right angles to the divider have names and that parallel streets be numbered.

Sockett's monthly work sessions were open for a year, but the final system was formally vetted at a June 21, 1933 hearing.

Thirty months after its start, the committee saw its recommendations win board approval on August 30, 1934. The county then reassigned house numbers. "Houses on the south and west sides of the streets would have even numbers and those opposite would have odd numbers," Kinnier wrote. They had to update and scrub all courthouse information and create signs at three thousand intersections. The appropriated funds totaled $7,500.

The new system took effect on July 1, 1935. The board passed an ordinance declaring that "if any majority of the citizens of one street did not like the name selected and wished to change it to some other name that would fit the ordinance, it could have the change made provided they would pay for the signs."

3
OLD HOMES AND SCHOOLS

Long-Vanished Falls Grove

The following are some fresh details on one of Arlington's most famous—and vanished—historic homes.

Falls Grove, built in 1852 near the intersection of North Glebe Road and Little Falls Road, was the scene of luxurious living and Civil War drama before its demolition in 1966. This author learned of one unsung effort to save it.

The two-story white wood home with a triptych bowed window and a six-columned porch was built in 1852 by Gilbert Vanderwerken (1810–1894). A Georgetown resident and coach line operator, he needed a summer residence and farmhouse where he could graze his horses. (Vanderverken's other role in Arlington was operating the first stone quarries on the riverbanks off what is now Potomac Overlook Park.)

The best research done on Falls Grove must be credited to historian Eleanor Lee Templeman. Her 1959 *Arlington Heritage* describes how, after the First Battle of Bull Run, Vanderwerken—who stayed safely in Georgetown—allowed Union forces to set up a hospital in his home as well as a construction staging area for building nearby Fort Ethan Allen. General Winfield Scott Hancock used its carpentry shop as a headquarters, and President Lincoln himself visited the ailing troops there.

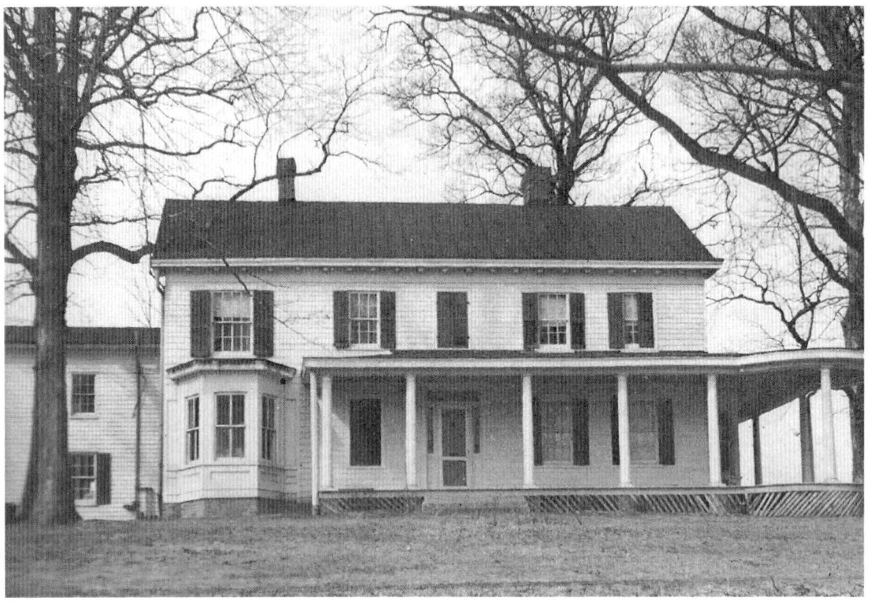

The Falls Grove house that hosted a Civil War hospital. *Courtesy of Eleanor Lee Templeman,* Arlington Heritage.

During that friendly occupation, Vanderwerken himself was once denied entry because he didn't have the password, forcing him to ride all the way to Alexandria for the army's help. After Lincoln's assassination in 1865, Templeman reported, soldiers ransacked the home, looking for the killer.

The pain and death of soldiers in the hospital later spooked the neighbors, who circulated ghost stories. But Vanderwerken recalled being pleasantly serenaded by the Fort Ethan Allen military band. In 1869, mounted army officers surrounded the house in a semicircle and Vanderwerken gave them all cigars.

With peace restored, the Vanderwerken family found the initials of hospitalized soldiers in the woodwork. The misspelled word "Hospitol" was carved on a door (only to later be painted over by a painter who was not historically minded).

Flash forward to the mid-twentieth century. Falls Grove owners George Truett and Lillie Hughes, listed at 3502 North Glebe Road, sold the property to the Yeonas Organization. Construction crews demolished the century-plus-old home on January 25, 1966, to make way for twenty modern homes. They're now on a cul-de-sac of North Thirty-Fifth Road, shielded by a wooden privacy fence on Glebe Road, across from Memorial Baptist Church.

In 1967, the *Northern Virginia Sun* reported on the new Falls Grove subdivision, calling Arlington "one of the most rapidly developing areas in the nation." One of the area's modern homeowners, George Varoutsos, told me his house has the same front-door footprint as the old Vanderwerken house and that Civil War artifacts are still discovered there.

Richard Malesardi, an Arlington architect (he was instrumental in construction of Dulles Airport in the early 1960s), told me in 2017 that back in 1966, he negotiated with homebuilder Steve Yeonas to buy and preserve the Vanderwerken home. He even drew up an alternative plan for the lots of the new homes. But in the middle of their talks, the wrecking ball hit. (When reached for comment, Yeonas said he has no recollection.) Malesardi did persuade the builder to retain the Falls Grove name.

"There was no hue and cry," I was told by John Stanton, researcher at the Central Library's Center for Local History, who helped with this author's research. "There wasn't much of a preservation movement at the time."

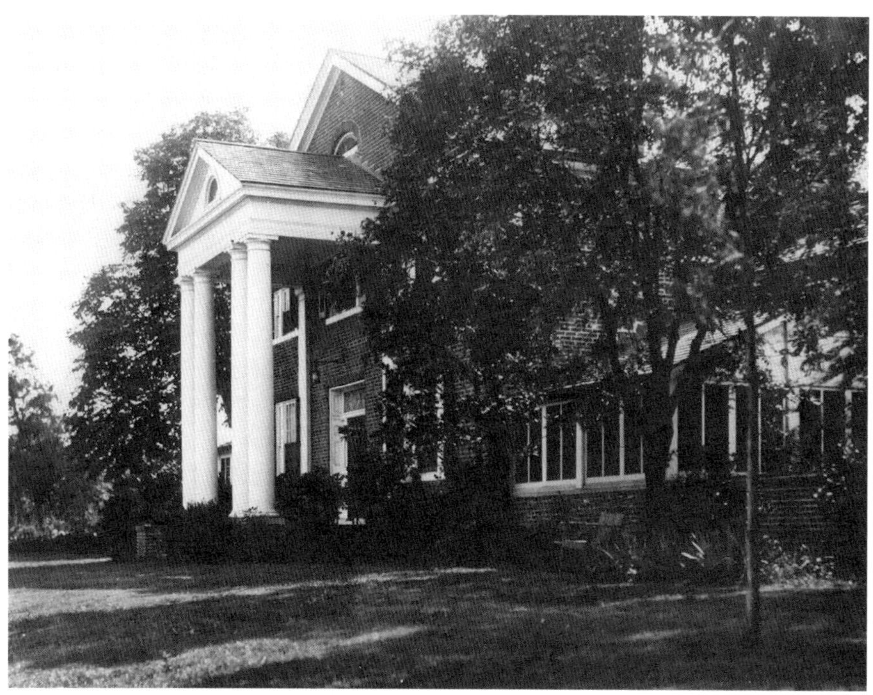

Brick contractor James Roach built Prospect House off today's Arlington Ridge Road. *Courtesy of the Center for Local History, Arlington Public Library.*

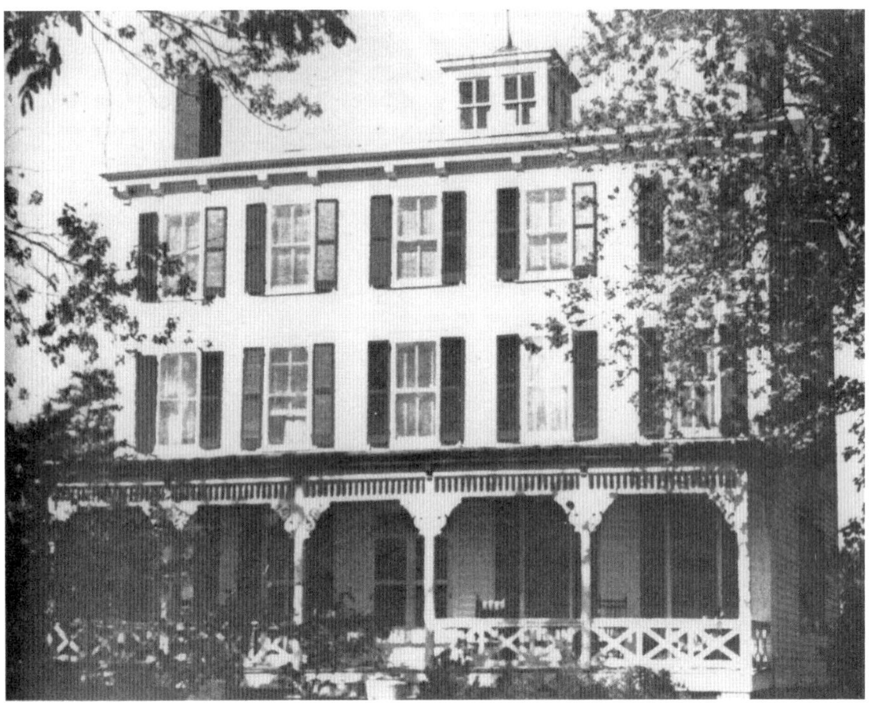

Fort Strong Villa was built in 1888 by gambling den owner John Walter Clark, who first paved Lee Highway. *Courtesy of the Center for Local History, Arlington Public Library.*

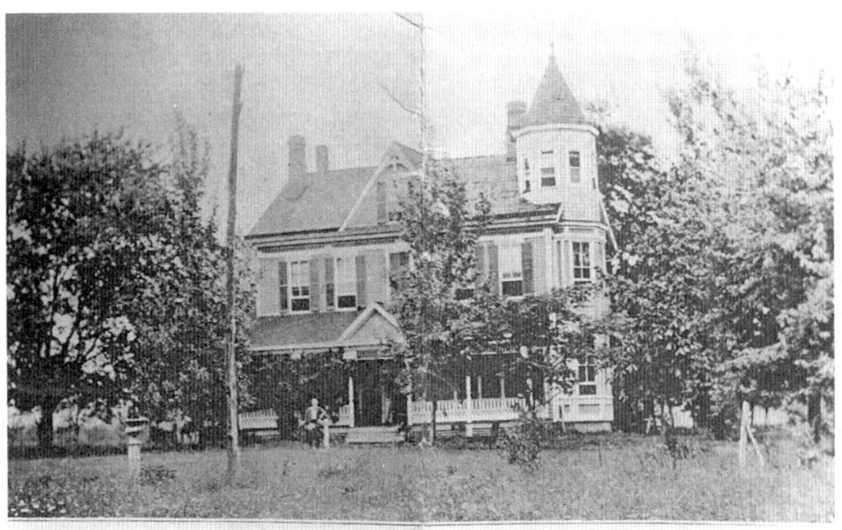

The home of prominent physician George Wunder, which was located at Lee Highway and North Glebe Road. *Courtesy of the Center for Local History, Arlington Public Library.*

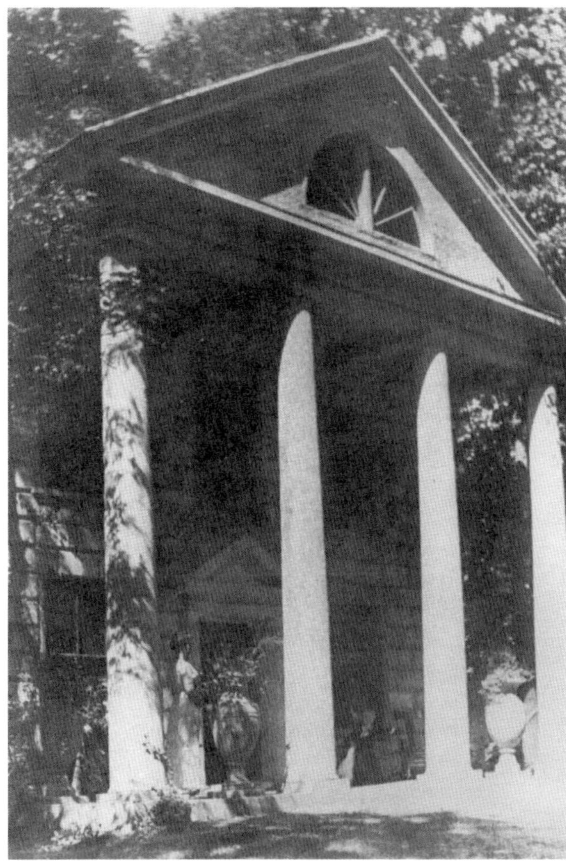

Left: Ellenwood, built in 1909 by illustrator Ellen Schutt as a fireproof house in Cherrydale. *Courtesy of Eleanor Lee Templeman,* Arlington Heritage.

Below: Kincheloe-Febrey House, a former sanitarium that became the Overlee swimming pool clubhouse before it was replaced in 2012. *Courtesy of Tom Dickinson.*

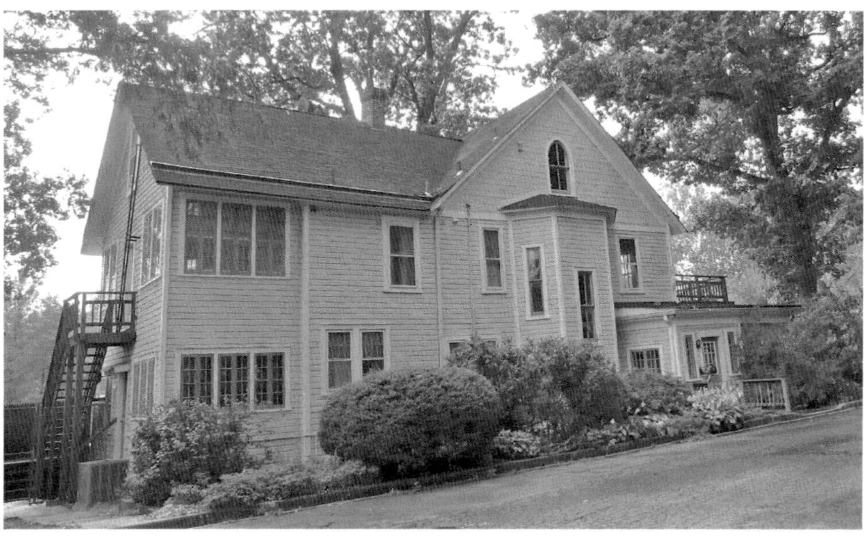

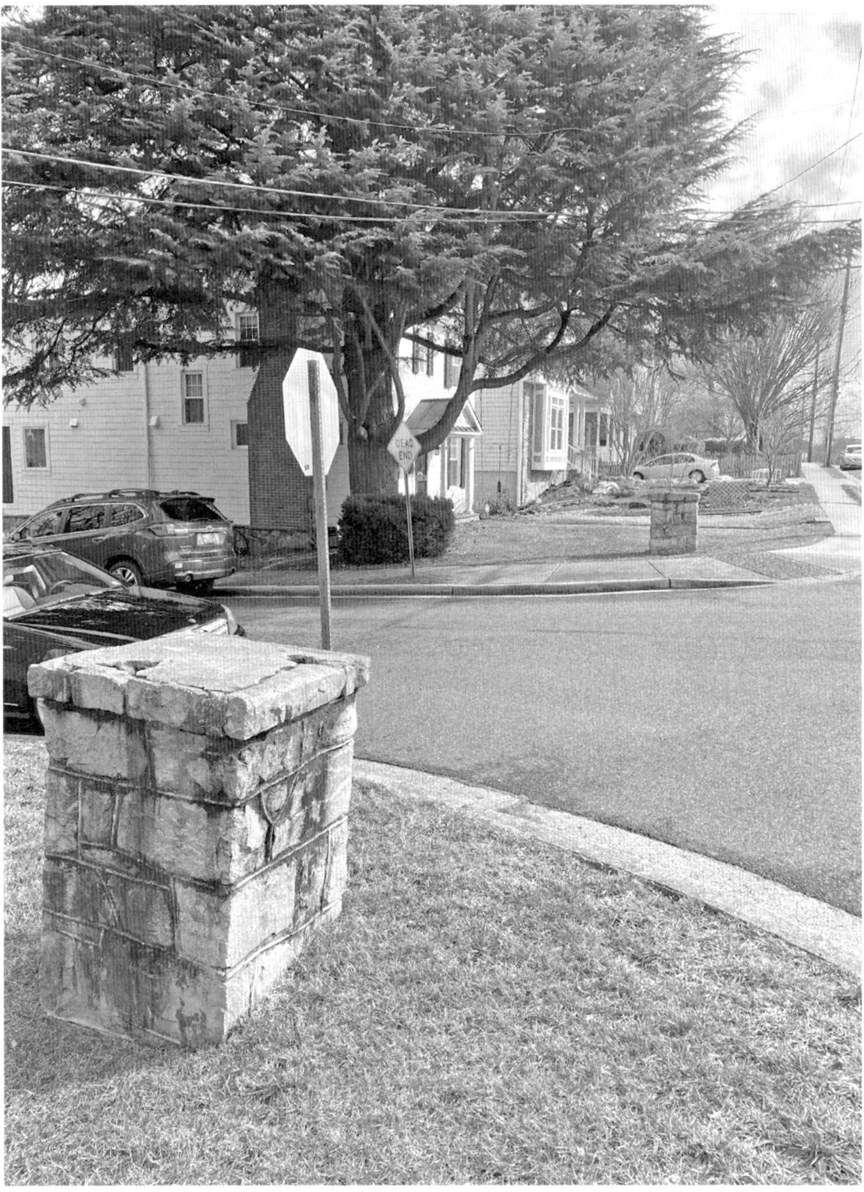

North Quantico Street remnants of the onetime gate of the 1850s plantation on North Powhatan Street, now called Maple Shade. *Author's image.*

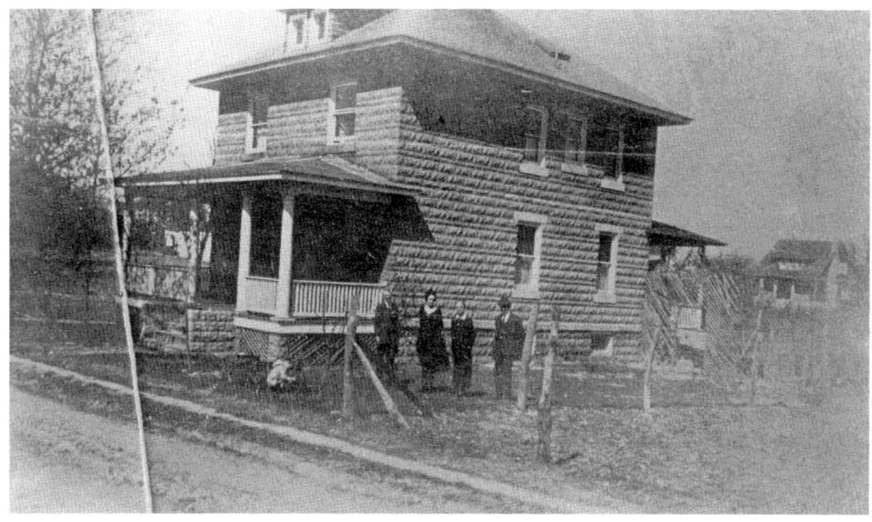

The Newman Sears home in Cherrydale. *Courtesy of the Center for Local History, Arlington Public Library.*

ROWS OF SEARS HOMES

Arlington was a prime customer for the construct-it-yourself homebuilding kits marketed by Sears Roebuck & Co. between 1908 and 1942. Probably one thousand homes of this type sprang up in Arlington neighborhoods, according to the Cherrydale historian Kathryn Holt Springston, who gives tours for the Smithsonian Associates. My favorite was the well-documented Newman home at 1823 North Nelson Street. Completed in 1910, it was inhabited by four generations of that family, and as descendant Robert Newman wrote in the 1987 *Arlington Historical Magazine*, Cherrydale Baptist Church began in its living room. As a boy growing up a block away, this author recalls hair-raising Halloween "scary houses" in the old home's basement. It was demolished in 2012.

OUR ROBINSON SCHOOLS

In July 2017, the 105-year-old Wilson School was reduced to rubble to allow for the construction of Arlington's first high-rise urbanized school, the H-B Woodlawn Secondary Program.

Preservationists were unable pull off their hoped-for miracle.

Weeks before, this author visited that underused utilitarian structure on Wilson Boulevard in upper Rosslyn and perused some documents to learn why passions had risen in this feud between Arlington's heritage and its future livability.

After years of hearings and debate about overcrowded Arlington schools, the school board voted on April 18, 2015, to press on with the Woodlawn move over objections from the Radnor/Fort Myer Heights Civic Association and a unanimous vote that January to restore Wilson by the Historical Affairs and Landmark Review Board.

The building that faced the wrecking ball was constructed in 1910 as Fort Myer Heights School, designed by noted Richmond architect Charles Robinson. It was the fruit of planning that dated as far back as 1902 by neighbors concerned that their children were attending a school using secondhand furniture in a former saloon in Rosslyn.

The two-story neoclassical structure boasted columns, a portico and a cupola, and it was renovated in 1925 to add a septic tank and an athletic field. That was also the year it was named for the recently deceased President Woodrow Wilson, who had spent happy hours cruising the newly paved

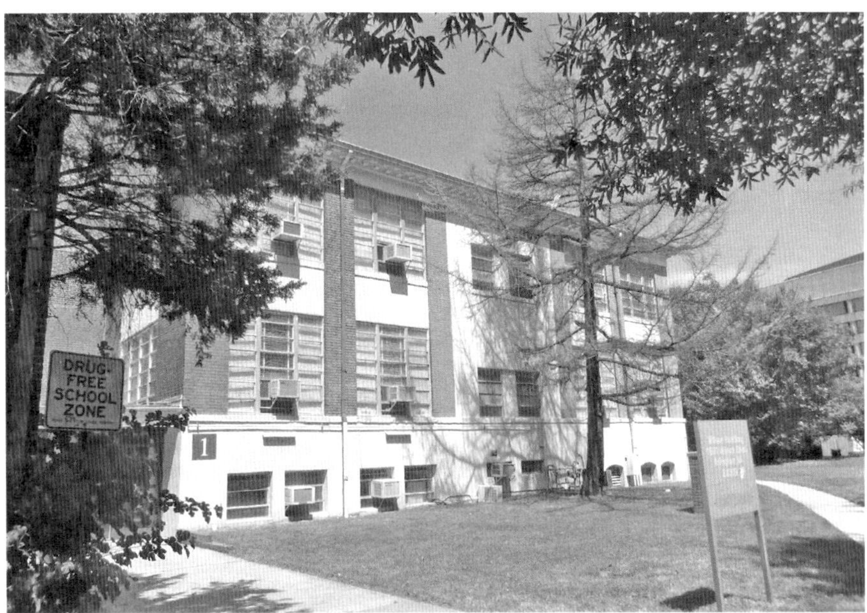

The Wilson School, designed by Charles Robinson, was demolished in 2017. *Courtesy of Tom Dickinson.*

Wilson Boulevard in his Pierce-Arrow, greeting the school's students. (The boulevard itself, previously known as Awbrey's Road and the Georgetown-Falls Church Road, was also renamed in his honor.)

Wilson Elementary School became a beloved alma mater and community gathering place. In August 1930, the Arlington-Fairfax Volunteer Firemen's Association hosted its annual carnival, parade and supper there. The structure was modernized again in 1957 (the fancy portico and columns were later removed), before elementary school classes there ended in 1968.

Ensuing decades saw the school used for employment training and temporary offices when it was not vacant. (It became the home of the Mongolian School of the National Capital Area on Saturdays.)

Civic association president Stanley Karson published letters arguing for a restoration of the "glorious building in its prime" to its 1910 appearance. It was he who approached the landmark review board after feeling "stampeded" by advocates of new high-rises.

Review board chair Joan Lawrence called for a blending of new and old, perhaps through the reuse of ceiling tiles and bricks and historic signage in an imaginative new structure for middle and high school students.

Preservation Arlington, in 2016, placed Wilson on its endangered historic places list, calling it "the longest operating school building in the county that is still owned by the county."

The site embodies a fascinating and well-documented history. When this author visited, the hallways and the multipurpose room made of old ceramic brick brought back memories of their own Arlington school days.

But the school system's current pressures make use of its existing land an imperative. And for the preservation of an Arlington school design circa 1910, one could point to a better example in the former Maury School that is farther west on Wilson (now the Arlington Arts Center).

The issue went before the planning commission, which backed demolition, as did four of five members of the county board. Karson had been lobbying board members, telling this author, "A building doesn't have to be beautiful to be historic."

That demolition left only the Arlington Arts Center near Virginia Square, the former Matthew F. Maury Elementary School that closed in 1975, as the last remaining Arlington structure designed by Charles Robinson. (It began as the Clarendon School in 1909.)

One of the commonwealth's most admired architects, Robinson (1867–1932) worked out of his Richmond firm's offices to design some four hundred education buildings in the early twentieth century. Those buildings included

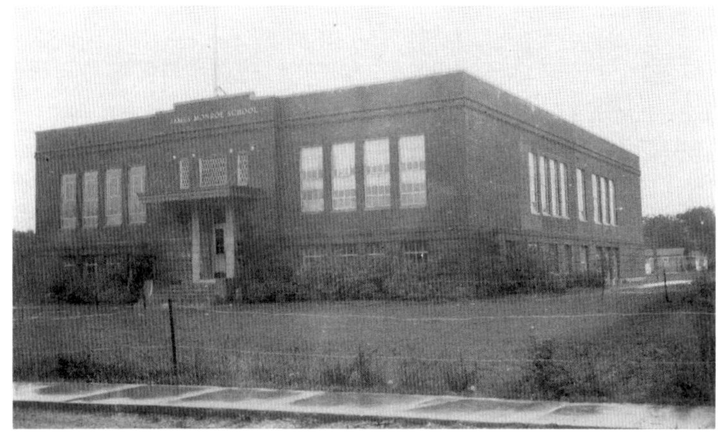
JAMES MONROE SCHOOL

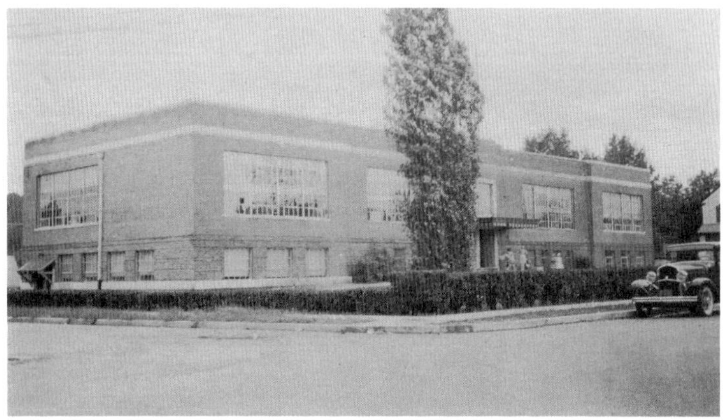

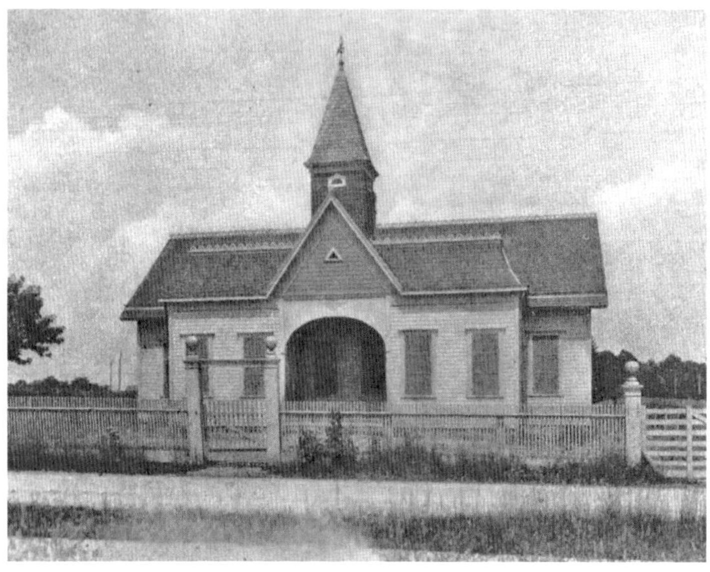

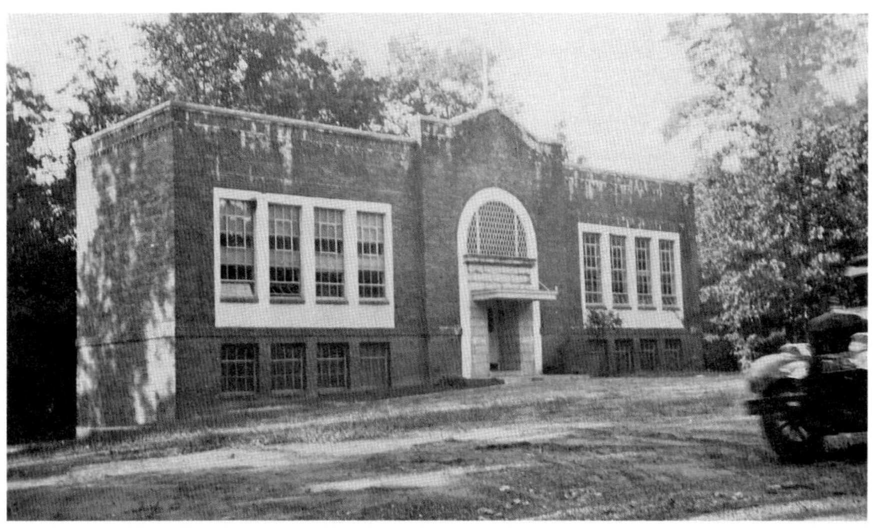

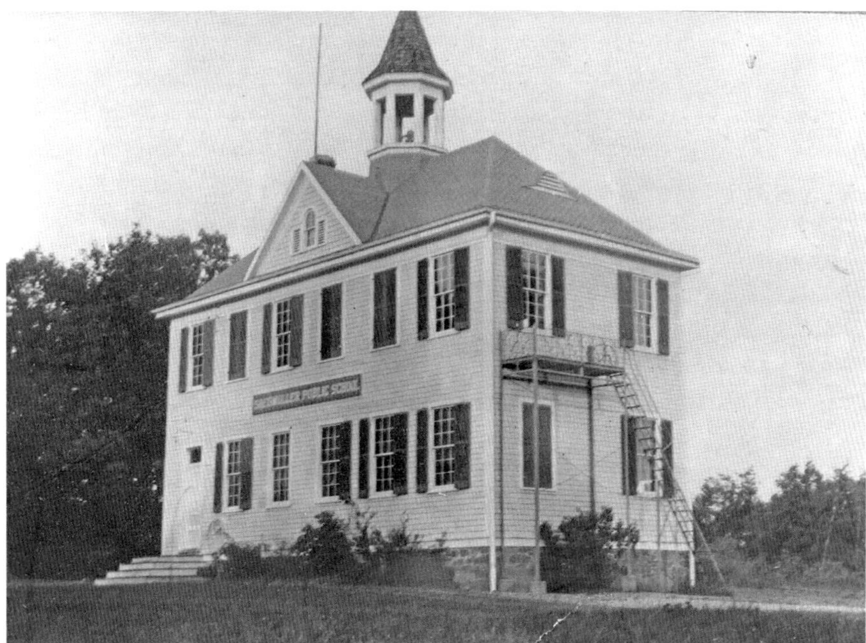

Opposite, top to bottom: James Monroe, Nellie Custis and Carne Schools. *Courtesy of the Arlington Historical Society.*

This page, top to bottom: Woodmont School. *Courtesy of the Arlington Historical Society;* Saegmuller School. *Courtesy of the Center for Local History, Arlington Public Library.*

many in the state capital and dozens on the campuses of what are today the College of William and Mary, the University of Mary Washington, Washington and Lee University, Virginia Commonwealth University, Radford University, Virginia State College, the University of Richmond, Bridgewater College and James Madison University.

But "Robinson Schools" were at the elementary level in counties and cities across Virginia. He designed five in Arlington (called Alexandria County until 1920). Besides Wilson and Maury, other Robinson schools that came and went included Cherrydale (1910), Ballston School (1914) and Barcroft (1924, later rebuilt but still thriving). Robinson also designed the now-defunct Fairfax County elementary schools: Forestville, Bailey Crossroads and Franklin Sherman.

Born in Hamilton, Virginia, the son of an architect, Robinson spent his school years in Canada. As a young man, he was mentored in architecture by notables in Michigan and Pennsylvania. He set up his own firm in Altoona in 1889 before taking his talents back to Richmond.

Though he was equally as prolific in designing sanitariums for public health, Robinson strangely is "relatively unknown today," as Sally Brown, curator of a 2019 exhibit on the man at the Branch Museum of Architecture and Design, told *Richmond Magazine*. "His inventiveness and philosophy of open-air school rooms was important then and now. He seemed to care more about the people and their well-being and the function of the building than many architects today."

Robinson's opus that became Arlington's Wilson School stood out for "its massing, materials [concrete and brick primarily], the alternating brick and window bays along the front facade, the wide frieze band, the decorative cornice with scrolled modillions, and the low-pitched hipped roof," read the Fort Myer Heights neighborhood's application for historic designation.

"Robinson had a rare ability to produce a huge amount of work at a consistently high level," architect Robert Winthrop wrote in *Richmond Architecture* in 2015. His structures "are always well built, logically planned, efficient and handsome. Robinson seemed to have a knack for creating architecturally impressive buildings for the notoriously stingy state, county and city school boards."

The Arlington Arts Center treasures its designated landmark that is listed in the National Register of Historic Places. "Robinson's design has withstood the test of time," said spokeswoman Blair Murphy. "We've worked with really talented artists, and it's wonderful to give them the opportunity to create in an environment with such a striking presence and rich history."

The Castle Called Bay-Eva

High on a wooded cliff near Rosslyn, overlooking the George Washington Memorial Parkway, stands a stone column. It is all that remains of a stunning stone vision once known as the "Bay-Eva Castle." Today, it is seen mostly by "in-the-know" hikers on a path off North Scott Street on the bluff that, during the Civil War, was Fort Bennett.

The moniker contains the first names of Dr. Bay Jacobs, a pioneer in women's medicine, and wife, Eva Harris Jacobs, who built it in the 1930s as a hideaway halfway between the Georgetown and Arlington Hospitals. He

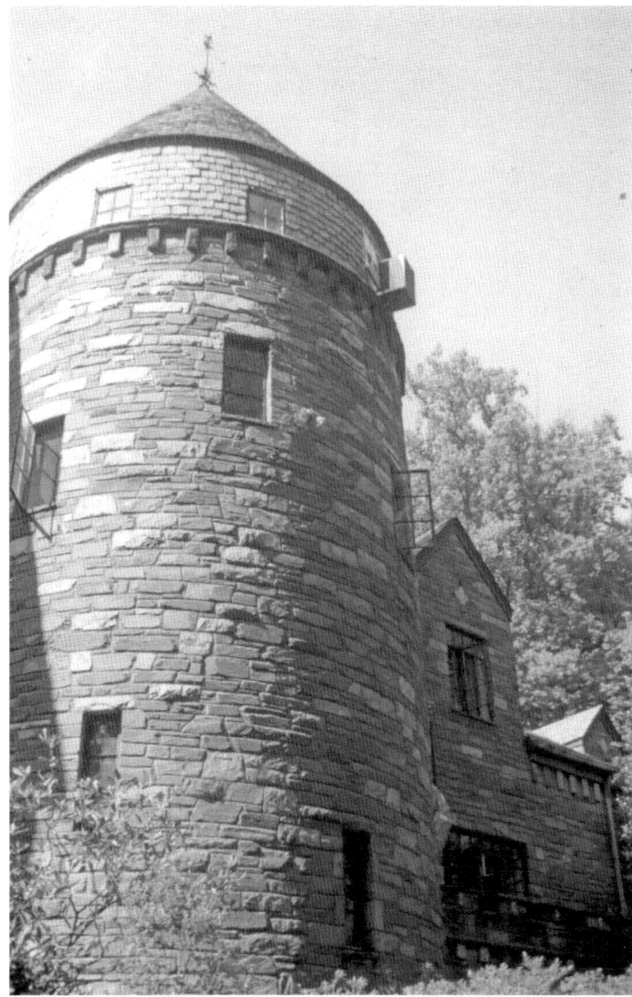

Bay-Eva Castle in upper Rosslyn, named for a couple's first names. *Courtesy of the Center for Local History, Arlington Public Library.*

was a leader as an OB-GYN, and she was the head of a women's business group and a novelist. Her concept for the American "castle" was inspired by medieval styles the couple saw on a trip to Bavaria. They purchased four acres from the Dawson family (Dawson Terrace, Arlington's second-oldest home, is a stone's throw away), as noted by the Center for Local History and a plaque on the site.

When completed, the couple's 9,200-square-foot stone spectacle boasted a slate roof, copper gutters, walls eighteen inches thick, oak flooring, an indoor fish pond and a wrought-iron staircase in the thirty-five-foot-tall central turret. The private couple decorated with French and Jacobean antiques.

Eva died in 1979, Bay in 1988. His heirs gave the property to the American College of Obstetricians and Gynecologists. It was then sold to a developer, whose plans for a community center never panned out. The castle was rented to a succession of twenty-somethings who enjoyed it as an opulent party place before the wrecking ball came in November 1994.

4
OUR RACIAL SAGA

The Notorious Bazil Hall

Nostalgic fans on Facebook, in May 2018, posted memories of passing the home of Bazil Hall, one of Arlington's infamous slaveholders. That's who attached his name to Hall's Hill, one of Arlington's vital Black neighborhoods.

Hall's mid-nineteenth-century farmhouse stood on the 1700 block of North George Mason Drive before it was torn down in 1999 to make a cul-de-sac of red-brick colonials. The two-story yellow farmhouse with eight columns was visible to patients across the street at Virginia Hospital Center.

It was the scene of much drama.

Hall (circa 1806–1888) was born in Washington, D.C. Before homesteading in Arlington, he was an adventurer on a Massachusetts whaling ship. That allowed him to tour South America and eventually California, where he met and married Elizabeth Winner, according to *Arlington Historical Magazine* write-ups by Willard Webb, Donald Wise and Ruth Ward.

In 1850, as a "trimmer of wood," Hall purchased 327 acres around what is now the swath between Lee Highway and North Sixteenth Street.

Hall raised six children (from two marriages) in a home on a four-hundred-foot-tall hill that was valued at $3,000. On the farm that was worked by enslaved labor, he raised fruit, potatoes, oats, cattle, hogs and clover. His worm fence was made of chestnut rails supported by cedar and locust posts.

Bazil Hall worked at his reputation for being hard on enslaved laborers. As contemporary Gaillard Hunt recalled, "Old Hall, as he is familiarly called in

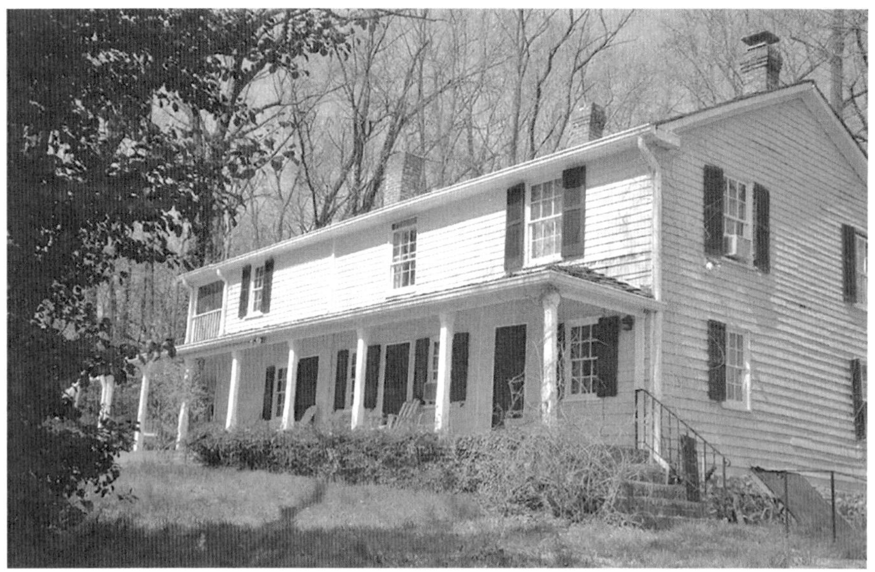

Home of Hall's Hill namesake and plantation owner Bazil Hall, demolished in 1999. *Courtesy of the Center for Local History, Arlington Public Library.*

the county, was a character well remembered because of violent temper and bad habits." He whipped many and shot one "Negro in bravado." A tragedy in Hall's household drew news coverage in the *Evening Star*. His wife clashed with an enslaved woman named Jenny Farr over whether to put more wood on the fire. The angry laborer pushed her mistress into the flames.

Elizabeth Hall died despite ministrations from their neighbor physician George Wunder. Jenny was hanged, and her fate entered Hall's Hill lore.

When the Civil War hit, Hall's life was upended. First, his farmhouse was shelled by Rebel forces from Upton Hill. But after the Second Battle of Bull Run, Union forces cut his trees to better view Upton Hill and Falls Church. They took his hay, corn and mules and burned his house. "My barn and other buildings were also burnt….I had not a bed to lie on nor a roof to put it under when I left the place," he later testified.

Bazil moved in with his sister Mary Ann, the downtown brothel keeper whose Arlington land became Marymount University. "I voted against the ordinance of secession at Ball's Cross Roads," he told Northern soldiers. "I go in for the Union, but I ain't no abolitionist, and any man of common sense will say that slavery is the very best thing for the South."

After the war, he made a $42,450 claim to the Southern Claims Commission set up by Congress. He was granted $10,729.

Hall became a justice of the peace. Beginning in 1866, his land tracts were sold to create what would become a Black neighborhood.

Hall died in that house in 1888 at the age of eighty-three. He was buried on his land with his two wives. But in 1930, the graves were moved to Oakwood Cemetery in Falls Church to make room for Arlington Hospital (now Virginia Hospital Center).

The Hall's Hill Wall

Black History Month brings volumes of hidden history out from Arlington's shadows. The author never ceases to be astonished at how much neighborhood lore they missed while growing up here.

On February 26, 2017, a crowd of 150 gathered for the ceremonial unveiling of the new marker for the "Hall's Hill Wall" at North Seventeenth and Culpeper Streets. Their podium, folding chairs and refreshments table were arrayed in front of an unprepossessing seven-foot-tall cinder block barrier. County and school board members and preservation officials joined with the Hall's Hill/High View Park Historic Preservation Coalition to admire the metallic sign that had just been installed beside the remnant of a once-longer racial divide.

The easy-to-miss structure dates back to the 1930s, when the White subdivision of Woodlawn Village erected it to avoid mingling with Black residents. In the late 1950s, Black children removed a chunk to clear access to a creek, and by 1966, with desegregation clearly the future's wave, most of the rest came down, the sign explains.

"A wall can't keep us from your love," said the prayer led by a clergywoman, which was followed by recollections from decades-long residents of Hall's Hill who grew up traveling to segregated schools back when George Mason Drive was called Frederick Street. "Hall's Hill, for 150 years, was a community where everyone knew everyone," said emcee Portia Haskins. "We helped raise each other's children."

"When I moved to Arlington in the 1980s, I didn't know anything about this," said County Manager Mark Schwartz. "I was stunned, but in a way, I'm glad there's a remnant—what is past is prologue."

For cultural and economic reasons, many Black enclaves in Arlington have come and gone outside of the consciousness of mainstream White residents. You can read about them in the *Guide to the African American Heritage of Arlington County, Virginia*, by John Liebertz of the county planning staff.

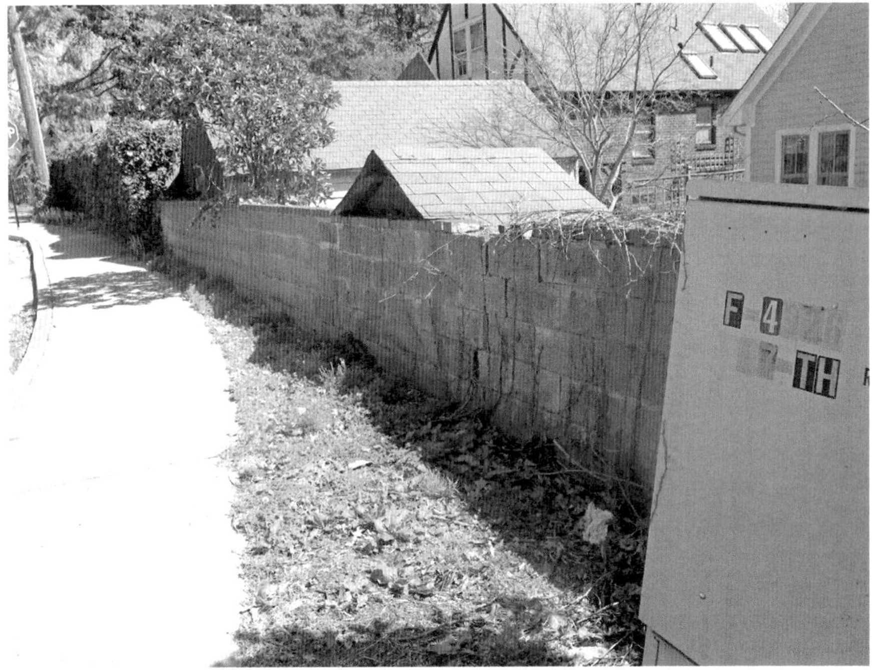

Remnant of a 1930s segregation wall in Hall's Hill. *Courtesy of Tom Dickinson.*

Several of these communities were recalled vividly by Dr. Alfred Taylor, an educator and historian of the Green Valley neighborhood who spoke on February 9, 2017, at the Woman's Club of Arlington. Besides Hall's Hill, there are numerous South Arlington offshoots of Freedman's Village, the 1870s community of free Black residents in what is now Arlington National Cemetery. The mainstay was Nauck (named for German landowner John Nauck), now called Green Valley (named for its beauty by another White developer).

South Arlington also brought East Arlington and Queen City near the Pentagon and Johnson Hill (Walter Reed Drive) and Penrose (also called Hatfield) off Columbia Pike. In Ballston, the Black reverend Galloway sold the land that became Parkington for $85,000 in 1950, Taylor said. There was a Black community on Moore Street in Rosslyn.

Among those that have vanished in recent decades are the Dunbar and George Washington Carver Homes, both projects supported by mutual home assistance societies, and the Arna Valley Apartments off South Glebe Road.

During Black History Month in February 2018, a commemoration of a different sort sprang up spontaneously on the Facebook page "I Grew Up in Arlington, VA."

Sydney Williams, a sixty-eight-year-old graduate of what was then called Washington-Lee High School now living in West Bay, Cayman Islands, lit up the site with bittersweet recollections of growing up in Hall's Hill, "a self-contained community": "As children, we did not have to venture out for much," wrote Williams, who has a master's in theology and worked in corrections in Virginia. "Ms. Allen's store sold everything a kid could want—two-for-a-penny cookies, cold soda, fried bologna sandwiches, chips. If you did not want to walk down from the playground, you could go to Mr. Montrose's bus (converted into a store). Hall's Hill [was] self-sustained, walled-off, isolated, safe and secure. Segregation was great!"

Williams did not mean that the Jim Crow laws and customs were fine. From 1950 to 1962, Hall's Hill was "like a county within a county. I could not go to the movies [or] the pools" or use the close-by Arlington Hospital, he noted.

"When I attended Stratford [Junior High], we still were not totally accepted as blacks," he wrote. "I was the only black on Stratford's basketball team....Every night, I had to walk through the white neighborhood in the dark by myself. I moved at a fast pace through dark places. I did not feel safe until I got to Lee Highway Peoples Drug Store."

Williams paid tribute to his grandfather Edward T. Morton, one of the first Black doctors from Hall's Hill. "We had black educators, professional racecar drivers, dentists, [and] excellent athletes," he continued. Other colorful characters were called Popcorn, Chick or Mother Goose and Pop Burrel. "Pop provided softball equipment for us before [the Recreation Department would]," he said. Often saluting, Pop "would dress in his World War II uniform and march to the playground with a burlap bag of balls and bats and gloves for everybody. The only catch to him providing the equipment was he had to umpire. He was the worst."

Several White respondents mentioned the historic plaque for the segregation wall. Another White member of the Facebook page recalled finding the 1951 deed to her North Arlington home that contained a covenant saying only "Caucasians and gentiles" could buy it.

Williams apologized for the unexpected discourse. "Even though it may appear that because of the racial climate of the times that it was hard or bad or unfair, that is not the case. Our parents prevented and shielded us from even thinking it was bad. Our childhood was wonderful, funny and interesting."

On November 13, 2019, the auditorium at Virginia Hospital Center rung with multigenerational music, nostalgia and tears of pain expressed by four who lived through Arlington's (ongoing) transition out of segregation.

As part of a multiday event funded by a Virginia humanities grant, the event titled "Learn From This Place: Bringing Arlington to Halls Hill" offered bittersweet recollections of the 1950s, when Black residents weren't allowed in Arlington Hospital, in movie theaters or on pony rides.

Wilma Jones Killgo, the author of a history of Hall's Hill, presented Black heritage songs performed on cigar box banjos by middle school students in career and technical education.

Traditional songs such as "You Are My Sunshine" and "Goin' Down the Road Feelin' Bad" were adapted to Hall's Hill memories of being forced to walk ten blocks to school after the Langston School closed and being late for faraway Little League games. To the guitar and harmonica strains of a blues duo, Junious Brickhouse performed a muscular dance.

Among the gray panelists was retired teacher William Vollin (who taught at Langston and Glebe, where he was also the principal). Born in the defunct Arlington neighborhood of Queen City, he recalled the Hoffman-Boston all-Black K-12 school with its "hand-me-down books" and no science lab. At Langston, the "food staff and custodians were like counselors," he said. Decisions on school boundaries were made by "racist" school boards so as not to "upset folks on the other side of Lee Highway." When asked by officials for the racial breakdown of Glebe Elementary, Vollin replied, "We're 100 percent human beings."

Michael Jones, one of the four Black residents tapped to integrate Stratford Junior High in 1959, said at Langston Elementary, "There was no remediation—we just fit in." Growing up with seven people sharing a bathroom "made us closer."

The adjustment to being "socially marginalized" at White schools was jarring after spending their early years in a Hall's Hill school "that taught us we had a lot to offer, to love, give and trust," said Kitty Clark Stevenson, now a human resources consultant. At Swanson Middle School, the drama teacher told her she couldn't appear on stage, and a counselor said she would "make a very good maid." Stevenson described "ragged" textbooks from which they had to "erase crude, profane language. Thank you, Arlington," she said, "for the best cuss words I learned."

Saundra Green, retired from Arlington Parks and Recreation, recalled "wonderful role models" in Hall's Hill, where "your schoolteacher may also be your Sunday school teacher," and a shopkeeper "your scout leader."

When switching schools, she had to give up her plans to be a cheerleader or sing in select chorus. When she came to work professionally as the director at the Lee Community Center, Green overheard a staffer calling her a monkey and being asked, "Are you the new custodian?"

She later became friends with that staffer.

Building Black Housing

The prominent name Syphax is associated by most Arlingtonians with education activist Evelyn Syphax, for whom the education center is named.

The family name is also intertwined with the history of Arlington House, where enslaved members of that family toiled and eventually became free and highly accomplished—their ancestor Maria Syphax, historians now recognize, was the secret daughter of plantation owner George Washington Parke Custis.

But there's another Syphax branch that merits fresh recognition. William Thomas Syphax (1920–1989) and his wife, Margarite (as of this writing, she is still living at the age of ninety-eight), from the 1950s to the 1980s, loomed as major figures in Arlington's business community. The Ballston-based W.T. Syphax Real Estate Co. and Syphax Management Co. landed the millionaires' companies in the nation's top one hundred Black-owned businesses in the early 1970s. They were written up in *Newsweek* and *Black Enterprise*. Margarite was invited for honors at the White House during the Nixon administration.

But as their daughter Carolyn Syphax-Young explained in 2020, they got their start battling to improve the substandard housing and water systems that were endured under segregation by many Black residents, both in Arlington and in the greater Washington, D.C. area. They built in William's childhood neighborhood of Arlington View (previously Johnson Hill), as well as Highland Park and Green Valley. The couple's first apartment complex was the seventy-seven-unit Arlington View Terrace, which had garden-style apartments on South Rolfe Street, near the Army Navy Country Club.

As noted in a Central Library Center for Local History exhibit, William and Margarite met while doing USO work during World War II. She was a dancer and an electronics engineer. After receiving a rich postwar education—William earned a master's degree in engineering administration from George Washington University and a PhD in behavioral philosophy

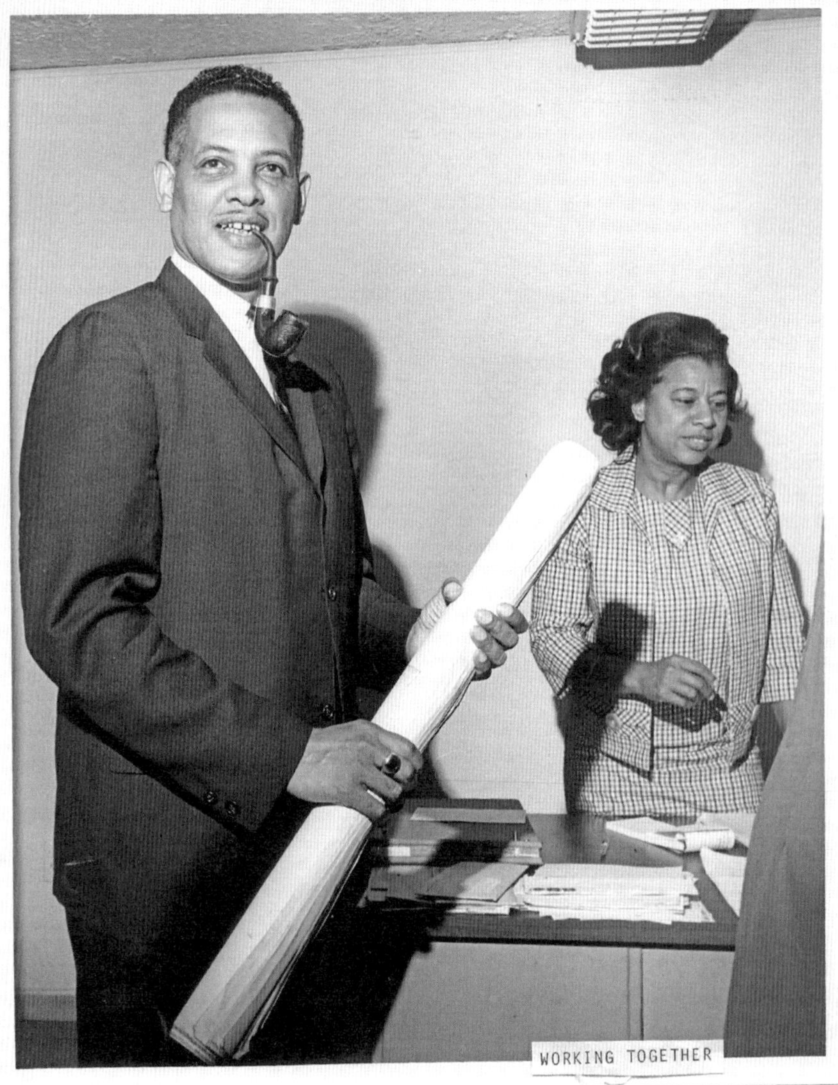

Housing entrepreneurs William and Margarite Syphax. *Courtesy of the Center for Local History, Arlington Public Library.*

from Pacific Western University—the couple moved to Arlington's South Queen Street. They set to work to plug a yawning gap in available housing simply by ignoring the practice of racial restrictions on renters—still common in the 1950s and 1960s. By 1959, they had built one hundred custom homes, too.

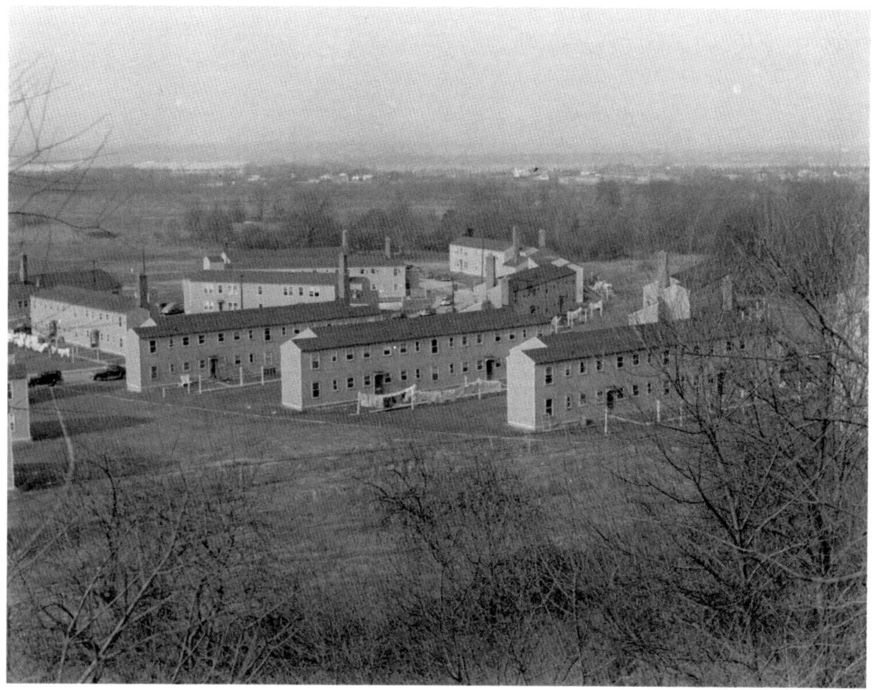

Fast-built wartime apartments that were open to White people were named for Confederate hero Jubal Early. Black residents were restricted to the nearby Carver and Dunbar Apartments. *Courtesy of the Center for Local History, Arlington Public Library.*

William was the developer and Margarite the secretary-treasurer, though she ventured out to work as one of the few females seen on construction sites. He became the president of the Virginia Real Estate Brokers Association, chairman of the Arlington County Building Code Board of Appeals and, at one point, the director of the Arlington County Red Cross.

She was one of the first Black businesswomen to earn the title of certified property manager from the Institute of Real Estate Management of the National Association of Real Estate Boards. She also served on Arlington's 1976 Bicentennial Commission.

This author read the history center's oral history interview with William, conducted in 1988 by civil rights attorney Edmund Campbell. He mentioned the property his ancestors received from Custis, stretching from today's Sheraton Hotel to the Marine Barracks, to one of Arlington National Cemetery's two mausoleums (see page 124). His father's dairy delivered milk to Fort Myer. He and Margarite were friendly with their neighbor Leone Buchholz, a county board member in the 1950s. He recalled that the streetcar line had a Syphax station and that some of his family members were buried in the graves on the former Odd Fellows property near Columbia Pike.

These Syphaxes were also philanthropic—William regularly befriended students at the segregated Hoffman-Boston Public School. He sent more than one hundred children to college, according to his daughter. "He was never the type to have a Cadillac."

A Lost Black Cemetery

In the mid-1960s, a fuss was made over the neglect of a "Negro cemetery" that was being moved from the intersection of Columbia Pike and Washington Boulevard. Thanks to reader Tim Kirk, the author was able to spot, hidden amid shrubbery near the Sheraton Hotel, a higgledy-piggledy array of dozens of graying tombstones. The 2009 Foxcroft Heights Neighborhood Conservation Plan suggests that they are likely leftovers of Black graves dating back to Freedman's Village days in 1870, after the firmer graves were relocated to the Alexandria section of Fairfax County.

By 2018, many of those same relocated graves had fallen into disrepair out in the Alexandria section of Fairfax County. An alarm was raised that summer by Dean DeRosa, then an interpretive park ranger for the National Park Service at Arlington House. He sent this author news clips and legal documents describing the clash that began in 1964. He expressed concerns over the "sad condition" of the Fairfax graves with names like Gray and Syphax that were so intertwined with Arlington House heritage.

The Black graves in plots at 1600 Columbia Pike, since 1880, had been sold and maintained by the Stevens Lodge no. 1435 of the Odd Fellows of Alexandria, Arlington County, Virginia. Details were spelled out in the *Northern Virginia Sun* in 1967 and in a write-up by an Arlington Genealogy Club's survey of local cemeteries.

Many of the founders of this Black lodge were formerly enslaved under George Washington Parke Custis and Robert E. Lee. They sold burial plots on two acres near what became the Marine Post at Henderson Hall for as little as five dollars. It eventually contained 700 graves, though only 164 were identified.

By the late 1950s—the last burial was in 1959—the Odd Fellows, whose headquarters had burned down, could no longer maintain the cemetery.

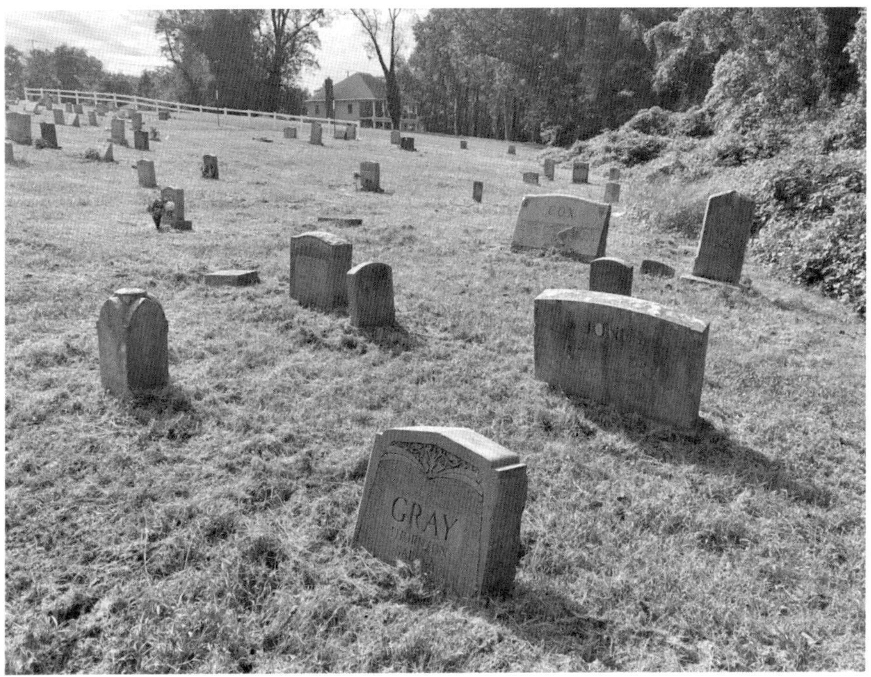

The cemetery of Arlington House's former enslaved workers in Fairfax. *Author's image.*

"Abandoned Graveyard Suffers from Abuse, Neglect," shouted the *Sun* headline. Reporter Deborah Sollers wrote of "flattened gray-green of yucca plants and an occasional clump of plastic flowers." Vandals had struck, a casket was showing through overgrown brush and neighborhood children had built a treehouse there.

In 1964, KCM Corp., planning to build what is the Sheraton Hotel today, applied to acquire the land from the Odd Fellows and was then eager to sell. A Circuit Court OK'd the waiver from a Virginia law against using cemetery land for other purposes.

The corporation paid $149,000 to move two hundred–plus graves to Fairfax (some graves were moved to Suitland, Maryland). Surviving descendants were compensated. Surveys also mention that some Black graves that were originally located at Calloway United Methodist Church at 5000 Lee Highway were also moved to the Coleman Cemetery.

The author drove to that cemetery in an Alexandria residential subdivision on 1900 Collingwood Road, near Hollin Hall. He found many headstones tilted and half-buried, their texts marred. He scoured to find markers for the famous Grays—Selina and Thornton, Harry, Sarah and Emma, as well as Ennis and Emma Syphax. Many headstones are unidentified.

The contacts this author made with local civic associations and the nonprofit Fairfax County Cemetery Preservation Association showed only that the cemetery was deeded in 1944 to the Churches and Fraternities Association of Alexandria.

This author learned that the same disrepair at Coleman was documented back in 1998, in surveys made by the Fairfax Genealogical Society and the Mount Vernon Genealogical Society. They noted no indicators of which graves had come over from Arlington.

There is no caretaker's office. A sign warns that without perpetual care, the grass will not be cut due to rising labor costs. Another sign posts a phone number for the Coleman Cemetery Association with a modern 571 prefix. This author traced the number online to Arlington, but it is inoperative.

So, there, in 2018, the trail of responsibility for Arlington's graves in exile went cold.

DIGGING UP BLACK HISTORY

Steve Hammond's ongoing retirement project is ferreting out new truths about Arlington.

A seventh-generation descendant of the Syphax family who came up from slavery at Arlington House, Hammond—still a scientist emeritus after forty years at the U.S. Geological Survey—in 2021 was busy with a flurry of presentations about his ancestry, reinterpretations of local history and policy advocacy.

His pandemic-era Zoom talks included an exploration of family patriarch William Syphax (circa 1773–1850), who bought his freedom in 1817 and set up a business next to the historic Carlyle House in Alexandria. This Syphax worked with a neighbor, Quaker pharmacist and abolitionist Edward Stabler, to save money to free the rest of his family.

Equally groundbreaking is Hammond's talk on ancestor Nancy Syphax (circa 1791–1880), her enslavement at Decatur House in Washington, D.C., and her being sold down to New Orleans. This author heard his lecture on Louisiana ancestor Peter Joseph (1842–1906), who was named an elector for the controversial 1876 presidential election.

Hammond supplements stories passed down in the family with census documents, manumission papers and news clippings. His "reconstructing a family narrative" approach is researched around his concept of FAN—family, associates and neighbors. A resident of Sterling, he gets help from his California cousin Donna Kunkel in keeping scattered Syphax descendants informed about Arlington House.

Joining the Arlington House Foundation helped Hammond pitch in when the National Park Service created its new exhibit on the enslaved community. The assertion that the plantation's builder, George Washington Parke Custis (1781–1857), fathered at least one child with an enslaved woman is explored in a 2018 talk Hammond gave to the Smithsonian's National Museum of African American History.

He is also conversant in the contributions of John Syphax (1838–1906), a leader among the formerly enslaved at Freedman's Village. That Syphax, in 1888, wrote to Secretary of War W.C. Bodicott to protest the "horrid" conditions at the government-run compound. The result: compensation for residents before the village was closed in 1900. (See page 38.)

Hammond helps create family trees, showing genealogical links between certain Syphaxes and Martha Washington via Maria Syphax's probable status as an illegitimate daughter of Custis. Her wedding in 1821 in the mansion and Custis's subsequent freeing of Maria and her children with a gift of land are clues that bolster the oral tradition.

The Syphax descendants still hope for collaboration with Lee-Custis kin to compare results of DNA tests as a sort of cooperative "truth serum," Hammond confides.

In the fall of 2020, Hammond boosted legislation to remove slavery-defender and Confederate general Robert E. Lee from the site's official name. Calling it simply "Arlington House" would make the park service memorial "more inclusive of everyone who worked, lived and died there," Hammond said.

And as Arlington's county board has empaneled volunteers to explore alternatives to the Arlington House logo, Hammond took a complex position. He doesn't buy one board member's notion that Arlington House, being federal property, isn't linked to our modern community. Yet, he would "encourage the park service to realize its responsibility to be more community-oriented and work with the county as a partner and stakeholder."

5
MODERN ARLINGTON LIVING

The Never-Was Bridge

Electronic signs for rush-hour toll lanes on ten miles of I-66 opened in Arlington and point to the west in December 2017.

Solo drivers who were willing to shell out a few extra bucks began to benefit—if they procured an E-Z Pass—from the commuter highway at peak hours.

The high-tech solution offered by HOT (high-occupancy toll) lanes would have been unimaginable to our forebears when they battled over an earlier "solution" to Arlington's clogged auto arteries: the proposal to build another span over the Potomac called the Three Sisters Bridge.

Named for those peeking mid-river rocks made legendary by the Natives, this project—which dominated Arlington politics in the 1960s—has a long history. Thoughts of constructing a bridge aligned between the Spout Run Parkway and Georgetown date back to the 1950s. (Actually, you could trace them to the eighteenth century, according to Wikipedia.)

The post–World War II period was a time of car worship (recall that I-66 itself was originally envisioned as a twelve-lane road with no sound walls) and little environmental consciousness. Federal proposals for the Three Sisters Bridge had the support of Arlington's Republican representative Joel T. Broyhill and Virginia Democratic senator William Spong. The notion was to capitalize on federal highway aid to unclog Arlington and speed the daily journeys of federal workers from Fairfax or Prince William.

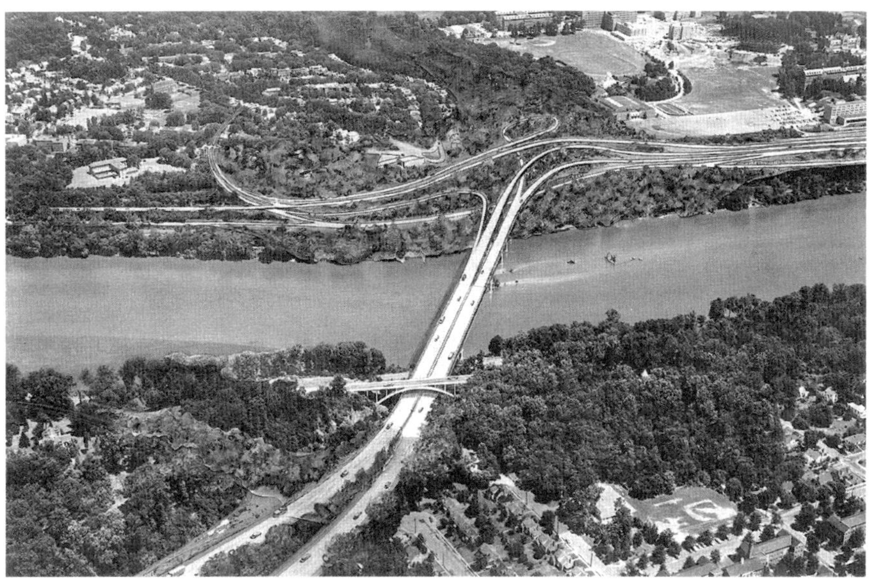

A transportation planner's vision of Three Sisters Bridge. *Courtesy of the District of Columbia Transportation Department, and courtesy of Ghosts of D.C.*

In a drama that lasted for more than a decade, the bridge was opposed by the Arlington County Board; many Georgetown and Washington, D.C. voters in a referendum; and grassroots protesters.

One lawsuit went to the Supreme Court, and a House committee chairman named William Natcher (D-Kentucky) held up funds to build the Metro for years, waiting for the Three Sisters to win approval. Arlington-based Broyhill tried to block the appropriation for the district if the Three Sisters wasn't funded. (Broyhill later changed and got the Metro funded.)

"Build the Bridge," admonished an editorial in the *Northern Virginia Sun* on August 28, 1968, slamming county officials for their lawsuit and requested injunction. "It is sad that parklands must be taken for feeder roads to the bridge," it wrote. But "if it is not, Northern Virginia's economy will be strangled simply because there will not be enough routes into and through the area."

Begging to differ was board member Thomas Richards, who said the project "would mean the loss of much of the beautiful Spout Run Parkway in Arlington and would mar the beauty of the Potomac Palisades."

Some five hundred protesters occupied the rocky Potomac islets that were accessible only by boat, the *Washington Post* reported.

Other opponents, including the fledgling Congressional Black Caucus, fought the Nixon administration, fearing the bridge and downtown roadways would destroy Black neighborhoods.

In the end, the final nails in the Three Sisters' coffin weren't hammered until 1977, when I-66 won final approval.

WHEN I-66 SHOOK UP ARLINGTON

Among the more vivid shared experiences of Arlingtonians in the 1950s through the 1980s was the drawn-out arrival of Interstate 66.

That divisive federal–state construction project required confiscation, under eminent domain, of 1,054 land parcels that contained homes, parks, gardens and dozens of businesses.

This confiscation effort was spread over four decades. Conflict over the eventual $275 million road lasted from the visioning that began in 1958, to the right-of-way finalized in 1966, to lawsuits and protests by environmentalists, to the downscaled compromise design in the 1977 federal Coleman report and the paving that allowed its opening in 1982.

Opponents—among the first to take advantage of the required Environmental Impact Statement under the 1970 National Environmental Policy Act—feared noise, pollution, dividing of neighborhoods and the unsightly twelve-lane concept behind the original design. Among the ringleaders of the resistance were Jim and Emelia Govan, who rallied a grassroots movement to the Arlington Coalition on Transportation.

John Reeder, speaking in 2019, recalled being active from 1976 to 1982 with a group called Continuing Action on Transportation and Environment (CONTACT), cochaired by Marianne Karydes. "Ted Neff of the Maywood neighborhood got that area designated as a national and local historic district to oppose I-66 demolition," Reeder said. At one point, he and a co-activist had a confrontation with a store detective outside the old Sears in Clarendon, where they were asking passersby to sign anti-I-66 petitions. The police were also called in, but CONTACT leader Karydes called a county board member and got the authorities to back off.

"Our original next-door neighbors, Mr. and Ms. Larry Potter, were active in opposition to I-66," recalled Cherrydale resident Bob Witeck. "They gave us their 'Stop I-66' bumper stickers and early 1960s photos of homes that were picked up intact, trussed securely onto trucks and moved a couple blocks away."

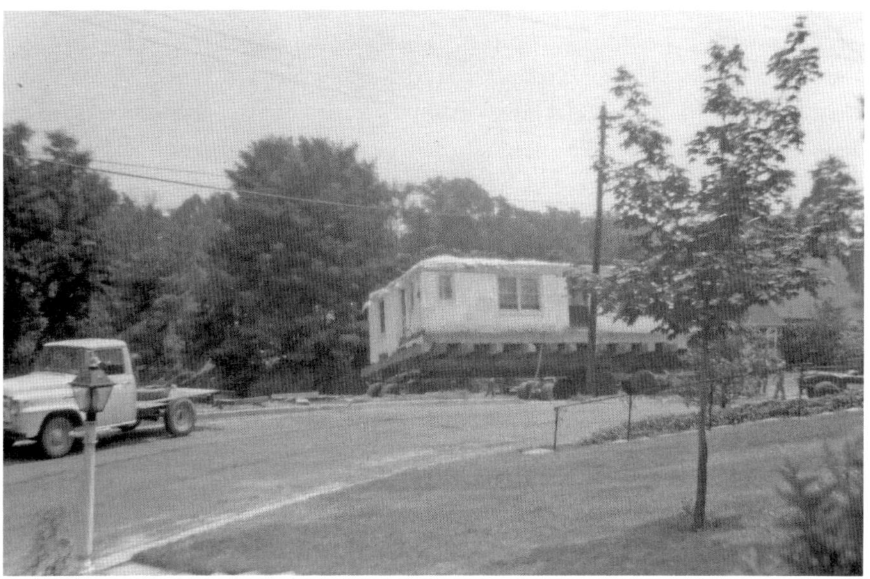

Homes were relocated to make room for a divisive new interstate. *Courtesy of Bob Connolly.*

There was a (largely) tongue-in-cheek contest to name the new highway, the *Arlington Journal* noted. The Arlington Historical Society proposed naming it for Black medical pioneer and onetime Arlingtonian Charles Drew. But many entries were cynical parodies from opponents of the highway, who proposed naming it after King George, Virginia governor Mills Godwin or Carter administration transportation secretary Brock Adams.

No one could argue that the advent of the much-debated I-66 didn't alter Arlington profoundly.

Retired Virginia Transportation Department land-use planner Tom VanPoole still owns a copy of one of the plans in the state's full collection of I-66 right-of-way plan sheets. It shows the site of the Frank Lloyd Wright–designed Usonian Pope-Leighey House, which was transported from Falls Church to Woodlawn plantation.

Former Maywood resident Sam Day, in 2019, recalled an array of stores around Kirkwood Road at Lee Highway that disappeared—Steve's Diner, the Village Market and Young's Bicycle Shop. At Arlington's Falls Church border, Ware's Pharmacy was forced to relocate, realtor Ed Downs remembered. And retired Fairfax teacher Carmen Clark Colliatie recalled how her First Church of Christ Scientist of Arlington was condemned and rebuilt on North McKinley Road.

Those who lost homes suffered the most anguish. "When the lawsuits got going, some people didn't move out, and maybe one or two people per block were left," said homebuilder Terry Showman. Phil Lord, who lost his house at 1409 North Utah Street, added, "It was strange to have so many vacant houses around—like no man's land."

Lynnette Yount, a leadership coach and minister's daughter, in 2019, said her "parents were truly screwed over" when the state offered a price that was "abysmally low. Luckily, my mother was a good financial planner, and my parents had saved enough for a lot and having their dream house built." But she was forced to switch high schools from Washington-Lee to Yorktown.

Jean McMahon told this writer of the "shock and disappointment" of her parents when they were told in 1963 that the North Twenty-Fourth Street house they'd owned and expanded since the 1940s was doomed. They, too, were offered "a very low amount" but got a lawyer to up it by a few thousand dollars. "I distinctly remember the 'rush' of trying to find a new home because of the new road," she says. But construction wouldn't start for nearly a decade.

J. Miles McFee and his sister Melissa McFee Stricker, in 2014, compiled a history of their parents' adventure of responding to I-66 by moving not once but three times.

"My father's comment was to name it 'that fricking road,'" Miles McFee said in 2019 about his homes near Williamsburg Boulevard and Westmoreland Street. "While he was not happy about the right-of-way taking our house and the corner of the property, he ended up buying the house back from the state for $600 (after they paid him $17,679) and moving it to the other side of the lot. He ended up buying two other houses close by along the way, which worked out well with respect to real estate investment."

Melissa McFee added, "Our dad, being a World War II veteran, decided to take the opportunity of the privileges given to veterans when buying a home with the GI Bill benefits. However, one of the requirements was we had to live in that house. In the spring of 1965, after only six months in the house on 27th Road, we moved back 'down the hill' into 6943 North 28th Street. The entire real estate adventure became our father's 'pension plan.'"

Diane Kresh, director of Arlington Public Libraries, remembered the surprise of losing her home at the corner of North Twenty-Ninth and Wyoming Streets. "The amount of money my parents were offered was maybe $17,000 or $19,000, and they were upset that the [similar] houses flanking theirs were valued higher," she said. "My family moved [nearby] during the week of the John F. Kennedy burial. The old lot remained vacant for years. There was a huge willow tree in the backyard that remained until the bulldozers started clearing for I-66 construction," Kresh recalled. "I still think about that tree…still sad it's gone."

REMNANTS OF OUR FARMS

What remains of Arlington's agricultural heritage? As "farm country" for the city of Alexandria, the area that is Arlington, in the nineteenth century, became a key supplier for Alexandria County as well as downtown Washington, D.C. markets. In 1840, the corn crops totaled 18,800 bushels, plus wheat, barley oats, rye and buckwheat, as noted by C.B. Rose. Arlington hosted thirty farms of one hundred to five hundred acres and forty more of fifty to one hundred acres, 1860 Census figures showed. Enslaved workers, leading up to the Civil War and emancipation, numbered 290 in the 1840 Census, with 235 "free colored" working mostly on farms.

The two family farms that would operate well into the twentieth century were run by the Reeves family (on two acres at today's Bluemont Park) and the Crossmans (their home still stands at North Underwood Street in East Falls Church).

Third-generation farmer Nelson Reeves was born in 1900 in the farmhouse. The operation known as Reevesland raised crops and dairy cattle. In 1932, the family began using modernized milking machines, staying in business until 1955, when, as the county's website notes, tank trucks replaced milk cans.

"Farming is a good life, although a hard life," a retired Reeves wrote in the 1975 *Arlington Historical Magazine*. "We had to get up at four o'clock in the morning. I started to help milking when I was big enough to sit on a milking stool and the old cow wouldn't switch me off with her tail." Reeves also worked for forty-six years with the Election Board, beginning in 1924 as a clerk in the Glencarlyn Precinct and then as a registrar, election judge and courthouse commissioner. The Reeves family, for decades, owned a special place in Arlingtonians' hearts. After Nelson Reeves gave it up in the mid-1950s, his land became a county park and Little League fields, the hill in front of his home prized for winter sledding.

In 2001, the county quickly bought the property, "enlarged the heavily used Bluemont Park and provided additional recreational opportunities

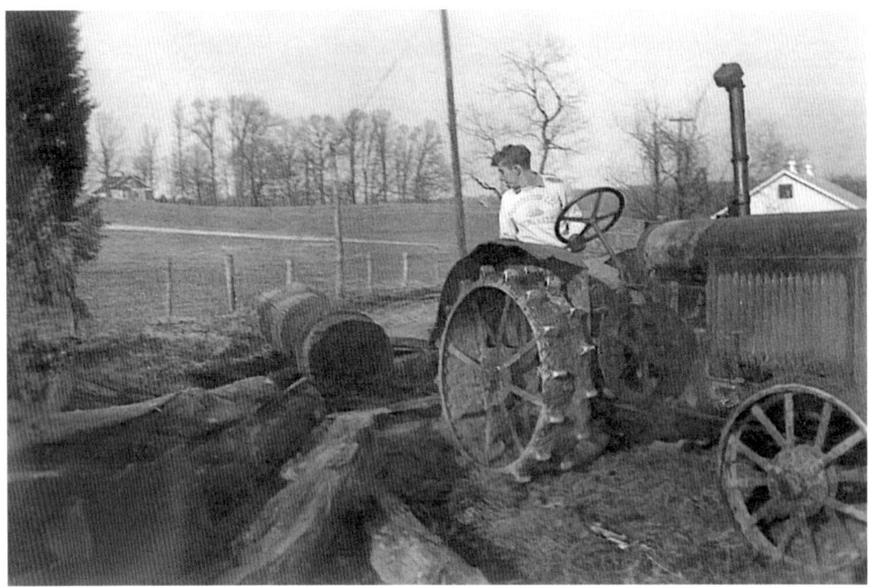

The last Arlington farmer, Nelson Reeves, at work. *Courtesy of the Center for Local History, Arlington Public Library.*

to county residents," as the historic preservation office phrased it. The acquisition of the 2.4-acre property protected the much-loved sledding hill, a neighborhood and school garden and milking shed, and it would (hopefully) preserve the remaining portion of the county's last dairy farm.

But there was indecision on how to use it. Could it be an education center—a wedding venue? After years of indecision, the county, in 2010, began looking for alternative private ownership. Neighbors and preservationists struggled for years to find funding and a partner. "Reevesland" needed an estimated $2.5 million in renovations. On March 21, 2017, the county board voted 5–0 to unload it. That left few happy.

The good news is that the chipped and weather-beaten house on the hill retained historic protection status. And the park containing the sledding slope and neighborhood garden remained.

But overall, "the neighborhood is disappointed in the Reeves outcome," this author was told by Phil Klingelhofer, the then-president of the Boulevard Manor Civic Association. "Many residents who personally knew Nelson Reeves still live here." Many in the association "think of the house as a treasure for the community and the country, and we're still hoping for some way that a nonprofit could come forward with resources that might allow the county to reconsider."

Flash forward to 2020. On February 25, county manager Mark Schwartz announced to the board his recommendation, and the board accepted a proposed multiparty funding plan for adaptive use of the home. It sets "the platinum standard for public–private partnerships," in the words of Chris Tighe, the new president of the civic association.

It was neighborhood leader Tighe who got the brainstorm of approaching the housing nonprofit HabitatNOVA, which rebuilds homes for sale to low-income residents. The fading Reeves house, which will require renovations and maintenance, "was too expensive for one family," this author was told by Noemi Riveira, HabitatNOVA's director of real estate development. So, HabitatNOVA hit on partnering with L'Arche Greater Washington D.C., a nonprofit that provides housing and support to persons with intellectual disabilities, which has experience in Arlington. Yet another partner was recruited to perform the renovations: HomeAid, the philanthropic arm of the Northern Virginia Building Industry Association.

The county board members were thrilled, though success still depended on HabitatNOVA raising 25 percent of the long-term estimated $2.3 million needed. And the modernized home that was to house four or five individuals from L'Arche must preserve features and satisfy the Historical Affairs and Landmark Review Board.

"The county has been super supportive," if a bit slow, Tighe said, noting that the house, over the years, "was basically a money pit."

Over in East Falls Church, George Grant Crossman built a home for his bride, Nellie, in 1892, on sixty acres. Their dairy farm would function until 1949 on the land that would become Tuckahoe Elementary and Bishop D.J. O'Connell High School. (The Crossman Stream remains an underground force to be reckoned with in today's flood-prone subdivisions.)

In 2018, grandson George Robert Crossman came to visit the homestead—which current owners, Buzz McClain and Leslie Aun, had restored to its original Victorian paint scheme. This Crossman recalled how he spent summers in the 1930s and 1940s working the dairy farm. He remembered his grandfather seeing Teddy Roosevelt speak nearby. And as a boy, he picked blueberries and blackberries near the creek. Crossman described the white-painted cow barn in the property's southwest corner. There, he would milk Bessie by hand, which meant he was excited when automatic electric pump machines arrived. After the crew had "partially emptied one cow," his uncle would move the pump down the row of cows; the hired help would drain the rest. The product was placed in huge milk cans that his grandfather would slowly lower into ice-water tanks for a truck

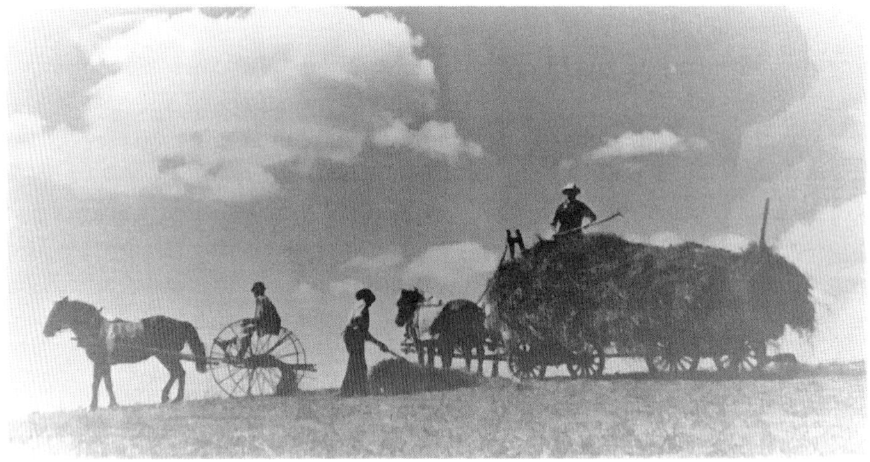

Working the Crossman farmland, now Bishop O'Connell High School. *Courtesy of Buzz McClain.*

to pick up—seven days a week, Crossman said. As a twelve-year-old, he wanted to explore the nearby (Tuckahoe Park) woods. But one day, his "cousin stopped me and marched me back to the house, saying 'never go down there again." The woods were where a Black worker had a cabin. That worker, Crossman recalled, was not permitted to enter the Crossman house, "and I wasn't allowed to get acquainted with him."

A third farmhouse exists to this day at the corner of North 16th and Lexington Streets with historic designation. The now-private Washington-Torreyson house is named for a Black man named James Washington, who bought the land (now in Westover) from plantation owner Bazil Hall in 1866 and 1875. The house was built around 1875 and was probably used by tenant farmers.

In 1905, it was sold (for seventy-five dollars) to Andrew Duke Torreyson (1866–1951), according to the county's preservation office. It was his father, William, who had first farmed the land that is now Swanson Middle School after the Civil War. The younger Torreyson, too, became a prominent dairy farmer, and he also became a land assessor and registrar for Alexandria County. He helped lead the Virginia Constitutional Convention in 1901–2, was the founder and first president of the Maryland and Virginia Milk Producers Association, a founder of Arlington's first bank and a founder of the Washington Golf and Country Club. He was buried at Oakwood Cemetery in Falls Church.

6
VANISHED BUSINESSES

Commercial outlets that supply Arlington with goods and services inhabit a special place in locals' memory banks. But we're not always conscious of the attachments until those businesses disappear. Like most vibrant communities, Arlington has witnessed the offerings constantly churning. The failure rate for restaurants is said to be nearly 50 percent after three years (according to a Cornell University study), a figure made worse during the 2020 pandemic. Each shuttered entryway represents the dashed dreams for a family or entrepreneur. But also—in some cases—they represent progress and modernization. The Facebook nostalgia site "I Grew Up in Arlington, VA" offers a steady diet of favorite storefront images, menus and matchbook covers, many of which jogged this author's memory. Let us pay homage here to some of the personalities, community fixtures and loyal providers of Arlington's yesteryear.

Clothing stores of this author's own youth in the 1960s included Herbert's Youth Fashions at Virginia Square, the Stag Shop in Parkington (now Ballston Quarter), the nearby Varsity Shop and Ted Lewis in Shirlington. Women favored Casual Corner at Parkington and Junior Sophisticates in Clarendon (which offered free Cokes to the little brothers who were left impatiently waiting).

Long before CVS and Rite-Aid, there was Peoples Drugs, Drug Fair and Dart Drug. For books, Arlingtonians shopped at Brentano's. Sponsors of Little League teams included Highlander Motel (torn down in 2021), Arlington Motors, Arlington Trust. Co. and Better Homes Realty.

Boys also favored athletic equipment from McQuinn's Sporting Goods in Clarendon, Sampson's in Ballston and Sport Fair in Cherrydale.

Hobbyists enjoyed Arlington Hobbycrafters, near Parkington, which offered the latest in Lionel and American Flyer trains; Wally's Aquarium at North Glebe Road, near Fairfax Drive (which later moved out to Annandale); and the Ski Chalet on Columbia Pike at Walter Reed Drive.

More practical was the Sleep Shop in Ballston and the nearby Carbone Animal Hospital. Some businesses were trendy—slot car racetracks like the one at Lee-Harrison Shopping Center in the late 1960s, at some point, looked like a good investment.

Hotels that bit the dust included the Twin Bridges Marriott, built in 1957 near the 14th Street Bridge. The world's first motor hotel, it was a favorite for high school proms and the site where rock singer Lowell George of Little Feat died. It was torn down in 1990. In 2020, Arlington lost the Americana Hotel in Crystal City, and in 2021, the county lost the Marriott Residence Inn in Crystal City to Amazon and the Highlander Motel on Wilson Boulevard to CVS.

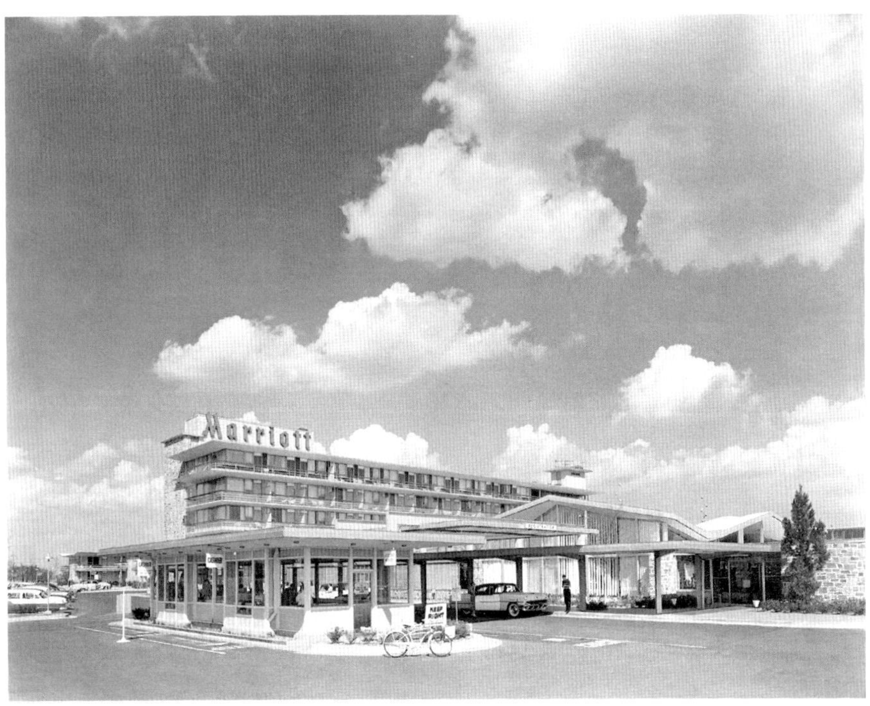

The Twin Bridges Marriott, the company's first motor hotel, near the 14th Street Bridge. It was demolished in 1990. *Courtesy of the Marriott International Corporate Archives.*

Vanished car dealers include Bob Peck Chevrolet at North Glebe and Wilson Boulevard, Kirby's Dodge, Cherner Ford and Mercury in Shirlington and Bob Rosenthal Chevrolet on Columbia Pike and South Glebe Road.

Early pioneers of the home delivery that, today, seems routine included the County Club Market on North Glebe Road, Chicken Delight in the parking lot at Glebe Road and Lee Highway and photographers who came to children's homes with a live pony and cowboy costumes.

Banking has always been a fluid industry. This author's personal accounts in Arlington shifted from his first childhood savings account at Clarendon Trust, to First American, Crestar and Suntrust, which is now Truist.

Inside Parkington was McCory's Five and Dime, near the Arcadian Garden. As a ten-year-old customer at its lunch counter, the author selected a balloon displayed on a clothesline. He popped it to find a slip of paper that entitled him to a one-cent banana split. The author can't claim that this vat of ice cream and toppings beat the overflowing tubs that were served for decades at the Arlington branch of Gifford's (on Lee Highway, near North Harrison Street). One rediscovered Gifford's menu from the 1960s lists those treats for just ninety-five cents and a jumbo hot fudge sundae for ninety cents. It also served fancy candies.

Entertainment included a 1950s standby Bernie's Pony Ring in Lyon Village (which had another pony ring at Bailey's Crossroads). Boat races on the Potomac were put on by Tommie Bartlett's Water Thrill Show. In Falls Church, locals enjoyed the Village House skating rink (now Kaiser Permanente) and indoor swimming in Cherrydale at the Northern Virginia Aquatic Club. The putt-putt mini golf course at the Ballston crossroads was the most famous, though those child-size links were also at what today is the Arlington Cinema and Drafthouse and Mario's Pizza.

Music clubs included the original Birchmere in Shirlington (now on Mount Vernon Avenue in Alexandria), Eskimo Nell's in Ballston and Bad Habits on Columbia Pike near Carlin Springs Road. We used to buy records at Swillers in Clarendon and Giant Music on Broad Street in Falls Church. Popular movie theaters, exploding in the post–World War II years, included the long-vanished Ashton (Clarendon), the Byrd (Near Fort Myer), the Wilson (upper Rosslyn), the Glebe (later the Dominion at Glebe and Lee Highway), the Crystal City and the Buckingham (which is still there but is now a post office).

Of the three bowling alleys from the author's youth, only Bowl America in Falls Church remains. Market forces in the 1970s took out the Skor-Mor ten pin alley across from today's Washington-Liberty High School, the Pla-

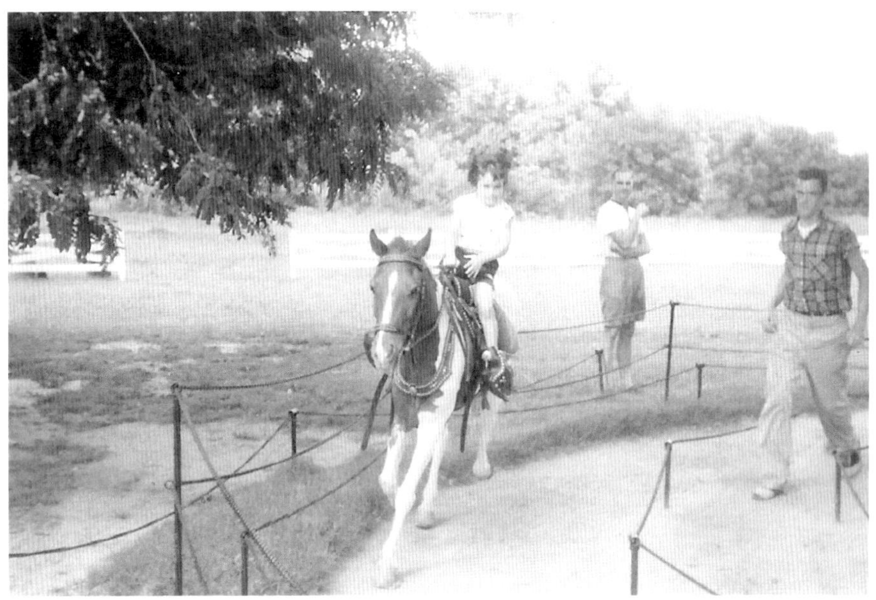

A five-year-old enjoys Bernie's Pony Ring in Lyon Village. *Courtesy of Jane Martin.*

Mor duckpin lanes at Fairfax Drive and North Glebe and the Nick Rinaldi Lanes on South Glebe, near Gunston Middle School.

Most locals frequent a favored gas station/repair shop. The Lee-Lex Shell Station, where country singer Jimmy Dean hung out in the 1950s, became an auto repair shop that folded in 2018 and hung a sign that said, "Thanks for 38 great years."

Restaurants that captured appetites for decades included Tom Sarris's Orleans House in Rosslyn, the Alpine on Lee Highway, near North Glebe Road (frequented by players from the old Washington Redskins) that was previously Frankenstein's and Evans Coffee Shop before that. The author also recalls early Tex-Mex at Speedy Gonzales in Ballston and the Colonial Restaurant in Crystal City. Lum's (fine mugs of cider) at Courthouse was replaced by Summer's, which died in 2020. And Little Tavern (its slogan: "Buy 'Em by the Bag") was located in Clarendon (now Goody's Pizza) and Lyon Village, next to the pawnshop.

The turnover in restaurants is encapsulated best by what some locals call the jinxed restaurant at Lee Highway and North Lexington Street. It opened in the 1970s as a Pizza Hut, evolved into an Indian health food purveyor, a Bolivian-Colombian mix, the Charleyhorse Grill, the Tap and Vine, Asian Kitchen, Misomen Ramen and, as of 2019, Sloppy Mama's Barbecue.

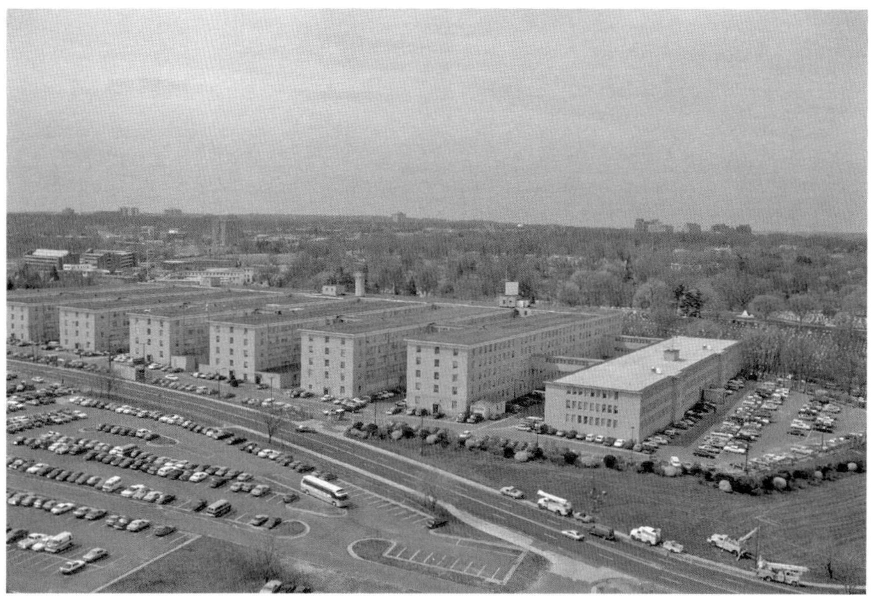

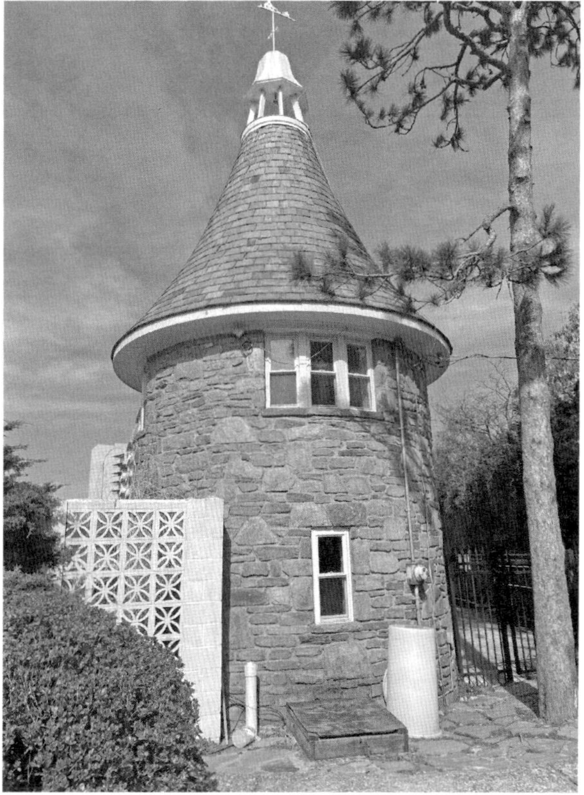

Above: The Navy Annex, built in 1941 near Fort Myer as a major federal employer, was demolished in 2012–13 to add land to Arlington National Cemetery. *Courtesy of the National Archives.*

Left: The remnants of the once-trendy Little Tea House restaurant still stand on Arlington Ridge Road. *Author's image.*

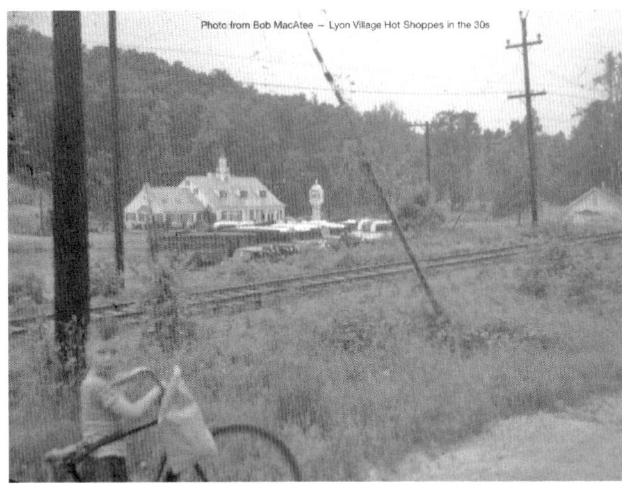

Howard Johnson's restaurant on Kirkwood Road in the 1930s with tourist buses. It later became Hot Shoppes. *Photograph by Bob McAtee, courtesy of John Cameron Peck.*

In April 2016, Latherow & Co., the stamp and coin shop that operated for decades at 5054 Lee Highway, announced it was going of business. There was some dispute with the landlord, a staffer said.

This author went over and found two cleaning ladies at work on the deserted shelves and counters, the handwritten sign on the door reading, "We are closed for good. Everything is gone."

Several times over the years, the author had stopped in the old-fashioned hobby shop—one of the area's remaining few—to donate items from his family's half-hearted stamp collection. In Arlington, that left only Philatelics Elite Inc., run by Chuck Hale in his basement at 222 North Park Street.

Many fine establishments moved on to that shopping strip in the sky.

ARLINGTON'S BREWERY

Long before Rosslyn Circle hosted the Marriott hotel, that site at the mouth of the Aqueduct Bridge was where beer was made. From 1895 until 1917, the firm originally named the Consumers Brewing Co. (but renamed the Arlington Brewing Co. in 1902) operated out of an intricate red-brick Gothic plant. (See cover.) While its neighbors in Rosslyn—pawnshops, gambling houses, brothels—were raided by ambitious commonwealth's attorney Crandal Mackey, the brewery survived until Virginia enacted its own version of Prohibition in 1916. As detailed in Arlington historian Garrett Peck's *Capital Beer: A Heady History of Brewing in Washington, D.C.*,

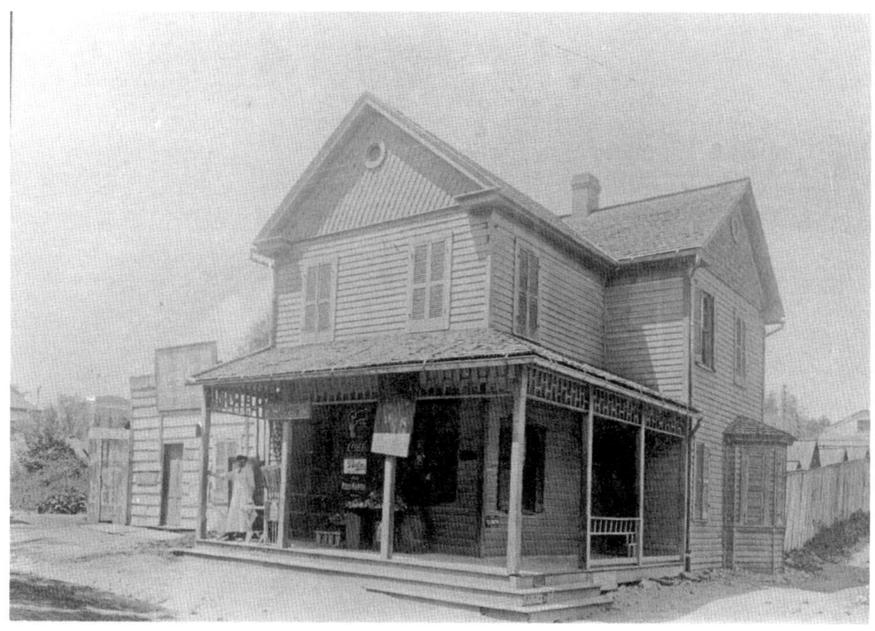

Cunningham's Sunday Bar in old Rosslyn. *Courtesy of the Arlington Historical Society.*

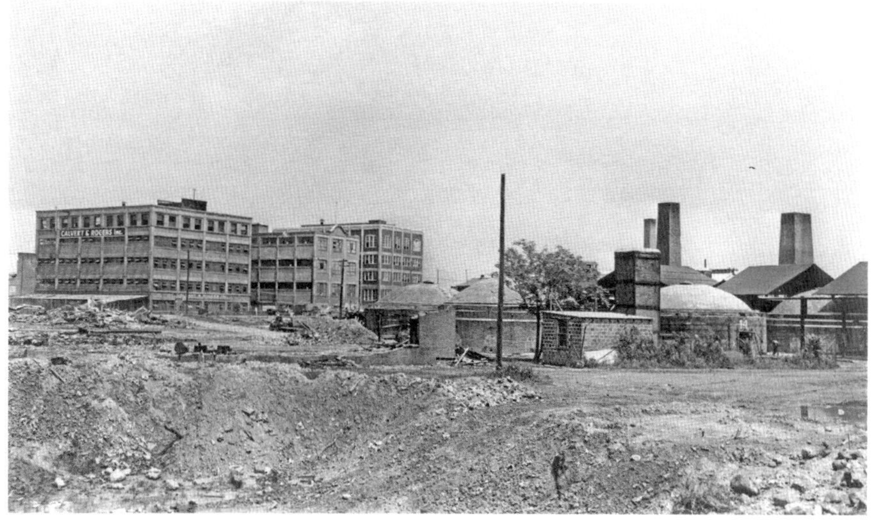

A century before Amazon sited its second headquarters in Crystal City, the Calvert and Rogers, West Brothers Brick Kilns flourished. *Courtesy of the Center for Local History, Arlington Public Library.*

moonshiners were active in and around Arlington. They transported twenty-two thousand gallons of their illegal product weekly along routes on Lee Highway and Columbia Pike.

Richmond, Virginia entrepreneur John Fowler bought the Rosslyn facility in 1920 to make syrup for a fruit-flavored soft drink called Cherry Smash. It became a soda fountain hit up and down the East Coast. The Arlington Historical Society, in 2014, put on an exhibit with the original bottles and bricks from the brewery, artifacts from the anti-alcohol temperance movement, as well as advertisements, postcards and other items from the Cherry Smash company, many of which were donated by a Fowler descendant. After Prohibition ended in 1933, Fowler tried to reopen beermaking with the Dixie Brewing Co. But it was a no-go. The building was torn down, and the J.W. Marriott Corp. bought it and opened a Hot Shoppes. That was replaced in 1959 by the Marriott Hotel, which, after renovations, stands today.

The Marcey Family Dairy

One of Arlington's premier land-owning families, the Marceys, trace their roots to the days of log cabins.

The clan is getting a fresh coat of history paint.

Descendant Cal Marcey, who was eighty years old in September 2018, spoke to this author from his home next to the family's land near Mount Olivet Church and offered a draft family chronology, complete with genealogy that can be traced back to England. He began his retelling in the 1970s.

A retired florist, Cal Marcey is worried over possible destruction of one of Arlington's remaining log cabins, to which his ancestors have ties. A new owner has purchased the early-nineteenth-century Birchwood cabin at the corner of North Wakefield and Twenty-Sixth Streets, and the plans for it—renovation versus teardown—are unclear.

Most Arlingtonians know the Marceys from Marcey Road, near Potomac Overlook Park. That area of north Arlington, located off Military Road, was settled by Cal's great-great-great-great-grandparents in the eighteenth century. Sam Marcey and his family came from the Blue Ridge Mountains and rented land from George Mason for $160 a year.

The family prospered on farmland around what is, today, the Church of the Covenant. You can find the Marceys on historic signs, and their marriages are often linked to other prominent Arlington families—the Balls, Donaldsons and Birches. Many Marcey graves lie at Mount Olivet, at an unmarked site off Marcey Road and Walker Chapel.

Civil War Union troops forced the Marceys to host campsites, where thousands of trees were leveled. (Arlington historian Eleanor Lee Templeman wrote of a soldier's buried treasure near Marceytown that was never found.)

Later Marceys worked at Arlington Cemetery as groundskeepers and as White House police and maintenance engineers, Cal said. The family ran the Arlington County Dairy at 2701 Wilson Boulevard before it closed in 1947. (Cal still has a dairy promotional calendar with photographs of the delivery trucks.)

Growing up on Marcey farmland in the 1940s, Cal said, meant he performed chores, like fetching water from a well before school, and his mother washed clothes using a three-burner stove. "We were in the sticks," he said of the Military Road land. "We called Cherrydale the city."

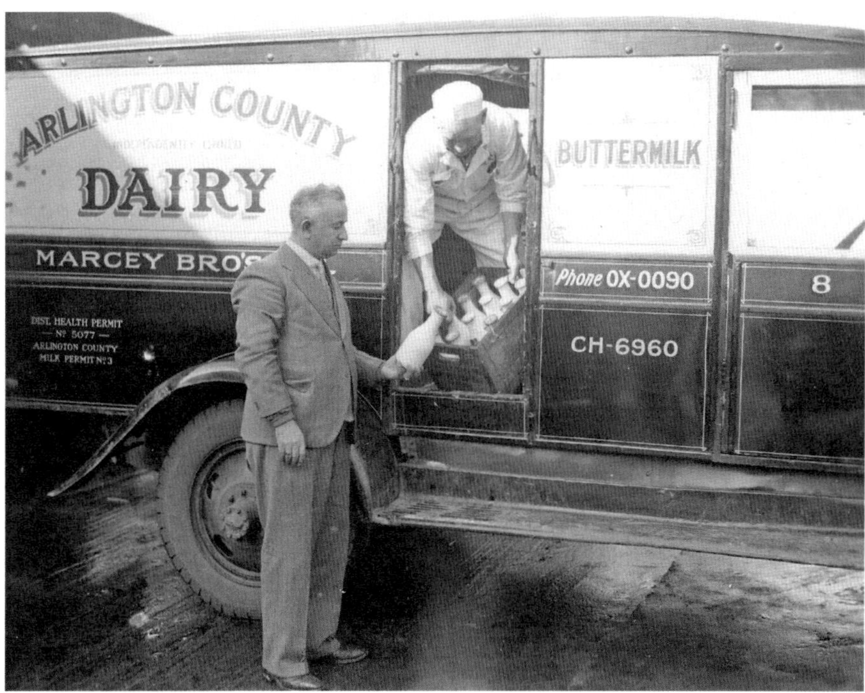

The landowning Marceys ran a home-delivery dairy business. *Courtesy of the Center for Local History, Arlington Public Library.*

Log cabins are intertwined with the Marceys. Cal recalled scavenging old Arlington brewery bottles from a cabin that was demolished in 1947.

But the most famous Marcey cabin was one from the 1840s that originally measured fifteen by fifteen feet, with chinked V-notched pine logs. One of his relatives raised thirteen children in the cabin after expansions.

In 1985, the cabin was famously transported to a historic neighborhood in Vienna, Virginia. "It had sat for a number of years, empty," after a housekeeper moved out (her relatives found $75,000 stored there), leaving little but a cellar full of snakes, Cal said. "The county didn't want it." So, the Arlington Historical Society offered it to attorney Charles Sloan.

Sloan's widow, Daphne, at first, said, "Over my dead body." But now, she fondly recalls the flatbed trucks and police escort (a $20,000 expense) required to move the roof.

One more cabin, later used as a toolshed and as Arlington's last smokehouse for butchered hogs, stood for decades near Cal Marcey's current home, on land that was originally a part of the Glebe House tract. It was on the Marceys' original ninety-five acres, which the family sold to make room for Glebe School (opened in 1971). The late Arlington sherriff J. Elwood Clements, born on the property, tried to save it from the wrecking ball.

The Eggs Man

During the grandiloquent debate in the twenty-first century over whether Arlington should allow backyard chicken coops, references were made to the glories of household egg production practiced by our forebears.

In January 2019, this author got to chat with one such natural foods practitioner: the almost-eighty-year-old Sam Day, an exemplar of our county's salt-of-the-earth workforce.

This author was also able to update him on county preservation developments in his own chicken coop story.

Growing up in the 1940s on North Kenmore Street in the Maywood neighborhood (at Twenty-First Avenue, "the only avenue in Arlington," he notes), Day helped with his father's egg business.

Behind the 1908 house in which Sam Day was born was the two-story "chicken house," built in 1920. "The chickens didn't run loose," he assured me. But the birds were fed well enough to support a basement egg distribution operation that endured for thirty-five years.

As a boy, Sam and his three siblings helped judge and grade the eggs (looking for blood spots, considered a flaw). The family sorted them—medium, large, extra-large, jumbo and double yolks. Then they packaged them, first in brown bags and later in boxes they made with a hand-operated machine. "Some eggs were brown," from Rhode Island Red hens, he said.

The Days would pack thirty dozen-sized crates in a gutted 1935 Dodge for delivery to regular customers in North and South Arlington, as well as across the Potomac. Because the customized car held only two people, Sam would catch the old Arnold bus at Quincy Street and Washington Boulevard, ride into Georgetown and transfer at Wisconsin Avenue to meet his dad at Massachusetts Avenue. They delivered eggs until 7:00 or 8:00 p.m. every day, except for Wednesdays and Sundays.

Customer demand exploded. So, his father began driving weekly to farms near Culpeper. "He bought them as is," Day remembered, "and while most farmers cleaned their eggs, one didn't." So, it was left to the Day kids to brush away the manure.

Sam played the egg man until he began junior high in 1951 at the still-under-construction Stratford building and then moved on to what was then called Washington-Lee High.

While the egg profits allowed his siblings to attend American University, Sam tried it but chose a different path. "I wanted a job where I didn't have to depend on anyone else," he said. First, he delivered eggs full time. Then he landed a job driving a delivery truck for Schlitz Beer out of a warehouse at Four Mile Run and Walter Reed Drive. Putting in sixty to seventy hours a week, Day married and, with two children, bought a house in 1964, mortgaged "for $169 a month."

His father retired from the egg business in 1968. When his mother died in 1995, the Kenmore Street house (their home for seventy years) was sold. The chicken house fell into disrepair.

In 2018, the home was purchased by Tom and Chrissi Gelson from Marion, Massachusetts. "We knew it was one of the oldest homes in Maywood, and the chicken coop one of the oldest agricultural outbuildings standing in Arlington," Tom told me.

During renovations—under strict guidelines of Maywood and the Historical Affairs and Landmark Review Board—they kept only the shed's brick chimney as a memory. "We wish we could have restored the chicken coop," said the new owner. "But much of it collapsed years ago because of disrepair."

ROADS LED TO GREYSTONE RESTAURANT

Arlington's Ballston crossroads, at the start of World War II, was hardly the neon commercial hub the county flocks to today.

So, when the Greystone Restaurant was first opened by an entrepreneurial family on North Glebe Road at Carlin Springs Road, it thrived as the sole eatery in that vicinity.

For nearly fifty years, the purveyor of refined comfort food served county officials, business and military leaders and families, invited by slogans, "All roads lead to the Greystone....Where you will like to eat and like what you eat."

In March 2021, this author traded recollections with ninety-six-year-old Beatrice "Bea" Root, now of Bethesda, Maryland, who worked the counter at her parents' restaurant while a high schooler. The grill launched in 1941 by Robert and Gertrude Goldman, managed by A.R. Parker, was a family affair, with Bea's aunt Mildred running the office and typing menus, her daughter Debbie later helping with hosting.

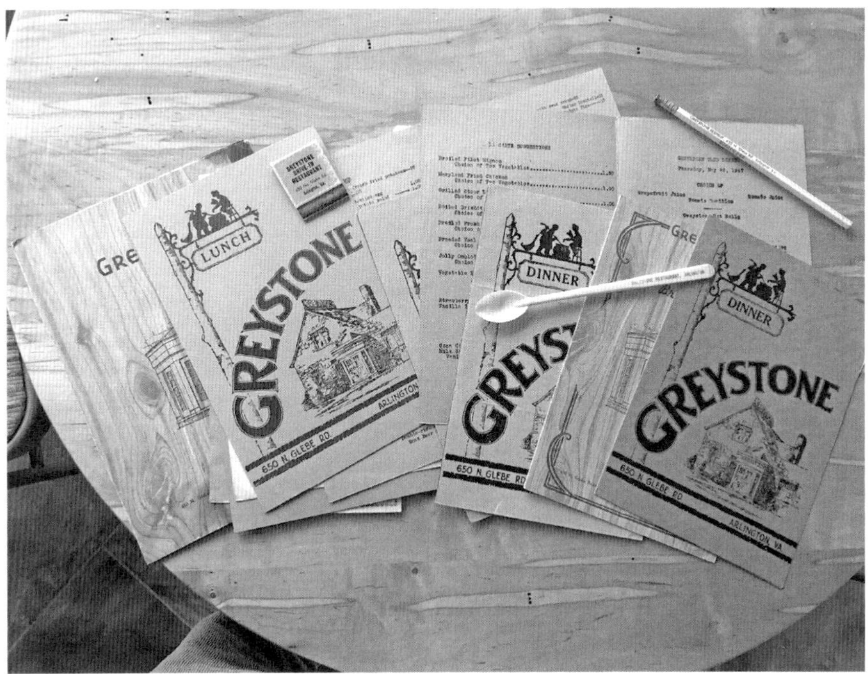

Artifacts from a popular hangout. *Courtesy of Jerry Root.*

"Two or three dollars bought you a complete dinner, with appetizer, soup, entree, two vegetables, salad, dessert and coffee," said Bea—rolls included.

The 1942 menu offered braised beef tenderloin tips for $0.60, fried jumbo oysters for $0.55 and grape nut pudding for $0.10. Then came wartime inflation. By 1947, the broiled filet mignon set you back $1.75, the breaded veal chop $1.15. A glass of Nina sherry cost $0.30; Pabst Blue Ribbon on draft cost $0.10.

Bea recalls the two rooms of booths, a bar, uniformed waitresses and a kitchen staff of five: Marion the chef; her assistant, Jack; and Becky, the pastry chef who produced fresh and homemade baked goods (except the hamburger rolls and bread). A family garden provided fresh produce.

The Greystone was celebrated on February 22, 1941, in a Washington's birthday newspaper advertisement signed by neighboring enterprises, among them Old Dominion Floors and Arlington Electric Co.

Because of the hardships of fuel rationing, Bea's parents bought a home next to the restaurant to avoid a commute from downtown. But Bea wanted to finish her senior year of high school (class of 1943) at Central (now Cardoza) High School, so she took the bus across the Potomac from the new Arlington digs. At Christmastime in 1944, she witnessed a frightening fire that burned the Greystone.

Insurance permitted remodeling. In 1948, she married Samuel Root, who worked at the jewelry store that was on Wilson Boulevard and later Nineteenth Street in Rosslyn. (Her son Jerry runs it today in McLean.)

Jerry Root still owns chairs (reupholstered) from the Greystone, plus matchbooks, plastic stirrers and business cards. His sister Debbie has dishes and a Greystone child's seat. Clippings show that Jacqueline Bouvier (Kennedy), as a young photojournalist, did an "Inquiring Camera Girl" interview at the Greystone. Another visitor was Chicago's world-famous eight-foot-two-inch-tall man, Don Kohler, who came to Arlington in 1952 to christen the Hecht Co.

Memories of segregation cloud the sunny recollections. When Bea caught the bus just outside the restaurant to go downtown, she would ride with Greystone staffers who were Black. By law, they had to sit in the back, as enforced by the driver. "But they were part of our family, so I sat as close to them as I could."

In 1988, after a brief new proprietorship, the Goldman family sold the Greystone and their house to Goodyear Tire. And that favored haunt in Ballston was no more.

WHAT SEARS HAD

"Sears has everything!" The old jingle rings quaint today. The once-preeminent U.S. retailer now has no space at the mall.

April 12, 2020, became the final day for the Seven Corners Sears, which had occupied the old Lord & Taylor building in Falls Church, Virginia, since 1998. The closure—accelerated by the coronavirus pandemic—was announced in February by the private Transformco firm.

The news stirred many memories of the Arlington Sears that stood at the heart of Clarendon from 1942 to 1993. After years as the Arlington Education Center at North Edgewood Street and Wilson Boulevard, that old building was dismantled to become the Crossing Clarendon. Sears's former garden center is now a Whole Foods.

News clippings about this Sears's opening during World War II were recently unearthed by those bird dogs on Facebook's "I Grew Up in Arlington, VA." The Sears group manager of the Washington, D.C. area advertised that he was looking to hire full- and part-time salespeople in hardware, draperies, rugs, paint, wallpaper, building materials and "ready to wear."

Arlingtonians of all walks responded, as the nostalgia buffs recently proved. Sue Meeder's mother worked there in "the '50s and early '60s," she posted. "She was a cashier upstairs in the main offices." Sydney Simmonds "worked there before I went into the army, setting up and adjusting TVs and stereos on the top floor."

Judy Munden "worked at that Sears in the late '70s for almost three years. Mom and Dad used my employee discount all the time. Dad with his tools and my mom with her appliances."

Gloria Moren told this author her uncle David Oddenino worked the Clarendon Sears as a jeweler/salesperson. "I would take my broken watches to him. After many years in the jewelry department, he sold appliances downstairs."

George Dodge recalled that, in the early 1970s, Sears "was virtually the only place remaining open after 6 p.m. for department store merchandise." It also maintained "an automotive area for oil changes (pre–Jiffy Lube)." David Ruiz remembered "walking to and from Sears with my mom from Lee Garden Apartments. Everything was calm during [the 1980s]; we didn't feel any fear."

Even before Sears's brick-and-mortar emporiums began to shutter, the national company, dating back to 1893, had become, for some, an object of derision. A bad driver in the sixties might hear a shout, "Where'd you

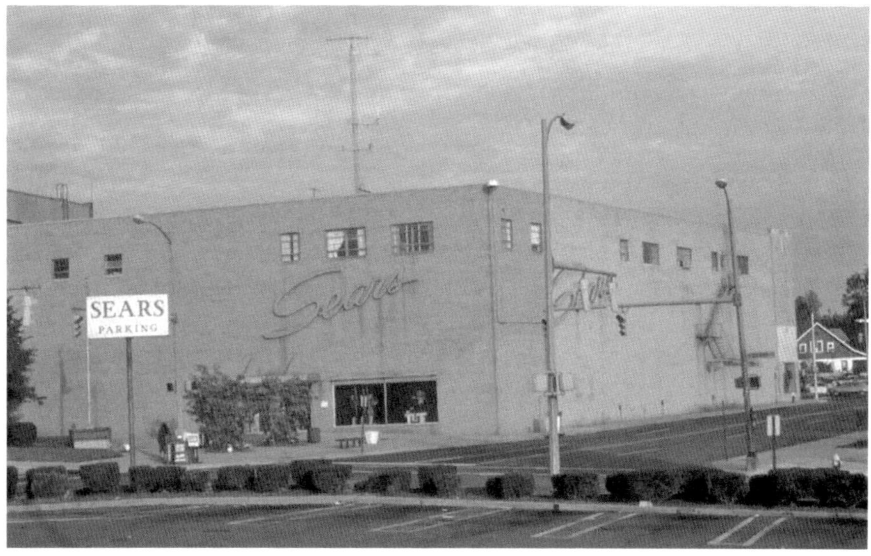

The favored "everything" store in Clarendon. *Courtesy of Michael Horsley.*

get your license—Sears?" But this author's household, in recent years, has continued to rely on Sears for kitchen appliances and services such as duct and carpet cleaning.

The author's personal memories of the Clarendon branch trace back to the musical instruments section. In particular, the Sears Silvertone twin-twelve amplifier provided reverb and tremolo to his well-intentioned electric guitar.

When the author was an eleven-year-old, that was his idea of Sears having everything.

Bonding Over Kann's Store

In March 2021, a red-brick windowless box known to long-timers as Kann's Department Store bit the dust.

George Mason University, which has used the Virginia Square building for multiple purposes since 1979, was creating space for its planned state-funded Institute for Digital Innovation.

Preparatory work on the interior began in November 2020, and construction fencing came up. "Select items were salvaged for potential reuse in the new building, including bricks and marble from the original structure, in the interest of honoring the history of Kann's," said Robin Rose Parker, a university communications strategist, to this author. The environmental impact report was quickly approved by county offices.

The Mason staff have long been sensitive to the special place for the old Kann's that beats in Arlington hearts—holding nostalgic gatherings for those who recall it as a law school. When this author posted photographs of the doomed building on Facebook's "I Grew Up in Arlington, VA," more than four hundred responses (and sad emoticons) appeared within forty-eight hours. "Sad to see it go. I went to law school there and fondly remembered getting my favorite winter coat there," said one commenter.

Built in 1951 to compete with the Hecht Co. in nearby Ballston, the regional department store Kann's became a three-story consumer adventure land for thousands. "Arlington Becomes Real Metropolis," read the *Evening Star*'s account of its $4.5 million construction. Suburbanites flocked there for dresses, coats, shirts, fabrics, cosmetics, intimate apparel, toys, Buster Brown shoes, tableware and fine candy, plus its gift-wrapping, beauty salon, photography studio and homey cafeteria.

Former employees recalled it fondly: "My sister worked in the lingerie department one summer, and my mother was assistant fashion coordinator. I was in a few junior fashion shows. Kann's was our go-to."

Another's "grandmother worked there until she was 84. Kann's was good about avoiding age discrimination." One alum "worked in the lamp department and Trim-a-Tree during the holidays." Kann's annual rooftop life-size Santa and reindeer became an anticipated annual spectacle.

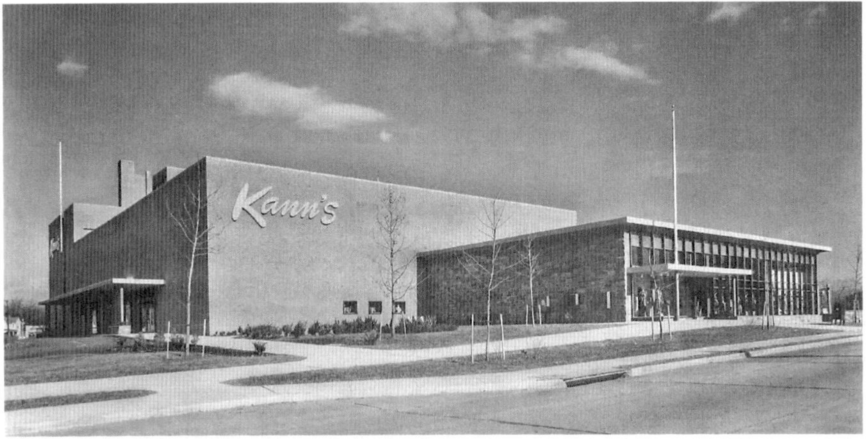

The vividly recalled Virginia Square emporium. *Courtesy of the Lionel Freedman Archives, under the care of Maya Myers.*

"I remember going there with my great-aunt when I was 4," one commenter reminisced. "What impressed me was the escalators, chimes and announcements over the loudspeakers. It seemed a cross between Disneyland and the zoo."

In the early sixties, one mother "would find items she liked and watch them get reduced, then go on sale, then on clearance. She'd end up getting things for a dollar or two…a role model in stretching a dollar." Another from that era got her first credit card from Kann's.

The downstairs "Kannteen" served tuna salad and "Cherry Smash, fries and barbecue on a bun," one commenter recalled. The eatery "had built-in 'loops' of counter space and you sat on stools," wrote another. "The waitresses wore uniforms…complete with aprons."

Perhaps the oddest memory: "The toilets that popped up into a magical rim of blue light that was supposed to disinfect them."

By far the most vivid memory involved the live monkeys in a glass cage in the shoe department. Reports are that the squirrel monkeys from Brazil were named Teeny, Weeny, Eeny and Miney. No one seems to have a photograph (WETA documentarians searched widely when they made the 2004 Arlington history *Heroes, History & Hamburgers*).

That special store also embraced community affairs: "Free hearing test, given by the Quota Club of Arlington," read the 1975 advertisement in the *Arlington News*. "Kann's Cares."

ROBERTSON'S FIVE AND DIME

Arlingtonions of a certain age spent their childhoods nickel and diming.

Sugar-coated memories of Robertson's 5 & 10 Cent Store, which greeted kids aged one to ninety-two for decades near Lee Highway and North Glebe Road, came to this author from scattered friends.

They have imprinted joys of wax lips, Lik-M-Aid, atomic fireballs, model cars and surly elderly sales ladies on the prowl for shoplifters in the grittier 1950s and 1960s.

Robertson's, located at 2213 North Buchanan Street (later Bill's Tru Value Hardware), was part of a six-store empire launched in 1935 by Falls Church resident William Robertson. When he died in 1987, his obituary recalled his claim: "We always say to customers that if you can't find it anywhere, you can find it at Robertson's."

In 2018, you could still spot the outline of his "5 & 10" sign on the chimney and its original aluminum lettering inside the hardware store run by Bill Ploskina from 1988 until his death in February 2021. Robertson's, in the 1950s, was located at 4447 Lee Highway (later a topless bar, now Hunan Village restaurant) before moving next door. Robertson owned several surrounding stores.

"I remember the dazzling array of candy inside on the right and narrow aisles crowded with goodies," said Jane. "I still have a collection of china and pottery knick-knacks [from Robertson's]."

Bob "had a pack-a-day candy cigarette habit at Robertson's."

The store "was a gateway drug and led me down a path to lifelong sugar addiction," said Chris, recalling her "first foray into pet ownership" at the store when she purchased "four goldfish, a bowl, blue gravel and a ceramic castle." A future professional singer, Chris also bought her first 45-rpm record at Robertson's—the Chiffons' "One Fine Day" and "He's So Fine."

Suze can still remember the store's layout. "The mothballs were on the far right as you walked in." Jean said she and her mom took sewing lessons in the basement.

Dave gorged on "root beer barrels and candy dots on sheets," while taking home lariats, balsa wood gliders and paper kites. The store with a wood floor had a "musty smell of things that had lingered on the shelves for years."

John came to Robertson's for wax pop bottle candy, gum and "cap rolls for our guns. It was the first store I could go to on my own," he said. "We couldn't understand why some things cost more than 10 cents."

Linda, as an employee there in high school, recalled Lynda Bird Johnson buying Carter's baby clothes. "I remember working with a woman who lived across Lee Highway. She barely had enough money to have lunch."

Nearby neighbor Mary, who went to Robertson's for licorice mustaches, Pixie Sticks and Life Savers, recalled a woman in charge named Birdie. "She had dark hair and glasses and was built like a fire hydrant, and she had a pretty good eye on all us kids."

Mary and Judy confessed to childhood shoplifting. "I went there fully intending to spend my hard-earned allowance (25 whole cents!) on penny candy," Judy wrote. "But I got so distracted trying to figure what to get, I somehow came away with an extra piece of candy." After agonizing, she returned and "discretely dropped a penny in one of the candy boxes, hoping I would not be taken to jail. It was a whole week until I had the nerve to go back again."

Once Familiar Sights

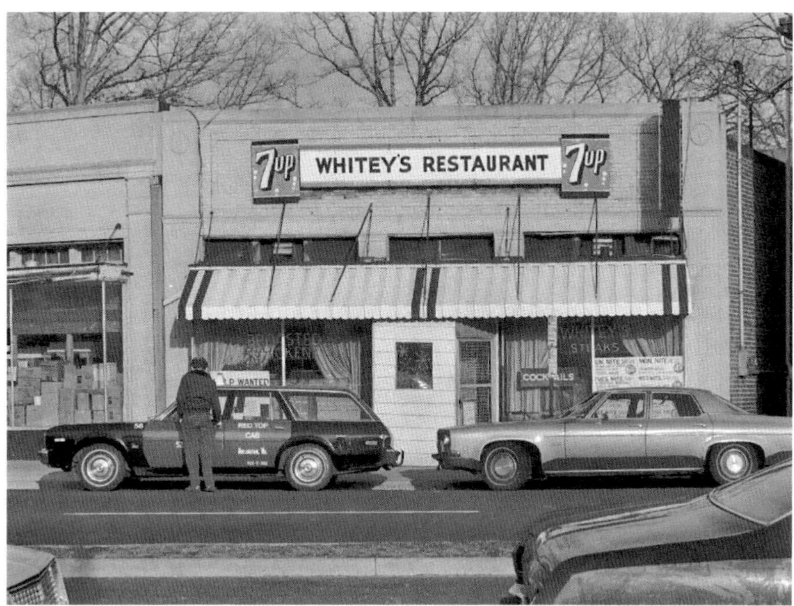

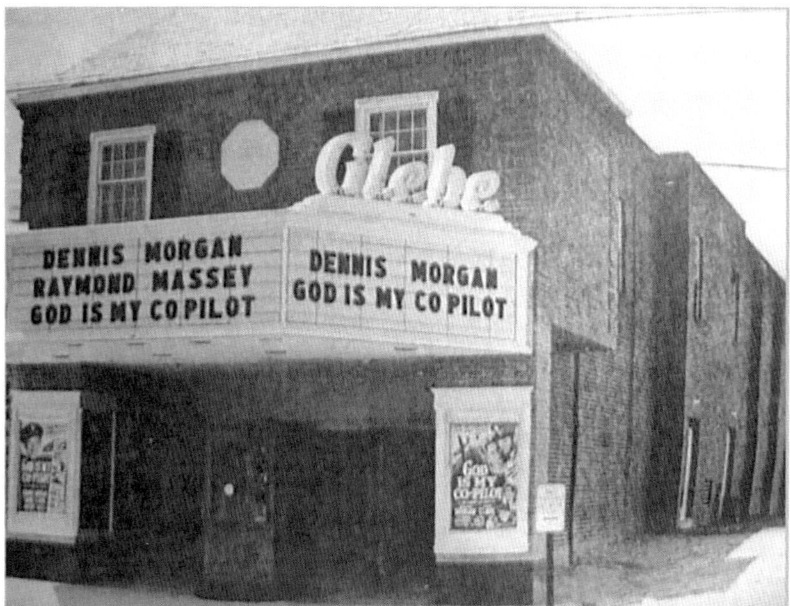

Top: *Courtesy of Lloyd Wolf; Bottom*: *Courtesy of Cinema Treasures.*

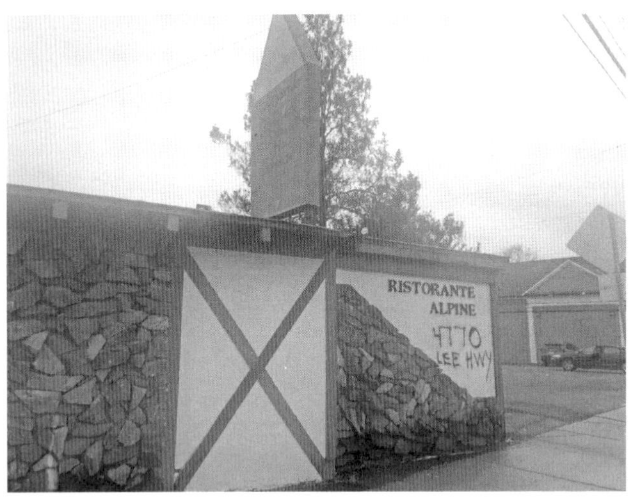

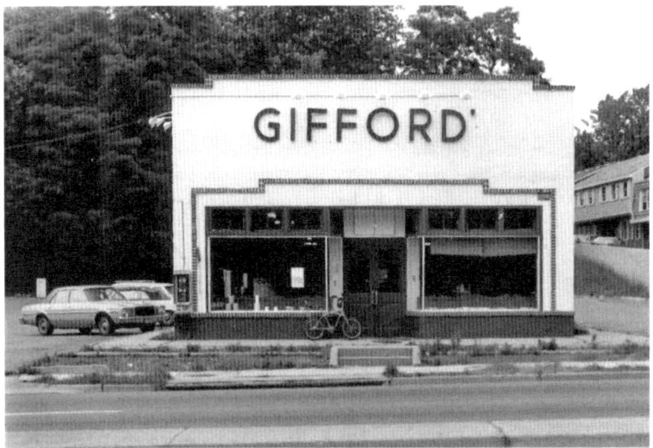

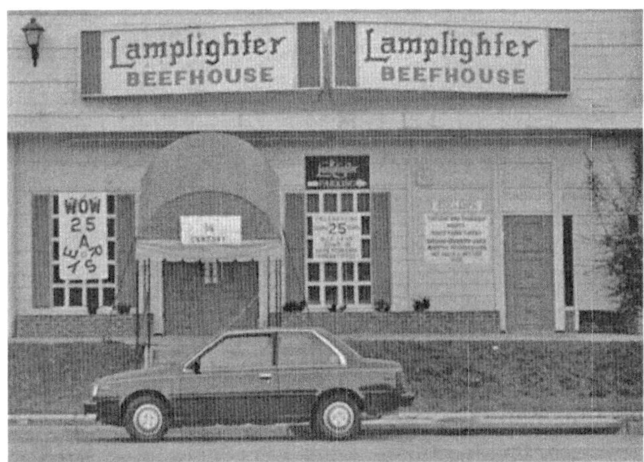

Top: *Author's image*; *middle*: *Courtesy of Lloyd Wolf*; *bottom*: *Courtesy of the Arlington Historical Society.*

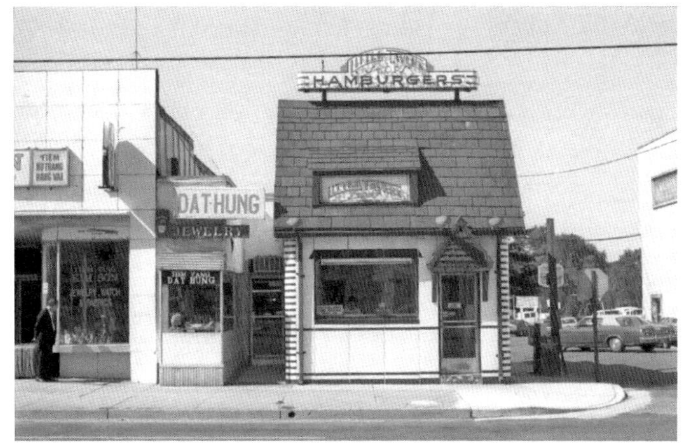

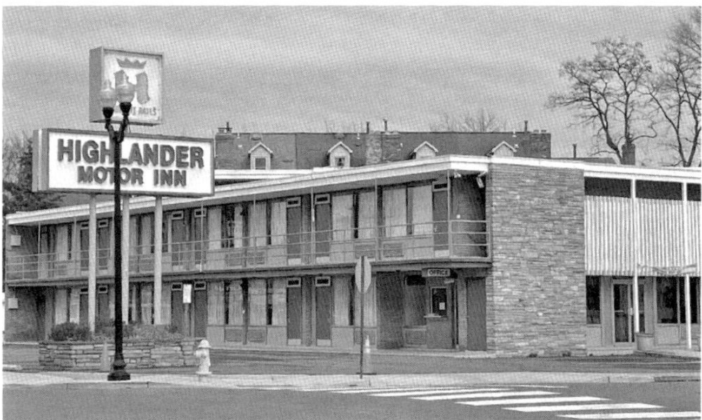

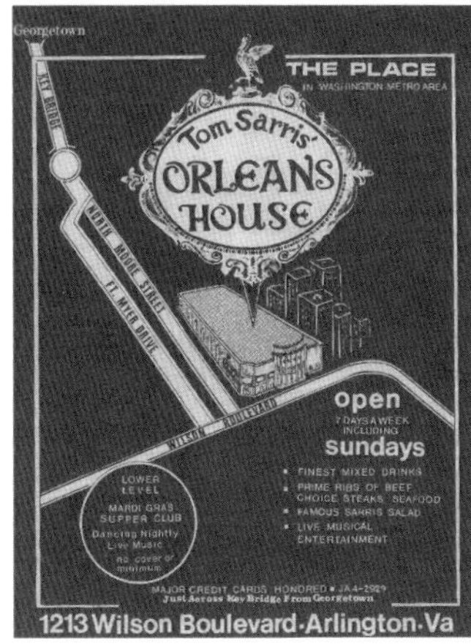

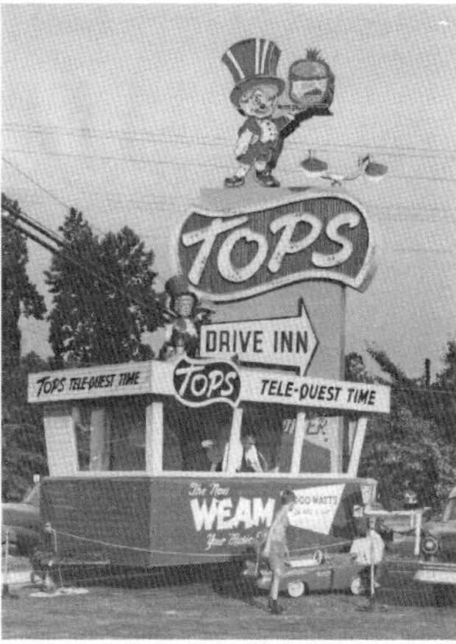

Top: *Courtesy of Michael Horsley*; *middle*: *Courtesy of Tom Dickinson*; *Bottom, left*: *From the collection of Greg Paspatis*; *bottom, right*: *Courtesy of the Matthews family*;

Piece of a Mausoleum

Arlingtonians in the know can find two remnants of an unusual burial temple that stood at Arlington National Cemetery from 1924 to 2001. The Abbey Mausoleum, a crypt for the well-to-do, was erected by the private U.S. Mausoleum Corp. near what became Henderson Hall at Fort Myer. It offered an elite spot for the remains of judges, senators and war veterans—about 283 people. The neoclassical building was later determined eligible for listing in the National Register of Historic Places because of its high artistic value.

But the burial company went bankrupt in 1957. Beginning in the 1970s, vandals had desecrated the property and exposed corpses, as the *Washington Post* reported in 2001. Even the best efforts of the marines and Arlington County Police couldn't stay the building's decline. In 1984, a relocation plan won approval by a judge. Scott Watson, an archaeologist with the U.S. Army Corps of Engineers, led efforts to find next of kin to arrange private reburials. But many of the bodies were reinterred at the National Memorial Park in Falls Church.

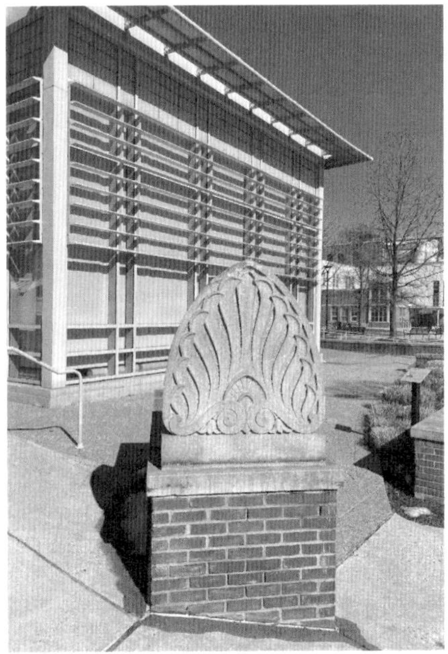

This vestige of the demolished Abbey Mausoleum, used from 1924 to 2001 at Arlington National Cemetery, now decorates the Westover Public Library. *Author's image.*

Some of the mausoleum's stained-glass windows were restored in 2004 and can be seen today at the Arlington Arts Center in Virginia Square. And Arlington County acquired another remnant: a granite acroterion that was created in 1926. In 2009, it was installed to decorate the refurbished Westover Library at the corner of Washington Boulevard and North McKinley Road.

Soleful Shoe Repairman

One depressing pandemic-era small-business casualty, Sam Torrey Shoe Service, was, for decades, a comforting continuity at Lee Highway at George Mason Drive. It dimmed its "open" sign at the end of July 2020.

The news pinged around the Nextdoor listserve, and more than 130 customers mourned the loss of the expert repair skills of Kervork Tchalekian, who, since 1986, had rescued countless favorite pairs of shoes, luggage, zippers and pocketbooks. (This author was a regular for heel plates, which he needed because he's slue-footed and wears down shoes fast.)

The pandemic's economic lockdown hastened Tchalekian's planned retirement to North Carolina's Outer Banks, which the fifty-six-year-old and his wife, a food industry cheese specialist, had envisioned for a decade later.

One Monday, during Tchalekian's multiday pack-up, this author reminisced with "Jo-Jo," as his Armenian family nicknamed him, as they stood amid stacked National Moving Company boxes, giveaway furniture and silent metallic machinery.

Still displayed on his vintage countertop was the black-and-white photograph of Sam Torrey's back when it shared a space in the Cherrydale Fire Department building, after Sam Torregrosa opened doors in 1945. Taped nearby was the familiar fix-it shop adage, attributed to English Victorian wise man John Ruskin: "There is hardly anything in the world that someone cannot make a little worse and sell a little cheaper, and the people who consider price alone are that person's lawful prey."

Jo-Jo insists you can't get quality without paying for it. But today's shoe market, with instant internet sales and disposable synthetics, has rendered the Ruskin philosophy quaint.

"The closing was unplanned, but COVID-19 made the decision easier," said Jo-Jo, who has run the business solo since March 2020, when he laid off his three craftsmen (plus some part-time customer service helpers). "I got them jobs," he said. That summer, "things had started to pick up a little, but it was not steady enough to call the guys in."

Jo-Jo then began working eighteen-hour days and, toward the end, started turning down work and calling pending customers to accelerate final pickups. The tins of shoe polish, shine kits and shoelaces he stocked remained on the racks, though he had given away or sold much of it. "I've already thrown away thousands of dollars in supplies," he lamented.

The movers were to transfer the "big, awkward" sander, trimmer, shining "all-in-one" machine "needed for any shoe shop," he said. The two stitching machines, five hundred pounds each, "are outdated and not easy to get rid of," he said. He'll keep one.

"The community has been great, and there are not enough words to express my gratitude," Jo-Jo said.

His landlord, Virginia Hospital Center, waived the lease, which wasn't supposed to terminate until November 2020. "He's been an institution in this area of Arlington" and will be tough to replace, given the parking difficulties, according to the hospital vice president for community relations Adrian Stanton.

The good news is that Sam Torrey's services continue online for those who want to "keep in touch" with his special capabilities; Jo-Jo has set up convenient shipping arrangements.

7
SOME SPECIAL FOLKS

Presidents in Our Midst

This author was inspired by the January 20, 2021 Inauguration Day image of former presidents Clinton, George W. Bush and Obama reflecting on U.S. history at the 101-year-old Arlington National Cemetery amphitheater.

Which of our forty-six presidents spent time in Arlington before or during their tenures?

Most, if not all, would have passed through during cross-Potomac travels, and in modern times, most visited the Tomb of the Unknown Soldier and the Pentagon. But which old-timers can we document?

We begin with George Washington, who, in 1774, bought land in what is now the Glencarlyn neighborhood and returned in 1785 to survey it.

Thomas Jefferson, who helped plan the Long Bridge, was seen, after being succeeded by James Madison on March 4, 1809, alone on horseback on Pennsylvania Avenue, riding south toward Virginia.

James Madison, while fleeing the attacking British during the War of 1812, came through Arlington via the ferry to what today is Roosevelt Island on his way to reunite with his wife, Dolley, in Fairfax.

Andrew Jackson dedicated his namesake Jackson City on the Virginia side of the Potomac in 1836. He, John Tyler and James Polk often visited nearby Abingdon as guests of Alexander Hunter, who lived there while serving as the U.S. marshal for the District of Columbia.

Franklin Pierce made several visits to Arlington House to see George Washington Parke Custis, and one visit was recorded in detail in April 1856.

During the Civil War, Abraham Lincoln visited Forts Corcoran (Rosslyn) and Albany (near Columbia Pike), a Union hospital at the Falls Grove home (now North Glebe and Little Falls Roads) and likely passed by Upton Hill (Wilson Boulevard at Patrick Henry Drive) on November 20, 1861, to review troops at Munson Hill, near Bailey's Crossroads. Among the young Union fighters stationed at Upton Hill were Rutherford B. Hayes and William McKinley.

Theodore Roosevelt, in the early 1900s, rode his horse for recreation near what is now the course at Washington Golf and Country Club. William Howard Taft came through by automobile caravan on July 21, 1911, on his way to a Civil War commemoration in Manassas (mentioned on a sign on Lee Highway at the Falls Church border).

Taft and Roosevelt, along with Woodrow Wilson, Warren G. Harding and Calvin Coolidge, were members of that country club, and Wilson was fond of riding in his Pierce-Arrow along what became Wilson Boulevard.

Franklin Roosevelt, on January 30, 1941, celebrated a birthday at the club, too.

Dwight Eisenhower, after he was appointed army chief of staff in 1946, lived at Fort Myer. And on November 10, 1954, with Vice President Nixon, he dedicated the Marine Corps Memorial Iwo Jima in Arlington.

Lyndon Johnson, as a young congressman in 1942, sent a Valentine's Day telegram from Los Angeles to wife, Lady Bird, who was living then at 22 North George Mason Drive (now the Arlington Oaks Condominiums), according to a telegram preserved by the LBJ Library in Austin. As vice president in February 1962, Johnson stationed his limo on North Harrison Street, across from Williamsburg Junior High (now Middle School), hoping that the wife of astronaut John Glenn—who, at the time, was making final preparations to become the first American to orbit the Earth—would receive the vice president (she declined).

Richard Nixon, while still vice president, came to National Airport on October 3, 1960, to speak at a program honoring his wife, Pat.

George W. Bush enjoyed Tex-Mex at the El Paso Café at 4235 North Pershing Drive.

Obama, in May 2009, enjoyed a meal with then–vice president Joe Biden at Ray's the Steaks restaurant in upper Rosslyn. And Obama spoke at Wakefield High School on September 15, 2009, and again on March 11,

2011. He shopped at One More Page Bookstore for Small Business Day on November 24, 2012.

Donald Trump, in 2017, gave a foreign policy speech at Fort Myer and went to his campaign headquarters in Rosslyn on June 11, 2020, and again that November 3. President Biden, on July 23, 2021, held an event at Lubber Run Park.

DOCTORS OF YESTERYEAR

Regional magazines enjoy success with cover stories showcasing the area's "best doctors."

Though this author would personally never indulge in formula writing, a dinner several years ago reunited him with a childhood physician. Dr. Bertram Snyder had offices first in Ballston, then in the group building at 601 South Carlin Springs Road. He inspired the author to survey friends and consult histories to give some ink to Arlington's medical notables from times when doctors still made house calls.

The area's first doctor, according to Arlington historian Dorothy Ellis Lee, was an eighteenth-century practitioner named Dr. Dangil, for whom Doctors' Run, near Four Mile Run and the park at 1301 South George Mason Drive, is named.

A pre–Civil War physician and Arlington local government stalwart was Dr. George Wunder. From his farmhouse near the intersection of today's North Glebe Road and Lee Highway, Wunder was summoned, in 1858, to the home of plantation owner Bazil Hall to treat (without success) the slaveowner's wife, who had been pushed into a fireplace in anger by her enslaved servant Jenny Farr.

After the turn of the twentieth century, the Arlington area's most notable MD was Williamson Welburn. Though he was born in Nashville, Tennessee, he married Mary King (who became Ballston postmaster) of Arlington's Glencarlyn neighborhood. Welburn practiced in the area for six decades, eventually becoming the county medical examiner. In 1905, he set up Arlington's first commercial pharmacy at Glebe Road and Wilson Boulevard, relieving locals of the burden of traveling to Georgetown for medications. According to his wife's recollections in the 2017 *Arlington Historical Magazine*, Dr. Welburn helped install, at the 900 Block of North Stuart Street, Arlington's first cement sidewalks.

The pioneer of Arlington's public health services was Henry Clay Corbett, according to Nan and Ross Netherton's pictorial history of Arlington. In the 1910s, this graduate of George Washington University mobilized against contagious diseases and improved our forebears' sanitation.

After Arlington Hospital was built in the mid-1940s, its chief of pathology, for a half century, was Dr. William Dolan (known as "Mr. Arlington Hospital," according to the author's friend George). Dolan was also the county's assistant medical examiner and a cofounder of the American Blood Commission.

Arlington, at that time, was still legally segregated. So, the MD who cared for much of the Black community in the 1930s was Dr. Edward Morton, who ran for county board. His practice was taken over by Dr. Harold Johnson. As recalled in Wilma Jones's 2018 book *Halls Hill: More Than a Neighborhood*, Johnson had an office in Falls Church with his partner, Dr. Oscar Ellison. Johnson lived in the mostly White neighborhood at 2901 North Lexington Street, but his children attended John M. Langston, the all-Black elementary school on Lee Highway. In September 1957, after he joined a lawsuit to desegregate Arlington schools, Ku Klux Klan members burned a cross on Dr. Johnson's lawn.

The author's inquiries to the Arlington County Medical Society produced a tip about Dr. W. Leonard Weyl, a surgeon in Arlington who became the president of the Medical Society of Virginia. "He was a motivator to get physicians involved in politics," said Dr. Edward Koch, a professor of obstetrics and gynecology who worked with Weyl in the early 1970s at Northern Virginia Doctors Hospital.

A surprising number of female doctors emerged in the fifties and sixties. This author's friend Eddie recalls pediatrician Dr. Ruth White, who partnered with her physician husband in an office on North Glebe Road, near Lee Highway (now the bakery Livin' the Pie Life). "She was a very serious woman who wore her hair pulled back in a tight bun," Eddie recalled. Another mainstay at Northern Virginia Doctors Hospital in the 1950s was OB-GYN Dr. Shirley Martin, who also had offices at Seven Corners.

Beginning in 1974, innovative orthopedist Dr. Robert Nirschl established "one of the first sports medicine facilities on the East Coast," says the website of his ongoing center. Nirschl then became the long-term team doctor for Yorktown High School.

Finally, the author's friend Mary recalled surgeon Dr. Leon Block, who, during her teen years in the late 1960s, treated her after a car accident. Block, who moonlighted as an admired jazz musician, performed "nine surgeries on my battered face," she recalled. Classmates were not kind when she came to school with bandages and black eyes. Mary said, "He became like a surrogate father and supported me through those tough years."

Social Life at Clarendon Fire Station

Tucked inside the Clarendon fire station on North 10th Street is a special closed-off room. By long-standing arrangement with the county, it is dedicated to honoring the station's decades of reliance on volunteer firefighters.

In 2019, the professionally staffed Fire Station 4 deployed "no active volunteers, but retains a volunteer presence," said Captain Richard Slusher III.

The walls where longtime volunteers continue to meet are lined with photographs of flaming houses and plaques that recall an era when Arlington relied on volunteer firemen to spring into action at all hours when tragedy threatened.

A stalwart of that era was Eugene Gordon, who is still an ambassador for the station at the age of ninety-six and who has made a second home at Fire Station 4 for seventy-seven years. When I visited him in 2019 at the Greenspring Retirement Community, he greeted me in a hat and shirt bearing emblems for Clarendon Volunteer Fire Department No. 4. His apartment's front door was decorated with model firetrucks and a Pentagon 9/11 patch.

Gordon showed me a wooden plaque honoring him for seven decades of service to the station he first signed on to on September 21, 1942. A separate certificate from 2014 proclaims him as sergeant at arms emeritus.

Arlington's firehouses, though utilitarian in ambiance, have hosted historical dramas. Fire Station 8 in Hall's Hill played a central role in ending segregation, and the Clarendon station, in 1974, made news when the nation's first full-time female firefighter, Judy Brewer, was assigned there.

Gordon embodies the willingness of average Arlingtonians to donate their time while holding down a day job in exchange for rewards that he says are mostly social. "We had no TVs, no smart phones, no computers," he said. "But it was easy to get young people to volunteer because there were lots of dinners and dances."

As a nineteen-year-old who grew up in the Clarendon neighborhood on what was Alexandria Avenue (now 9th Street), Gordon enlisted in the navy after World War II broke out. His goal was to be an aerial gunner, but after training in Maryland and Florida, he flunked the eye test. As a machinist mate on liberty, he began helping out at the fire station, where there were five paid firemen and some twenty volunteers.

Back then, "we had no radios, though Clarendon was first to get one," Gordon said. So, volunteers would hear a siren from home and hustle on foot to, say, a coal plant in Rosslyn. "There was no way to tell if the fire was out before you got there." Many home fires were caused by someone smoking in bed, he noted, and firemen could never be sure a mattress wasn't continuing to burn.

Gordon's paying jobs included making venetian blinds and installing asbestos insulation. But he valued his fireman's life for its sense of community—the fast-pitch softball leagues, the group outings to Washington Redskins games.

Chuck Satterfield, the station's president who joined in 1962, called Gordon "a mainstay," whose "counsel we always take."

Both men express astonishment at how neighborhoods like Clarendon and Ballston have evolved from "shotgun cottages" to high-rises, as Satterfield put it, causing both of them to occasionally get lost in their own hometown.

Gordon laments that today's firehouses "have trouble finding" volunteers.

Though he no longer drives, Gordon appreciates that his car repair shop honored volunteer firemen. "They gave me 10 percent off."

Thrills of a Batboy

"Wanted: Senators Batboy." That poster at James Madison Elementary School in the early sixties spawned envy among the author's peers with the idea that you could quit school and be tutored while mingling daily with heroes like Eddie Brinkman and Chuck Hinton.

Bill Jett got to live that dream, both for the original Senators, starting in 1958, and for the expansion team that arrived in 1961. The 1961 graduate of Washington-Lee (W-L, now Liberty) High School said he began ushering at Senators games in the old Griffith Stadium. He was recruited by fellow W-L graduate Ralph Schleeper. From his view from the left-field foul line, "there wasn't much of crowd" toward the end of that downtown venue's life, "so they let us go home early," said Jett, who played baseball, basketball and track at Thomas Jefferson Junior High and W-L.

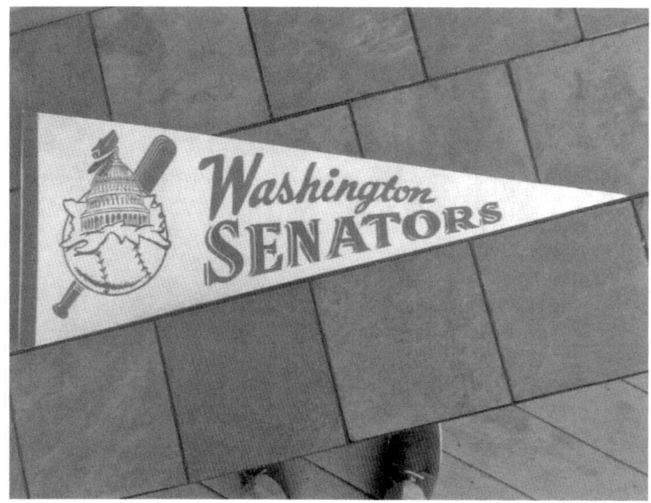

An old Senators pennant. *Courtesy of Bill Jett.*

But he did see "a lot of great players, and I saw Harmon Killebrew hit a deep home run" off Herb Score of the Cleveland Indians in May 1959. He was particularly friendly with outfielder Bob Allison, whose fan club Jett joined. One time, Allison struck out three times, and the star was so angry in the dugout, he wrenched a water faucet out from the wall.

Jett continued on staff during college, after the Senators moved to the new D.C. Stadium (renamed RFK Stadium in 1969), also pinch-hitting as a batboy. He already "knew all the ushers, and the captains knew me." Being older and already trained, he didn't need tutoring, and was available for day and night games—due to flexibility from bosses at his new job at the FBI.

A few times, he served as batboy for the visiting team, recalling sitting in the dugout near the Detroit Tigers' batting star Al Kaline. But more often, his job included running the lineup card from the Senators' manager Gil Hodges to the press box and *Washington Post* sportswriter Bob Addie. He got to know slugger Frank "Hondo" Howard and, later, Senators manager Ted Williams. Both were "real nice," Jett said.

He even had a U.S. Secret Service clearance that allowed him to be one of the few ushers with access to the president's box, which hosted VIPs (he remembers Ike's grandson David Eisenhower, for one). Jett got to know the photographers, who gave him signed photographs, which he still has, and he picked up gossip on players' futures from team physician George Resta.

Senators second baseman John Schaive gave the teenage Jett his game hat and shirt when the player left the old Senators.

Now retired in Gainesville, Virginia, after a career in commercial and mortgage banking, Jett, who was seventy-eight in 2020, blends his love of the game with memories of his youth in Arlington, where he also ran maintenance operations at Greenbrier Field for the county recreation department.

The most memorable Senators game Jett witnessed, he said, was the June 12, 1967 historic milestone that went on for a record twenty-two innings (six hours and thirty-eight minutes). Finally, at 2:30 a.m., Nats catcher Paul Casanova hit a single to win the game against the White Sox. Jett reported: "I got about three hours of sleep that night before I had to get to my day job."

Struggling Fraternal Lodges

For decades, the fraternal organizations, lodges and service clubs that once dominated civic life in Arlington have been rowing against the current. Their efforts in recruiting among baby boomers, Gen Xers, millennials and Gen Zers is like pulling teeth for the shrinking roster of community activists who were such joiners in the post–World War II period.

In 2020, this author's chats with doers of good works from the Optimist Club of Arlington, the Kiwanis Club of Arlington and the Woman's Club of Arlington showed they're struggling against more than the "Bowling Alone" trends among youth who prefer fellowship online.

The pandemic has also crimped the style—if not the generosity—of the luncheon groups (and their international bodies) that do so much for needy students, the food insecure, young athletes and Christmas tree buyers.

The North Arlington Kiwanis, who usually lunch at Knights of Columbus, have been meeting by Zoom, said stalwart Edd Nolen. The current membership of 48 is tiny compared to the 140 he recalls in 1994. "My first awareness of the Kiwanis was my dad's activities in my hometown in Alabama," Nolen remembers. "That's how a small town like Arlington functioned—if you didn't belong to the Kiwanis or the Lions, you were not going to go anywhere in that community. I sensed the same thing around here."

But today's Kiwanis have had to discontinue their annual pig roast after the workload became too heavy. "The decline in community spirit is because people are busier today and doing things in a different way with the internet, emailing and texting," Nolen added. "Now, people may help with a food drive but then move on to something else, without real long-range commitment."

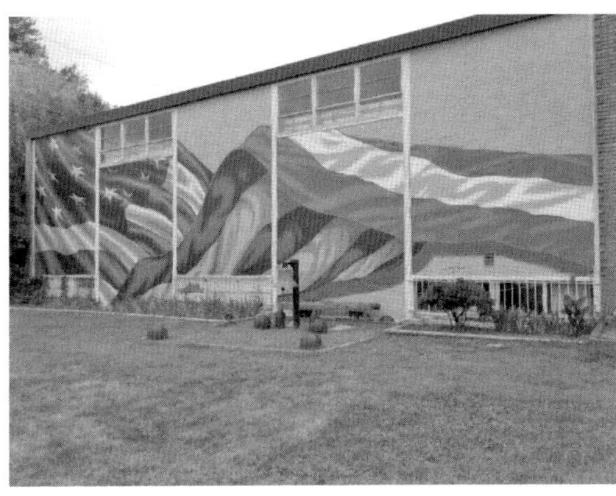

American Legion Post 139 club near Virginia Square. In 2018, it was torn down and converted to affordable housing for veterans. *Courtesy of Bob Romano.*

The Woman's Club of Arlington, said president Deneise Boyd, has been "fairly steady with 23 active members," down from 120 at its peak after World War II. The club, with its own building on South Buchanan Street, has continued its outreach but has confined its meetings to Zoom (not all members participate). "Keeping our members engaged has been a goal," she said.

Longtime member Sandy Newton said the Woman's Club "has been fortunate that other organizations have sought us for use of our parking lot for dancing, acting, flea markets and food distribution for Barcroft families." In October 2020, a "Traffic Garden" was installed on club property so that kids could learn rules of the road. "It was only in August that some of our renters returned with strict social distancing," Newton said. "We are hoping to attract more members by being relevant in their lives through activities that might draw them in."

The local Optimist Club, which recently, as of the writing of this book, resumed in-person (but socially distanced) lunches at Washington Golf and Country Club, has forty-one members, probably half what it attracted in the 1950s or 1960s, according to member Frank O'Leary, the retired Arlington County treasurer. The group's "socializing strategy has been unsuccessful, because no one wants to physically get together," he said. "So much of this is out of date," in that young people don't "hang out physically but in chat rooms, and they have a far larger set of people with whom they're interacting."

It isn't just service clubs that suffer, O'Leary added. "Any organization I've been in has the same problems—today's veterans do not join the VFW or go to the hall. The formula doesn't work because of changes in society. It may be the twilight of these sorts of organizations."

8
PRESERVATION BATTLES

Current-Day Teardowns

Dateline: September 2015. It was demolition derby time for Arlington's churning housing stock. On every residential block, it seemed, there's a teardown on ever-more-valuable land.

Ranch- and Cape Cod–style homes erected during our county's post–World War II boom were increasingly deemed obsolete. Demolition permits, county figures show, rose from 91 applications in the first half of 2013 to 129 for the same period in 2014 and 124 for the first six months of 2015.

One teardown that was in progress on North Potomac Street poignantly exposed the wallpaper of some kid's bedroom that was surely once held dear.

All this crashing of bricks and dust means steady work for prospering homebuilders. But many Arlingtonians are less than thrilled. They watch $400,000 or $600,000 homes give way to $1.3 million formula mansions that tower over more modest neighbors. "Can middle-income people in their thirties, first-time buyers, still live in Arlington?" asked Margie Bell, who gets letters weekly from builders seeking to buy her home. "Many people I have talked to who sold directly to developers never even talked to a realtor or considered the impact of their decision."

Paul Donaldson, an agent with RE/MAX Allegiance, said the shift toward luxury dwellings harms neighborhood cohesion. "These people don't need the space, it's the status," he told this author as they toured a new eight-bedroom customized home. (It was being shown fully furnished, with a rented grand piano, and included a home theater.) Most of these wealthy new arrivals are seldom home, he said. "You never see them walking around."

"I don't think anyone minds when a rambler is popped up to a two-story home," Donaldson added. "But there are things builders could do that wouldn't change the neighborhood character."

The one Arlington builder who returned the author's call, New Dimensions Inc. president Jennifer Landers, said her company works with landowners to keep the new dwelling affordable, adding that it's not easy in the current market to unload an expensive home.

Bell asked county board member Libby Garvey for solutions. She forwarded a staff-created list of reasons why there is little policymakers can do. Property owners can sell to whomever they choose, it said, and "encouraging owners to sell to first-time buyers will likely have little impact; sellers and real estate agents' primary considerations are the sale price and the amount of risk associated with an offer." The missive acknowledged that many builders follow "the letter of the law" rather than consider neighborhood character.

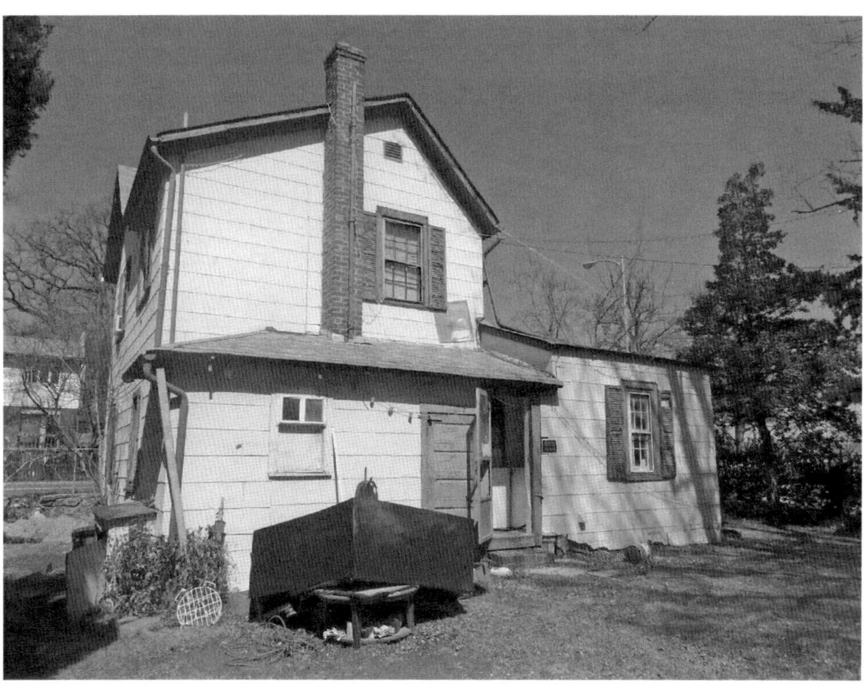

The century-old farmhouse at 4210 Washington Boulevard was demolished in 2015. *Courtesy of Tom Dickinson.*

But because historic preservationists worry about losing vintage homes, the teardown trend is being monitored.

Bell was disappointed. "The county can do something creative to encourage preserving just-right-sized houses, though I know they prefer the extra tax dollars for the huge houses," she said. She favors a public service campaign to encourage homeowners to resist suspicious offers from builders that emphasize "no hassle, no commission" and list with an agent more sensitive to buyers' needs.

County board candidate Katie Cristol (later elected), who loves to label herself a millennial, told a September 8, 2015 forum that the most common complaint she hears is from longtime homeowners who say they couldn't afford to buy here today. "The economics of teardowns versus preservation," she said, "don't make it easy for property owners to improve their homes to age in place or for new owners to get a foothold."

TREE WARS

The teardown trend in our home sales market continued apace in 2017. But a few mighty oaks may have begun to slow the demolitions that have put much real estate beyond the financial reach of average local American dreamers.

Arlington's tree stewards—a label far more sophisticated than the epithet "tree hugger"—in July 2017 banded together under the banner of the Arlington Tree Action Group.

Several dozen residents from neighborhoods across the county gathered in a leafy private home alongside the lush setting of Donaldson Run, laying out plans to confront the county government that views itself as green.

"It breaks our hearts to see old [Civil War–era] trees torn down," said one. "Big developments are destroying the beauty of Arlington," said another. A big decision to loosen zoning requirements "made by a few people in the county a decade ago is being carried out despite new information and citizen concern."

Group members know that Arlington's Urban Forestry Commission and well-intentioned staff are devoted to environmental protections of the tree canopy that is so vital to air quality and water drainage—not to mention aesthetic grandeur.

There's a feeling that powerful market forces exploited by builders have tied the hands of county leaders who, some say, are addicted to tax revenues from newly built luxury homes. In the Penrose neighborhood, one participant said, two acres of virgin forest were bulldozed, inviting in mice and rats.

One Yorktown High School student said tree protection was a good place for Arlington to start to address climate change.

Solutions aren't simple. The action group would start by assembling a critical mass to apply pressure.

"Some very active negative publicity" for developers who clear-cut trees could be spread, for example, along with requiring permits to chop trees of a certain size; challenging builders whose homes exceed the 40 percent lot allowance; prodding the county to appoint a tree ombudsman; creating a builder-financed tree preservation fund.

The tree group has blitzed the planning commission, and members filed comments to help update the public spaces master plan.

County Board vice-chair Katie Cristol told this author she is sympathetic, citing teardown moratoria elsewhere.

"Unfortunately, current provisions in the county code—which includes a tree preservation ordinance—maximize the state's enabling authority for tree preservation," Cristol said. "I don't think this means our hands are tied, only that we have to be more creative in giving alternatives to an activity we cannot outright ban. If residents, or new owners, of a property can more easily add value to an existing structure, they will have options other than a teardown." That means accessory dwellings and zoning improvements for non-conforming homes.

Such ideas were echoed by board candidate Erik Gutshall, who made middle-class housing a theme. (He won the election but died in April 2020.) There is a connection between losing tree canopy and housing stock, he said. The most doable solution now is exploring "voluntary incentives." For example: "You petition the county with an application to have it designate one or more trees on your yard as 'specimen trees.' That protects them from removal or injury even after the home is sold," Gutshall said.

Gutshall also investigated real estate tax breaks within property assessments for homeowners who preserve trees. Builders could be given credit for keeping trees as part of their stormwater management plan.

"We can't change the fundamental equation," Gutshall said. "But there's more we can do on the margins," all to honor God's trees.

Contrasting New Homes with Old

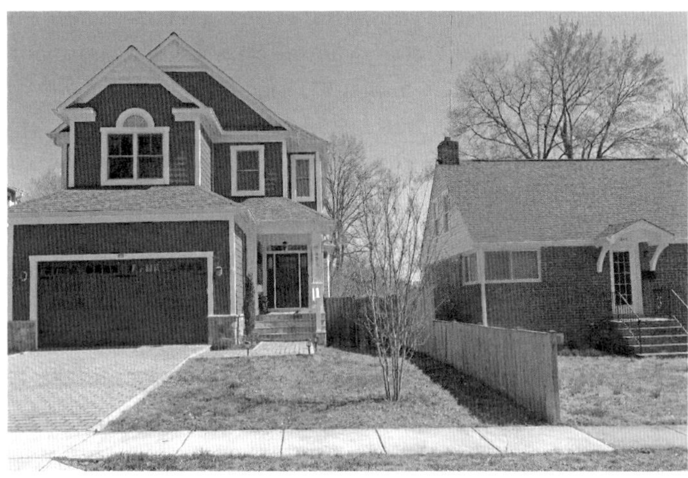

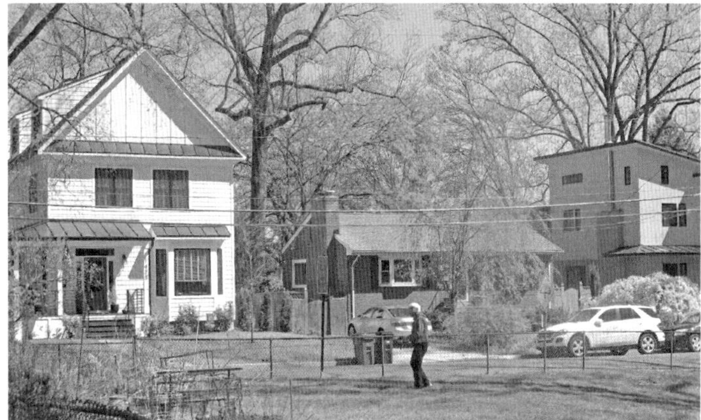

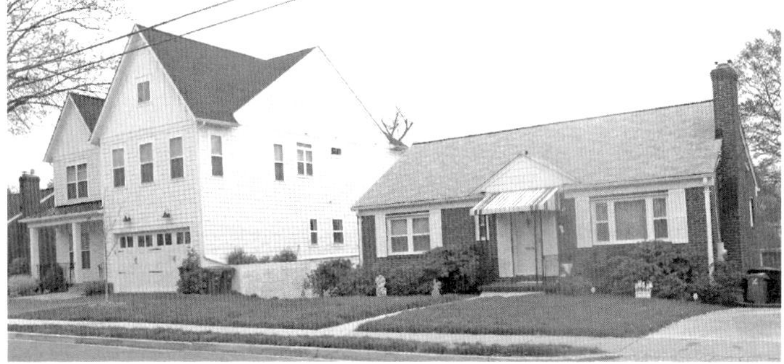

Photographs by Tom Dickinson.

In June 2018, the teardown bulldozers were headed for a familiar mansion at 3260 North Ohio Street, the site of a famous annual flower display.

More alarming, said activists in the Arlington Tree Action Group, is that the builders who were taking over from the deceased owner were planning to remove deep-rooted trees to make room for two homes. One in the front yard that was slated for the buzz saw was an award-winning dawn redwood that is one of Arlington's champion trees. County board member John Vihstadt reached builder Ross Richmond to request a change in plan. But the dawn redwood and the house came down in August 2018, where two luxury homes now sit.

SUCCESSFUL PRESERVATION

Arlington's ambitious growth and rising population during and after the two world wars created demand and revenue, which enabled county preservation acquisitions. Some of the best examples follow.

The Hume School on Arlington Ridge Road was built in 1891 on land purchased by the Alexandria School Board. It was named for a local landowner and Confederate colonel who was wounded at Gettysburg and came back to the area as a developer (for six hundred acres) and philanthropist. Lessons were given in that schoolhouse until 1958. Then the Arlington County Board, in 1960, deeded the site to the Arlington Historical Society, which opened its museum there in 1963. And it continues today.

There was also the Gulf Branch Nature Center at 3608 Military Road. Its building began as a stone retreat, shielded in the woods in the 1920s. When the last private owner, John Davis, departed in the early 1960s, the county debated its acquisition during the earliest days of the environmental movement. "What the devil is a nature center?" people asked Girls Scouts executive and future county board member Dorothy Grotos, who advocated for it. She teamed up with board member Thomas Richards, who, cognizant of the Arlington's coming economic growth, sought to balance concrete and steel with new open space. In 1964, $135,000 from the General Land Use Plan account were offered to Davis for six acres. The Nature Center opened in 1966.

A similar situation unfolded at the Long Branch Nature Center at 625 South Carlin Springs Road. It was the home of William and Mae Hickman, both bird and animal lovers, for twenty-seven years. The county, again with

Richard's impetus, bought the six acres in four lots gradually between 1963 and 1966. That center opened in 1972.

Another fertile period came at the start of the twenty-first century. The county acquired the Reeves farmhouse in 2001 (page 99) and the 1913 vintage Fraber House at 1612 North Quincy Street in 2002. William Fraber (1881–1945) wasn't historically prominent—a veteran of the Spanish-American War, he was employed by the Washington Navy Yard. But the house on three parcels (two of which are now Oak Grove Park) was deemed a good representation of an intact and classic early-twentieth-century bungalow. After documenting the house's features, the county, in 2013, sold it to private owners.

Perhaps the most ambitious and successful preservation effort—one that continues to benefit the county—was the 1994 acquisition of the Hendry property. That nineteen-acre site of Civil War fort C.F. Smith, near Spout Run Parkway, still contains a handsome 1927 home built by physician Ernest Hendry. He married Anne Pearce in 1939, and they decorated the property with exotic ornamental and specimen trees, as the National Park Service report noted in a 1999 report on Fort C.F. Smith. The property "has survived the intensive development of the region and is an island remnant of Arlington's early twentieth-century landscape," it said. "The estate is locally significant as an early-twentieth-century estate without peer in Arlington and as physical evidence of the former suburban character of Arlington."

Numerous times in the 1950s, Hendry applied unsuccessfully to the county for rezoning, as property taxes on the nineteen acres were high. He died in 1976. By the 1980s, his widow and son Ernest Jr. had begun renovations to convert the home to a bed-and-breakfast, as laid out in Sherman Pratt's *Arlington County, Virginia: A Modern History*. Instead, they engaged with developer John G. Georgelas and Sons and real estate broker George Bonaface to subdivide the land. The plans called for forty-one new homes in the Woodmont neighborhood and possibly a retirement community overlooking the Potomac.

The neighbors were unhappy. More than five hundred showed up for a September 29, 1985 meeting, and the Parkway Citizens Association (now the Woodmont Citizens Association) objected to the new homes. The whole roster of players got involved: the Historical Affairs and Landmark Review Board, the Planning Commission, the Parks and Recreation Commission and the Arlington Historical Society. It was an uphill battle for preservationists—in 1979, a bond referendum to acquire the property had suffered a rare rejection by voters.

"It was really a question of funds," recalls then–county board member Mary Margaret Whipple. The large Hendry tract, well situated near the Palisades, "had always been a property the county thought it would add to the park network in a meaningful way. But any capital purchase has to be really thought out as to whether the value to community is worth the expenditure."

The Historical Affairs Board concluded that acquiring the land would be a "unique opportunity; a site of this potential may not be found again in Arlington."

On February 28, 1987, the county board voted 5–0 to approve Historic District Designation for the Hendry tract's ninety-two thousand square feet of open space. And on September 9, 1994, the board voted to acquire the property as public land for $5.25 million from the Anne P. Hendry Living Trust and Ernest and Judith Hendry. The developer later sued Anne Hendry for lost income.

Fort C.F. Smith Park opened in October 1996, and the Hendry House, after suitable renovations made it even handsomer, opened as a long-contemplated event venue, rentable by payments to the county.

Perhaps the challenging complexity was worth the trouble.

The following are examples of preservation efforts that didn't pan out.

The Doomed Blue Goose

Sometimes, Arlingtonians grow attached to the least likely of community institutions. In the early 1960s, an eight-story "modern movement" office building rose at Fairfax Drive and North Glebe Road as one of that now-teeming neighborhood's first high-rises (next to a duck pin bowling alley and a palm reader). It would house staff from the Federal Aviation Administration and the CIA. Because of its distinctive—some would say utilitarian—blue metallic panels, the building designed by John M. Walton and erected by M.T. Broyhill and Sons became a landmark. The press popularized it as "the Blue Goose."

But Arlington's Marymount University, whose main campus is down Glebe Road, bought the Blue Goose in 1993. Eager to expand its Ballston satellite facilities linked by bus, the growing Catholic university used the Blue Goose for its School of Business Administration; Center for Global Education; Departments of Physical Therapy, Forensic Psychology and Counseling; Verizon Information Security Lab; and graduate admissions office.

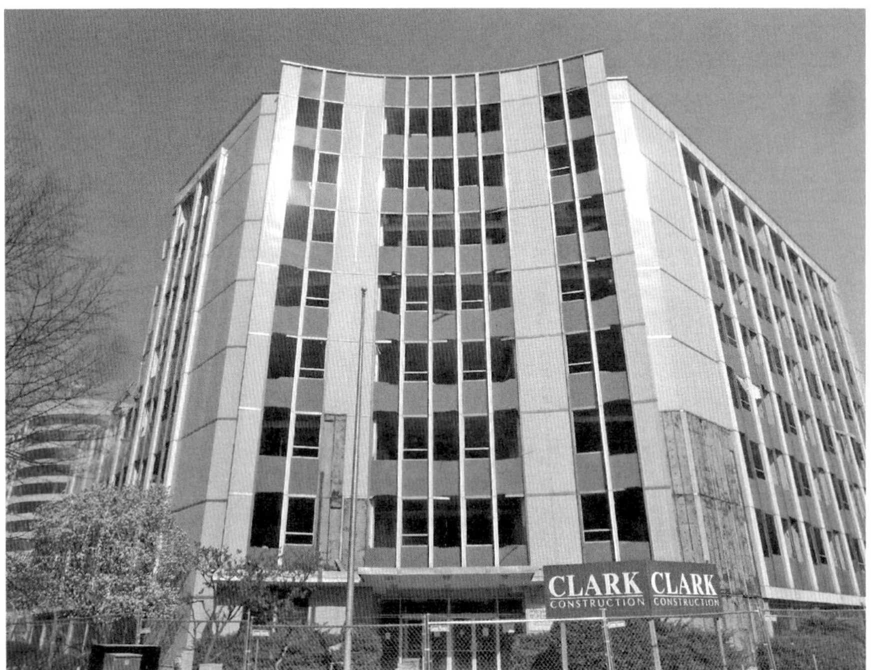

The "Blue Goose" in Ballston housed federal officials but was called ugly. *Courtesy of Tom Dickinson.*

The expansion continued. Matthew Shank, the president of Marymount University from 2011 to 2018, said in an interview with the *Arlington Catholic Herald* that the first time he beheld the Blue Goose, he called his wife and called it "pathetic" and one of the "ugliest" buildings he'd ever seen.

So, beginning in 2013, Marymount teamed up with the Shooshan Co. to create a nine-story academic office complex with residential condos (fifteen stories, called the Rixey for Admiral Presley Rixey, on whose land Marymount was built), a plaza and parking facility. Then–county board chairman Jay Fisette welcomed the planned $75 million project as "attractive and energy-efficient and will come with many benefits for our community," including leadership in energy and environmental design (a "gold-certified green building") and some units of affordable housing. But Joan Lawrence, the then-chair of the Historical Affairs and Landmark Review Board, was not excited. "This project represents missed opportunities," she told the board on October 28, 2013. "Not only does it not even remotely acknowledge or relate to the historic structure that will be demolished, but it does not provide a distinctive gateway structure likely to age well to replace the existing distinctive historic structure....While the use of historic markers may be helpful, they fail to provide the same sense of history of place that can be achieved by a building carefully designed to respect that which has been lost."

The bulldozers came in March 2015. The ceremony, as the *Sun-Gazette* reported, was led by a "sledgehammer-wielding Roman Catholic nun whaling away at the side of an office building." That was Sister Jackie Murphy of the Religious of the Sacred Heart of Mary.

One has to give Marymount credit for good public relations. Rather than consigning the Blue Goose to the dustbin of history, the academic institution followed with a new vision. The public plaza for its new complex would "retain some flavor" of the old Blue Goose, with blue seating and moody blue lighting. To boot, campus historians created historical panels in tribute to the old building that had won the hearts of some—though not all—who beheld it.

Goodbye to John Glenn

Since the early 1960s, Arlingtonians have been proud that astronaut John Glenn lived across the street from Williamsburg Junior High, which his children attended. In January 1962, while Glenn was in Florida, preparing to become the first American to orbit the Earth, his shy wife, Annie, was left at home to deal with a phalanx of reporters and camera crews at the 1950s rambler at 3683 North Harrison Street.

The Glenns moved to Texas in 1963 and later settled in Ohio, where John Glenn was elected to the U.S. Senate. He died in 2016 and was buried in Arlington National Cemetery. The Discovery Elementary School, which now shares the land with Williamsburg Middle School, was named implicitly to honor Glenn. Annie Glenn died in 2020, and days later, after her Arlington home had been sold to a builder for $1 million, it was demolished to make room for a modern replacement.

Historic preservationists were miffed that the county didn't plan a marker, and tree preservationists were dismayed that the new home builder cut down two huge oaks. But preservationist Tom Dickinson visited the lot during demolition and salvaged the telephone connector box. Those wires, he had noted, carried voices from President Kennedy, President Johnson and Soviet premier Nikita Khrushchev.

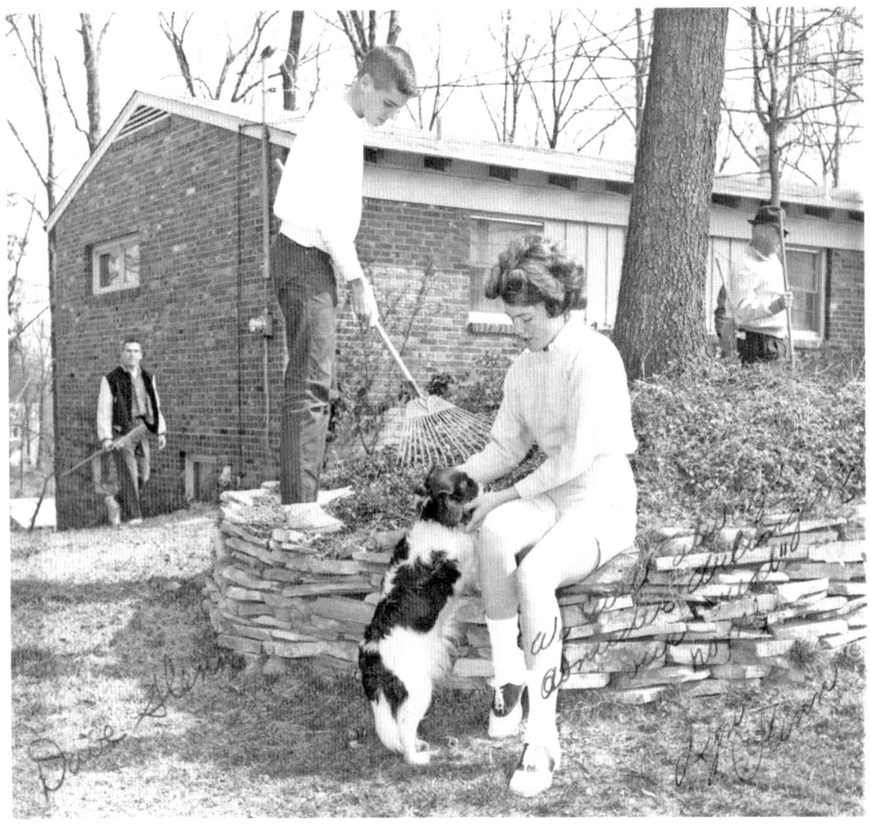

Astronaut John Glenn and his family work their yard near Williamsburg School. *Courtesy of the Arlington Historical Society.*

A PERSISTENT PRESERVATION ACTIVIST

Many of the alarm bells over preservation in Arlington are raised by Tom Dickinson. A Wisconsinite who came to Arlington in 1980 as a motion picture and television producer/director for the air force at the Pentagon, Dickinson has been on the board of the Arlington Historical Society since 2005 (he was president from 2010 to 2012) and chaired its Historic Preservation Committee. Previously, he was on the board of a group called the Arlington Heritage Alliance, which morphed into Preservation Arlington. "When I arrived in Arlington, I was shocked by the routine and pervasive demolition of older houses and commercial buildings," he said in 2021. "For some, it was a sign of progress. For me, it was a lack of respect and appreciation of our community's rich historic past."

Dickinson bemoaned Arlington's average of four hundred demolitions a year for the past three decades. In his Wisconsin hometown of Edgerton, where houses date back to the 1880s, teardowns are rare. He got the preservation bug soon after his arrival in Arlington, when he noticed the doomed shopping center at Walter Reed Drive and Arlington Mill Road. That old strip contained the original Birchmere Music Club (now in Alexandria), an A&P Grocery, a laundromat and a favored Chinese restaurant. That once-funky site is now the Heatherlee Townhomes.

Armed with his camera and determined attitude, Dickinson has since taken more than ten thousand photographs of more than five hundred buildings that are now lost. "Arlington," he laments, "is a target-rich environment." (See sampling page 140.)

Dickinson sometimes rubs property owners the wrong way, and he can be impatient with the government's occasional passivity. But here's what he and other preservationists are up against.

The county's Office of Historic Preservation has a small staff. Its veterans are proud to have helped establish designated historic sites from Civil War–era forts to churches and cemeteries. Arlingtonians can pass and read eighty-one historical markers the office helped erect.

Program coordinator Cynthia Liccese-Torres could rightfully note, in 2021, that in her twenty years with Arlington, she saved a Lustron home from demolition (and oversaw its display in New York City's Museum of Modern Art in 2008, then its 2011 donation to the Ohio History Connection in Columbus). She successfully completed three National Register of Historic Places nominations and five local historic district designations while she authored more than a dozen Arlington historic markers. "We are striving to broaden the focus of historic preservation beyond just architecture and historic buildings," she said, "by exploring cultural history, personal stories and connections, and celebrating our diversity."

Still, the broader challenge, notes Jackie Barton, a consultant helping Liccese-Torres revise the preservation master plan in 2021, is "not about stopping time or preventing change but helping manage change."

The best advice on preservation is supposed to come from the volunteers on the Historical Affairs and Landmark Review Board. But its carefully researched nominations for protection by historic designation can be ignored or overruled by the county board.

That leaves the elected board. And preservation appears low on its 2021 list of priorities that includes setting tax rates and budgeting for law enforcement, public health, schools, building regulation, transportation and housing

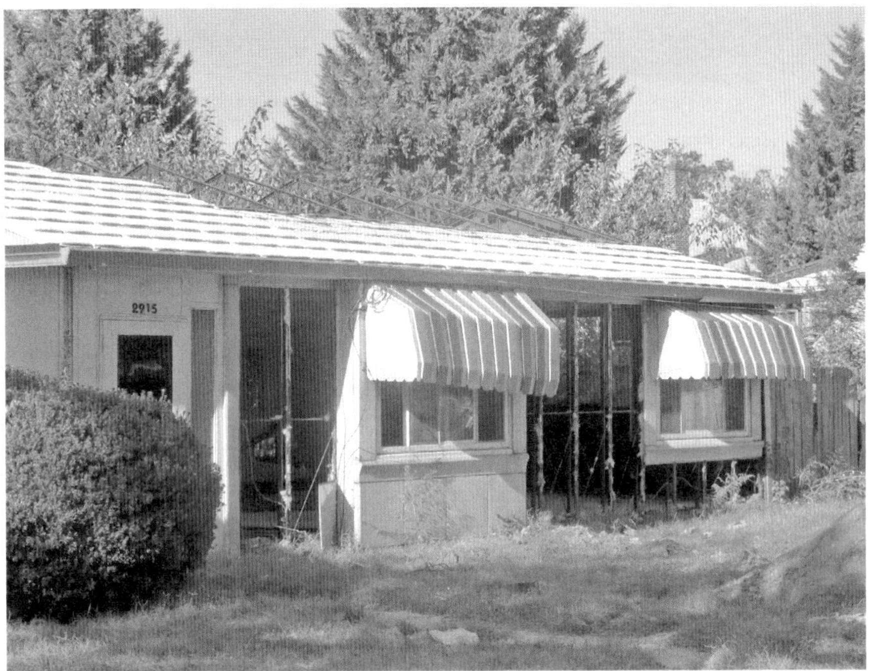

A now-demolished prefabricated steel Lustron home; Arlington had eleven, but it now has two. *Courtesy of Tom Dickinson.*

challenges. The county board doubtless felt burned by its ill-fated ownership of the Reeves farmhouse in Bluemont Park, purchased in 2001 for $1.8 million and designated as a historic district three years later. But it was left empty for two decades while there was indecision on how to make use of it.

In 2021, the county board members were excoriated by Dickinson and dozens of street-protesting preservationists who were upset at the board's failure to block the demolition of the 170-year-old Febrey-Lothrop house. That Colonial Revival–style home on Wilson Boulevard and North McKinley Street had been flagged as a "generational site" in the county's master parks plan since the 2017 death of its owner. Inquiries were made for it as a potential school or park site. But budget-conscious officials delayed action until they were outfoxed by an aggressive trust and homebuilder.

That gray-shingled house on 9.5 acres, with a swimming pool and ancient outbuildings, was occupied until 2020 by Michele Rouse, the widow of homebuilder and equestrian Randy Rouse. His first wife was the late actress Audrey Meadows, who, in the late 1950s, commuted to New York City from Arlington to tape the TV hit *The Honeymooners* with Jackie Gleason.

This author was treated to drinks with the Rouses in the home while doing research for the house that was built by nineteenth-century school superintendent John Febrey. It was purchased in 1893 by Alvin Lothrop of department store fame.

In the spring of 2020, news broke that the party that was best able to afford the Febrey-Lothrop house was a private builder with plans for dozens of new homes.

"Trustees have not actively marketed the property," read the statement given to the author on April 27, 2020, by CPA Sid Simmonds, representing the Rouse trust.

> *In spite of not marketing the property, we received a number of unsolicited offers. The trustees had a fiduciary duty to review each offer. We retained a consultant to assist us in reviewing the offers and provide analysis and recommendations. We did not retain an agent. Most offers were filed away to revisit if the trustees decided to actively market the property. However, the trustees did receive one unsolicited offer that we felt must be pursued. The offer was from a reputable party, but it includes a confidentiality requirement, and we cannot provide further information.*

The push for the county to buy Rouse's property was expressed in 2020 emails from civic activist Suzanne Sundburg. She complained that the county resisted because the land is "not suitable" for a school and because of its proximity to Upton Hill Regional Park, even though it "has a beautiful, open, flat lawn space that could be perfect both for passive and active recreation," she wrote.

The proposal to acquire it was seconded by Peter Rousselot and the nonprofit Arlingtonians for Our Sustainable Future, which filed a Freedom of Information Act request for county deliberations. The Dominion Hills Civic Association's position was that it "would prefer that the property be preserved as open space for parks," said acting president Brian Hannigan. "But if that is not possible and the owners pursue development, we will insist that current R-6 single-family zoning be maintained."

Then–county board chair Libby Garvey told this author in the spring of 2020 that what seemed more realistic, given the competition from homebuilders and the current pandemic, is that the property "is not at a price the county would want to pay right now."

Then entered Tom Dickinson. He had the foresight to file an application to designate the home as a Local Historic District. Arlington's Historic

Preservation staff deemed his application complete and sent it for review in the fall of 2020 to the Historical Affairs and Landmark Review Board.

The solution Dickinson personally favored was for Arlington to adopt a resident curator program, authorized under a 2011 state law, in which a long-term tenant occupies a publicly owned property for free in exchange for maintenance and repairs. "It's a win-win-win proposition," argued Dickinson, who has pushed for a curator program during debates over the fate of such historic properties as the Reeves farmhouse, the Birch cabin and the recently demolished home of astronaut John Glenn. The advantages include "preserving historic properties and providing residential housing at no cost to the occupant/tenant."

Curator programs have been successful in Maryland, Massachusetts and, most locally, Fairfax County. This author spoke to one of the main instigators, Ted McCord, an associate professor of history at George Mason University. For twenty-four years, McCord has occupied Mount Gilead, a "middling" eighteenth-century tavern in Fairfax's Historic Centerville Park. (By coincidence, he knew the Rouse property because his father, in the late 1950s, was the physician of Randy Rouse and his then-wife, actress Meadows.)

The reason the legislation sailed through is that the bill required no money, McCord said. Rather than being a "one-size-fits-all" solution, the law allows jurisdictions to "assess each property on its own merit." The best properties are those that go back centuries, are a rare example of architecture or were once occupied by "someone important."

The downside is that the bureaucracy "can be a pain," McCord said, noting restrictions against using his old home's fireplaces and the parks authority's occasional desire to tear down homes to make room for tennis courts or golf courses. The best resident curators are those with "deep pockets" (they won't gain equity in the property), who "like to restore old properties," either by themselves or through contracting. And "it's really taking it out of the public domain" if the residents don't allow public visits. "But if you get a builder with a little imagination to preserve an old house," McCord said, "it can add to the identity of a neighborhood."

Arlington is not currently entertaining the admittedly admirable idea, countered spokeswoman Elise Cleva. A curator program would "require significant planning, plus investments of staff resources and public funds," she said. "The county would need to evaluate considerations, such as initial funding, potential inventory of eligible properties, zoning amendments, tenant coordination and need for additional staff."

In January 2021, Dickinson circulated an online petition at www.moveon.org, urging the county to protect the home. It drew more than 1,400 signatures, ambitiously calling for the suspension of a recent demolition permit, the acceleration of a county study of eligibility for historic designation and the purchase of some or all of the property for a public purpose.

Dickinson brought in two activists in local history. "Based on new research and accessibility to digital records, it is becoming evident that [nearby] Upton Hill, Fort Ramsey and the Febrey property were all connected to a major part of U.S. history," wrote Civil War researcher Peter Vaselopulos during an email debate. "Thousands of Union soldiers camped on Upton Hill, including two future presidents, Rutherford B. Hayes and William McKinley. Newly discovered letters and diaries from northern soldiers reveal a unique and untold perspective."

Sketches of the home from the 1860s were submitted by Luke Burke, who cited the home's "scenic view of Washington, D.C., and the surrounding area…including the possibility that part of the original 1860s house remains and could have Civil War inscriptions."

The importance of the land-owning Febreys to nineteenth-century Arlington was stressed by descendant Michael Febrey, who wrote, "To allow this house to be torn down would diminish the history of the county." Soon, the Arlington Historical Society took a position in favor of preserving the home.

Skepticism was heard from history activist Karl VanNewkirk. "It's been stated that we need more parks. But Upton Hill Regional Park is across Wilson Boulevard, the skatepark is only a little further away and half a mile down the hill is the Four Mile Run valley, basically one continuous park for miles," he wrote. "The house is not as old as commonly thought. The Civil War connection is minor."

A similar downbeat note came from former county board member John Vihstadt, who noted that in tight-budget times,

> *The fate of the estate is a multifaceted debate with no perfect answers. It isn't practical for the county to save the house, unless it could quickly facilitate a well-capitalized for-profit or nonprofit to make a major investment. The most economically viable outcome could have been—and maybe, with the right public and private leadership, could still be—a combination of neighborhood-sensitive, context-driven redevelopment, including housing for a range of incomes, modest commercial uses and recreational open space. A simple but informative nod to the history could be done through markers.*

Drawn into the discussion was Dick Woodruff, chairman of the Historical Affairs and Landmark Review Board. "The way forward is to persuade the owners to protect the house and some surrounding viewshed property in the context of the single-family home development they intend to build there," he wrote.

> *The home, plus an acre or two, would be a historic district and sold to a private owner who wants to live in it and fix it up to preservation guidelines. The owners could be talked into selling the house and then building respectfully around it—which would add to the attractiveness of their neighborhood. We wouldn't get a big new park, but unless someone comes up with $20 million, that isn't happening.*

The builder applied in December 2020 for permit to cap off the property's sewer lines. Then the (still unnamed) firm applied for a demolition permit in January 2021. It was approved on January 25 but could not be issued until the historic designation permit was approved. Meantime, on January 27, the HALRB recommended unanimously that the property receive local historic district designation and that a study process be expedited. But the county board "does not have the legal authority to prevent the owners of the property from demolishing the structures," said new chair Matt de Ferranti on March 3. The board agreed only to advertise the issue and take it up in April.

But it was too late. Workmen, on March 20, 2021, were seen preparing the Febrey-Lothrop house for demolition. That didn't stop several dozen pandemic-masked protesters, who gathered and carried "Save the Febrey House" signs to the honks of cars passing on Wilson Boulevard. "It's all about the money," one complained about the builder's plan to raze the nineteenth-century structure.

Organized by civic activist John Reeder and Dickinson (and attended by Civil War historian Vaselopulos), the protest was more likely to generate debate over future policy than to block the teardown. There were several scolding letters to the editor, some accusing the board of valuing tax revenue from "McMansions" over historical landmarks. And Dickinson told the board:

> *Remember, that while your eyes are focused on the future of Arlington County (to your great credit), the eyes of history are fixed on each of you. She will be kind and favorable to your legacy as a leader of Arlington County should*

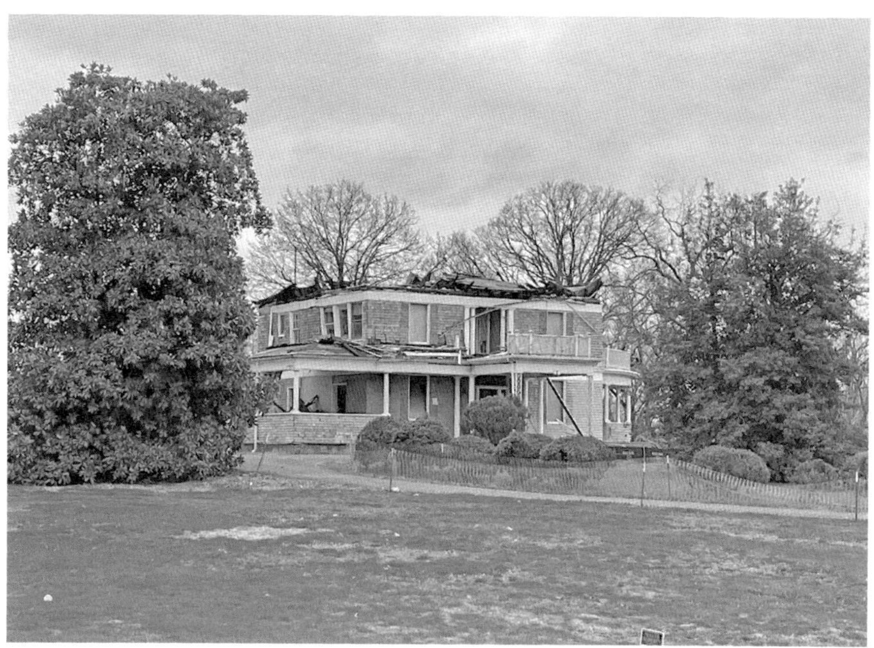

The partially demolished Febrey-Lothrop historic house. *Author's image.*

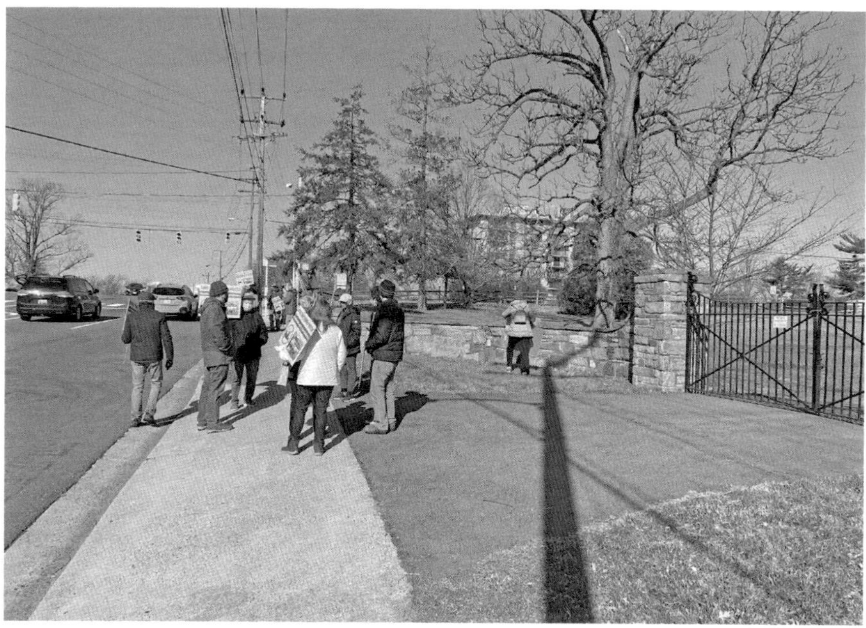

Preservationist protest outside the owner's "no trespassing" signs. *Author's image.*

> *you choose to support, preserve, protect and defend her now, at this time, in this cause, in her time of need. History is watching this matter of national impact, as represented in this unique, historic piece of Arlington's renowned past, in hopeful aspiration that you will all choose to align yourselves with her for the benefit of present and untold future generations of Arlingtonians.*

In the end, county preservation staff members were permitted a last-minute visit to photograph the home's interior. In early April, the main house was demolished.

"I'm disappointed Arlington County didn't step up," Dominion Hills president Hannigan told ARLNow.

> *Personally, I've been advocating for the county to target this land and acquire it for years, but those pleas have fallen on deaf ears. Two years ago,* [the] *county did put the site on the Parks Master Plan as generational and unique opportunity for acquisition. The language they used was appropriate—that if it goes on the market, it's gone forever. Well, that's what happened.*

9
A SPATE OF RENAMINGS

Shifting Names for Arlington House

Arlington's own Robert E. Lee is posthumously back in the news. Powers in Richmond, Virginia, in 2020, prepared for the removal of his statue, eighteen months after the Confederate hero's name was excised from Washington-Liberty High School.

Then came a proposal to remove "Lee" from the county's flagship "Arlington House, the Robert E. Lee Memorial." First, the proposal came in a letter to the *Washington Post*, then from Black activists and legislation introduced by Representative Don Beyer (D-Virginia).

That mansion, built between 1802 and 1818 by George Washington Parke Custis, was known by multiple monikers: Mount Washington, Arlington House, the Custis-Lee Mansion and the Lee Mansion. The author's study of this tortuous history surprised him. The fights over Lee's legacy were as passionate in the 1920s (when Arlington's first high school was named) as they are today. Arlington House, attached to Arlington National Cemetery, was in disrepair as the 1920s dawned.

As noted in a 2013 National Park Service historic registration application, Lee's reputation had made a comeback—even among northerners. Forget the originator, Custis, who lived there for fifty-five years, compared to just the few his son-in-law Lee lived there. Congress was intent on restoring the property to honor the southern military tactician as a postwar conciliator.

This was also when a statewide Lee Highway was created, along with a slew of Confederate monuments and a rising Ku Klux Klan (whose Ballston office was listed in the phonebook).

A consensus didn't come easy. Some northerners wanted to convert the home into a museum for Union soldiers; others wanted more Custis themes. But the tide was turned by an influential author, Frances Parkinson Keyes, the wife of a senator who strategized with the United Daughters of the Confederacy (UDC) to devote Arlington House to Lee. In 1925, Congress resolved that the secretary of war be directed to "restore the Lee Mansion in the Arlington National Cemetery to the condition in which it existed immediately prior to the Civil War and to procure, if possible, articles of furniture and equipment which were then in the mansion and in use by the occupants thereof."

Yet Charles Moore, the secretary of the Commission of Fine Arts, was wary. "There is no real demand from the South that a Lee shrine be established in Arlington Cemetery," he argued, noting Lee's memorial at his burial place at Washington and Lee University. Plus, "extreme care must be exercised in preserving [Arlington Cemetery's] art values."

The association of veterans of the Grand Army of the Republic sent a protest to Congress, calling Lee a "traitor." Senator Porter Dale (R-Vermont) introduced a bill to make "the Custis Mansion" into "a museum in which shall be kept trophies and emblems of the Union army and navy of the United States during the Civil War." The National Society of Dames of the Loyal Legion protested against allowing the UDC to make the site a Lee shrine.

Because of the controversy, money wasn't appropriated for renovations until 1929. Flash forward to 1955, another period of racial strife. Arlington's Republican congressman Joel Broyhill introduced the resolution that honored Lee's "high character" and "grandeur of soul." It officially named the property the Custis-Lee Mansion but established it as a national memorial to Lee. It took new legislation in 1972 to officially demote Custis, but it compromised with "Arlington House, the Robert E. Lee Memorial."

Many don't realize, said Matt Penrod, who retired after twenty-eight years as a park ranger at Arlington House, that the creation of the memorial and its full name were to keep it from becoming a Confederate shrine.

De-Confederatizing a High School

Two hours south of Arlington, on August 12, 2017, a "unite the right" rally was held in Charlottesville to protest the city's planned removal of a statue of Robert E. Lee from a park. The torch-lit nighttime parades by White supremacists and the daytime killing of a female counter protester via automobile horrified the nation. (The Lee statue finally came down in July 2021.)

In Northern Virginia, the event energized an ongoing movement to de-Confederatize the names of schools and roads. Arlington School Board chair Barbara Kanninen opened a discussion on removing the name of Lee—associated with Arlington for much of his adult life—from Washington-Lee High School.

Deleting Confederate symbols was not a new phenomenon. Back in the 1990s, Arlington Schools removed the name of Old South-celebrating author Thomas Nelson Page from an elementary school, now called Science Focus. The name of Stonewall Jackson was similarly removed from the building that houses Arlington Traditional School (before its recent move). But those steps were carried out quietly.

After Charlottesville, the clamor for changes got noisier, and the Arlington schools staff dove in deep for the community engagement process. In September 2017, it named a twenty-one-member committee (students, parents, faculty, neighborhood groups, historians, an outside facilitator) and studied principles set out by colleges that have renamed buildings. Eventually, more than one hundred alternative names were suggested. Criteria were established to guide future renamings—one sample principle: people (enslavers) are cruel, not the plantations. If entities named for plantations were targeted, that would result in a slew of local excisions: Abingdon, Ashlawn, Gunston, Wakefield, Westover and Kenmore.

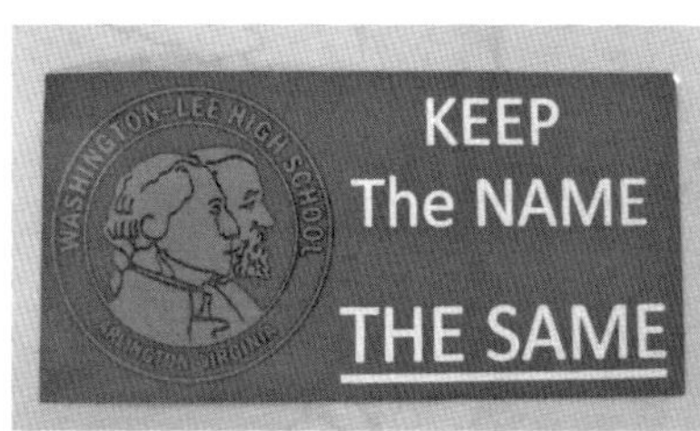

A bumper sticker circulated by the Washington-Lee Alumni Association. *Courtesy of the Washington-Lee Alumni Association.*

As the process continued, the school board took what might be seen as a preliminary step. It removed the name of "Stratford" from a building that was constructed as a junior high in 1950 and named for Robert E. Lee's birthplace in Westmoreland County. Instead, officials relabeled the slated-for-renovation middle school, which, in 2016, the county board had protected as a historic site, as it was the first Virginia school to be integrated, back in February 1959. The school board voted on December 21, 2018, to call it Dorothy Hamm Middle School, after one of the Black parents who fought the legal battle for integration.

But no change created more local controversy than the two-year debate over renaming the county's oldest high school. Thousands of loyal alumni opposed the decision, and they did not go quietly.

Washington-Lee High School opened in 1925—an era of revival for the Old South and the "Lost Cause." The combination of Virginians George Washington and Robert E. Lee's names was considered an act of reconciliation between the North and South, sixty years after the Civil War. Through its ninety-plus years, Washington-Lee went on to graduate thousands of proud alumni—including accomplished actors (Shirley MacLaine, Warren Beatty, Sandra Bullock, Gina Rowlands and Forrest Tucker). It won state sports titles and earned world fame by sending a rowing team to the 1964 Henley Regatta in the United Kingdom. The Arlington Historical Society, in 2020, displayed an exhibit showing the *Virginian*, Washington-Lee's first yearbook (changed to the *Blue and Gray* in 1927). The school's newspaper remains the militaristic *Crossed Sabres*.

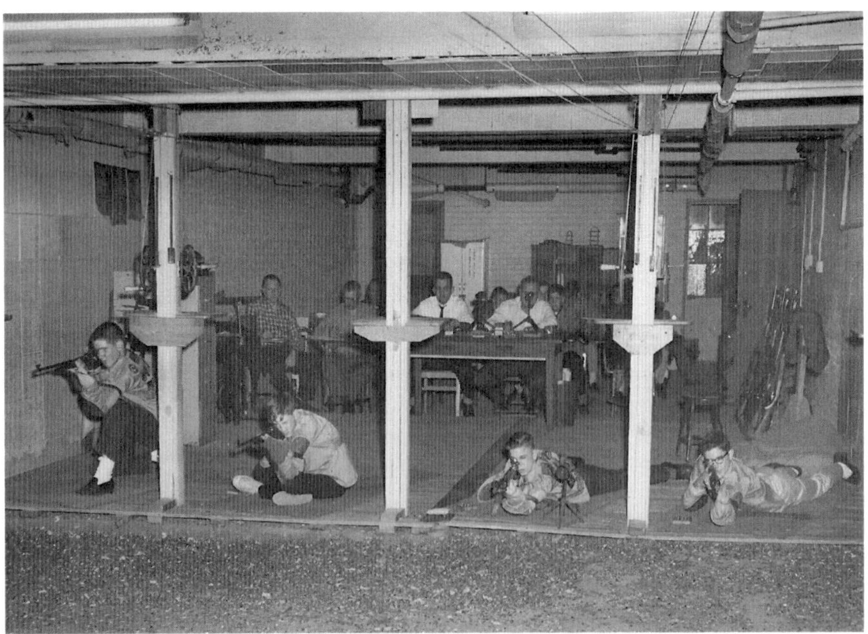

Post-Columbine, it's hard to imagine Washington-Lee's on-campus rifle range in the 1960s. *From the collection of Fred Gosnell.*

So, it was no surprise that the Washington-Lee Alumni Association, formed in 1999 and growing to forty thousand members, organized to preserve the name. They printed yard signs and lapel badges. Some eight hundred endorsed a letter to the school board. Vocal opponent Dean Fleming, class of '75, estimated that alumni sentiment ran 10–1 against a change. Alumni also attacked the process, calling for a referendum, eventually filing a lawsuit against the board (unsuccessfully).

Also active was Washington-Lee basketball star Edward Hummer (class of 1963). In a twenty-four-page missive sent to the school board in December 2017, he described his experiences during the groundbreaking integration of Stratford Junior High. He included a Washington-Lee football program from 1962, pointing to the school's first Black players. Hummer did a credible job in gauging the complex character of Robert E. Lee, painting him as a man of his time, but declaring that he, on moral questions of patriotism and racism, fell short compared with Abraham Lincoln.

As an alternative to erasing Washington-Lee's ninety-three-year-old name, Hummer suggested keeping it as a learning tool and naming a coming new high school for William Harvey Carney, a former Virginia slave who became a Civil War Medal of Honor winner.

Also speaking in opposition was John Cameron Peck, the unofficial school historian from the class of 1996. He cited the school's reputation among the nation's finest, listing its accomplishments in academics, sports and wartime sacrifice, speaking on a panel staged by the Arlington Committee of 100. "I don't even think of the name" when admiring Washington-Lee's attributes, Peck said, adding that he wouldn't mind if Lee's profile came off the logo. "The portraits mean nothing, it's the legacy." (Peck later changed his mind, he told this author in 2021, on the strength of a classmates' testimony and the decision to keep the sports records and nickname the "Generals.")

But modern-day critics noted that the naming of what began briefly as Central High School came just as the Virginia General Assembly enacted the Racial Integrity Act, which banned interracial marriage and defined White persons by blood purity. Back then, the Ku Klux Klan was growing. Michael Beer, a Maywood neighborhood parent and cochair of the civic federation's schools committee, told that the same panel that "hateful and damaging names should be changed as soon as possible to put the needs of children first," he said. "Stamping out racial supremacy" can also be "a wonderful opportunity to bring people together."

How did the students themselves feel? Current Washington-Lee senior Malcolm Douglass, who favored changing the name, told me students

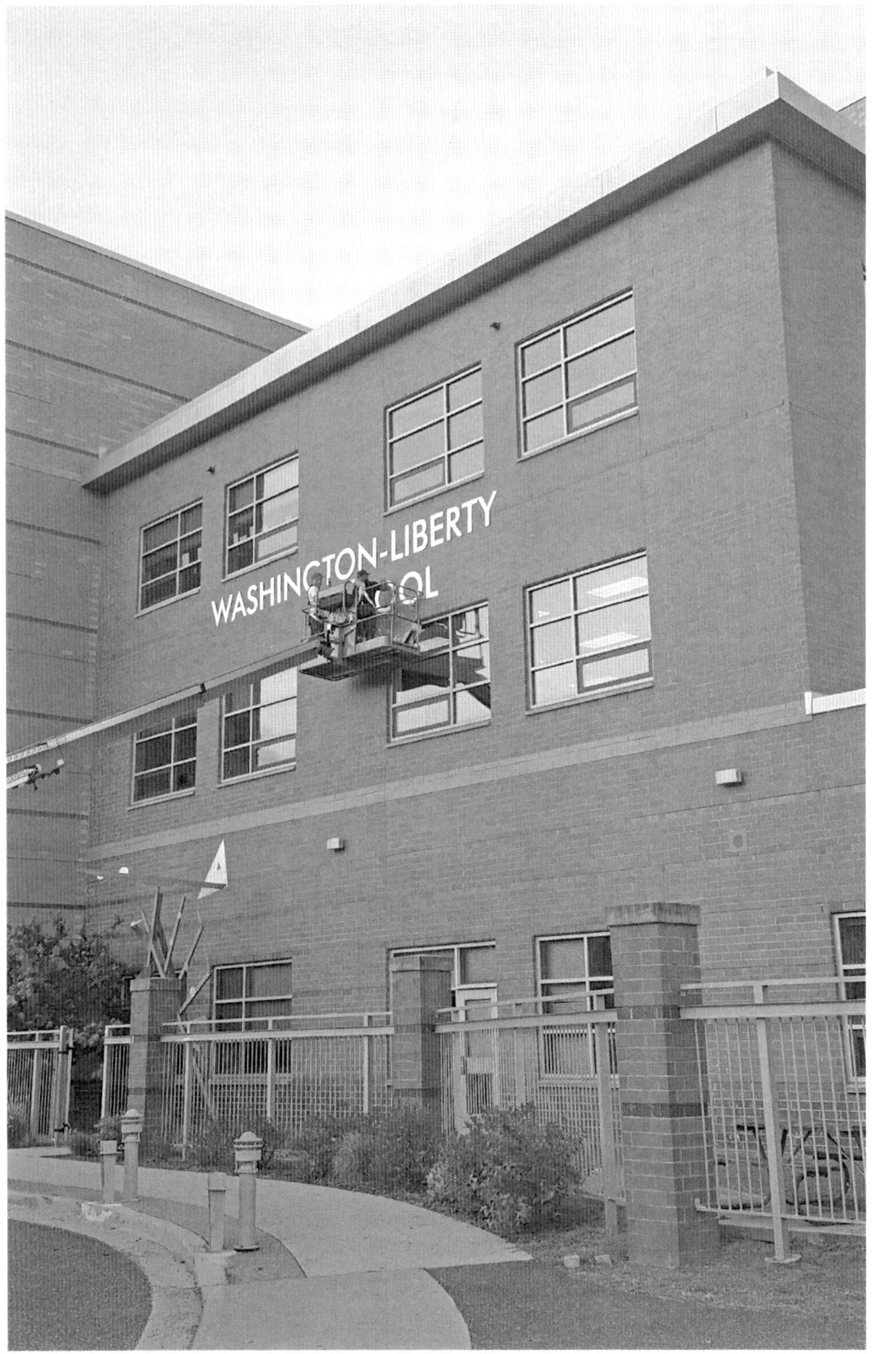

An Arlington Schools crew makes the hotly debated name change. *Courtesy of Eric Dobson.*

were "more willing to have the conversation." Washington-Lee staff were under instructions not to talk. But in a November 2017 op-ed in in the student paper, student Julia Van Lare summarized the arguments, quoting a Black Lives Matter activist student who said Lee is not a good role model. She challenged the notion that changing the name would be painful and expensive. "Maintaining the 'L' may help ease the change, Van Lare wrote. "It would enable the school to maintain many of our logos, uniforms, supplies." Principal Gregg Robertson said, "It may also be a nice compromise."

On December 20, 2018, Arlington school staff formally presented the board with a proposal to drop Robert E. Lee and, instead, honor Richard and Mildred Loving, the pioneering interracial married couple from Caroline County, Virginia, who won their landmark Supreme Court case in 1967.

So, at a dramatic packed Thursday night meeting, on January 10, 2019, after hearing eighteen speakers, the school board voted 5–0 to accept a modifying amendment. They would call the school Washington-Liberty High School as a symbol of hope, diversity and inclusion, beginning in September 2019.

At the January 25, 2019 high school basketball game between Yorktown and Washington-Lee, an unusual ritual unfolded. In a nod to the fight over renaming Washington-Lee, the Yorktown Patriots taunted the Generals by sporting T-shirts that read "Beat W-L?" They chanted, "What's your name?" Apparently unfazed, Washington-Lee students in the opposing bleachers shouted back, "Lib-er-ty!"

Goodbye to Jeff Davis Highway

The de-Confederatization of twenty-first-century Arlington proceeded.

On September 5, 2019, county board chair Christian Dorsey joined Delegate Mark Levine on Route 1 in Crystal City to fold up one of the dismantled signs that, for decades, honored Confederate president Jefferson Davis.

The county's Transportation Division set to work over the following days, replacing all of the Jefferson Davis signs, the sight of which, county manager Mark Schwartz confirmed to this author, had irked merchants and development planners in the Crystal City area that joins with Alexandria (which, earlier, had also changed its Route 1 stretch to the more-neutral Richmond Highway).

"Jefferson Davis had no known connection to this region," Dorsey said at the media photograph opportunity. "The very designation was a direct and antagonistic response to the proposed [nationwide] Lincoln Highway. It symbolized White supremacy in a Jim Crow South."

The defenestration of Davis, endorsed in a letter to Arlington leaders from Virginia governor Ralph Northam, cost $17,000. Though it was pursued for years, it occurred only after newly acquired permission was given from Richmond, where legislators, since the 1920s, had guarded their efforts to enshrine names like "Davis" and "Robert E. Lee" in conspicuous locations.

Southern romantic hero Lee, of course, enjoyed special status in Arlington, given his thirty-year affiliation with Arlington House.

But the county's patriotic local leaders, in the 1920s, went overboard, in this author's view, when they joined a southern regional push and put Lee's name, not just on the new Lee Highway portion that ran through Arlington, but also on a parallel road they called Lee Boulevard. Due to easily predictable confusion, that one was renamed in 1952, as we know it today as Arlington Boulevard or Route 50.

The Lost Cause crowd remained influential in 1935, when Arlington recast most of its street names. A comparison between the old and new names shows the leaders removed the names of several Union officers—Grant Avenue, Sherman Avenue, Sheridan Street. (Because they could, they also renamed a Pocahontas Street.)

10

HONORING HISTORY

The World War I Centennial

On April 6, 2017, Arlington joined others around the nation to mark the one hundredth anniversary of the United States' entry into what we now call World War I.

Some sixty officials and citizens gathered in the county building (a rain threat canceled plans to assemble at the war memorial in Clarendon).

The grand-scale horror a century before—to which Arlington has a slew of strong connections—caused 38 million deaths, including those of 116,000 U.S. soldiers. Among them were the 13 Arlingtonians who are listed—segregated by race—on the American Legion's War Memorial that was erected in 1931.

Five fallen soldiers from Cherrydale had already been honored on a 1926 Daughters of the American Revolution monument off of Lee Highway. One, Lieutenant John Lyon, became the namesake for Post 3150 of the Veterans of Foreign Wars.

Another 2,100 U.S. dead were brought to Arlington Cemetery in 1921 for a record-size expansion and reburial—a move that inspired the cemetery to build the Tomb of the Unknown Soldier and an amphitheater.

In March 2017, the national cemetery's visitors center mounted an inspiring exhibit, with World War I photographs and artifacts grouped by themes of combat, technology, mobilization and the role of women

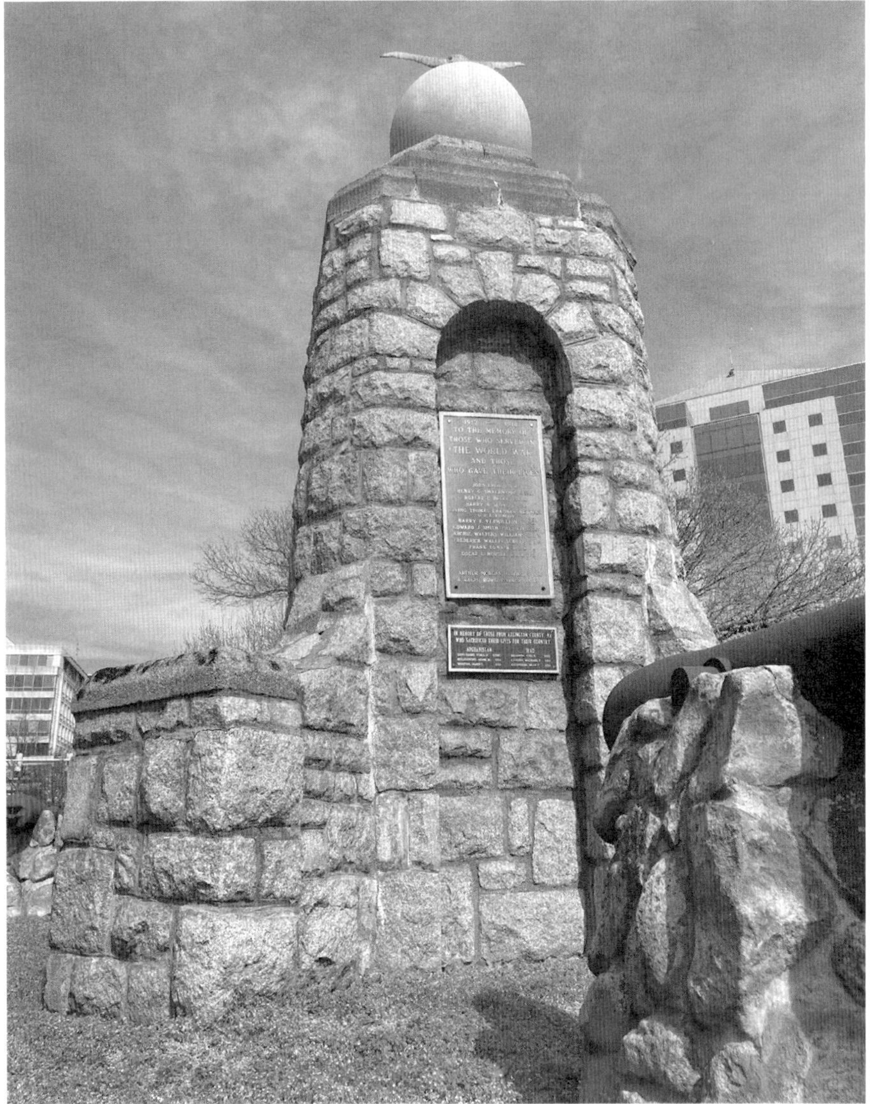

The 1930s Clarendon war memorial was updated with added signage. *Author's image.*

and Black Americans. It noted that Arlington National Cemetery's plots, for decades, were racially segregated but that the U.S. cemeteries overseas were not.

Cocurating the exhibit was the American Battlefields Monuments Commission, which was created in 1923 to care for graves overseas and is now headquartered at Arlington's Courthouse Square.

At a Pentagon commemoration on April 6, 2017, Army Chief of Staff Mark Milley asked his audience, "Are we that much smarter than those who came before us one hundred years ago today?"

The county's ceremony kicked off its World War I Commemoration Task Force's planning of a nineteen-month series of events aided by schools and nonprofit organizations. At a podium bedecked with a doughboy helmet and poster with the slogan "Remembering the Spirit of 1917," county board member John Vihstadt said the war helped convert Arlington "from a sleepy rural community to a modern urban county."

Five-decade Arlingtonian Ed Bearss, historian emeritus at the National Park Service, described the horrors of poison gas and machine gun warfare. His father fought in the war with the marines and seldom discussed it—its drama overshadowed by World War II, Bearss said.

Task force chair historian Allison Finkelstein laid out goals of engaging diverse groups, encouraging community service and confronting "the more difficult issues wrapped up in memorializing this war, chiefly, [its] racial legacy." One of her consultations was with Karen Nightengale, president of the Arlington NAACP. Nightengale had weighed in months earlier with a proposal to update the 1931 plaque that listed "colored" veterans Arthur Morgan and Ralph Lowe below the eleven White heroes. Nightengale told this author her goal was to have a new marker that "does not distinguish between Negro and White." But she acknowledges the hesitation to remove the plaque that has been there for eighty-six years. "I understand why the original was put up the way it was," she added, impressed that folks in the 1920s even "had the due diligence" to include the "colored" dead.

Eighteen months later, nearly 150 residents, bundled up on a chilly Veterans Day Sunday in 2018, packed the sliver that is Clarendon Park for Arlington's marking of the one hundredth anniversary of the end of the "war to end all wars."

Somber reflective remarks and rituals combined with light lyrics of "Over There," sung by the Arlingtones, as traffic whizzed by on three boulevards.

Arlington's event stood apart from the countless others with the unveiling of a new interpretive panel that addresses the delicate issue of the local memorial's segregated tribute to fallen troops. A color guard marched, wearing doughboy uniforms.

"If you were on the battlefield in 1918, these are some of the sounds you would hear—until 11:00 a.m.," said emcee Linden Dixon of Arlington's American Legion Post 139. There followed a recording of explosions and rifle fire, followed by birds chirping.

At precisely 11:00 a.m. came the moment of silence, followed by a traditional bell ringing, then a three-volley salute by Arlington police riflemen and a bugler playing Taps.

"The brave Americans memorialized behind me on this monument," Dixon said, "in 2018, are especially significant because, unfortunately, we know today the guns are not silent." He mentioned ongoing combat in Afghanistan and Iraq.

The event that was staged by county staff, the World War I Commemoration Task Force and veterans groups drew a crowd of all ages and ethnic backgrounds, including stalwarts from the Arlington Historical Society. Veterans of Foreign Wars came from as far away as Danville, Virginia.

All appreciated the doses of century-old culture—the Opera Nova singer performing "God Bless America" and Arlington poet laureate Katherine Young reciting the poetry of World War I veteran Archibald MacLeish. All seemed receptive, as speakers noted how "intertwined" Arlington is with the Great War through Arlington Cemetery, Fort Myer and the Marine Corps Memorial.

Marvin Chadab, the past president of the Great War Association, wore a doughboy uniform. He knew Frank Buckles, he told this author, the last surviving World War I veteran, who was buried at Arlington in 2011. But Chadab was disappointed that Buckles didn't lie in state in the U.S. Capitol.

The unveiling of the interpretive panels came as task force chair Allison Finkelstein expressed the hope that the addition will "breathe life into this too-often overlooked memorial park." Sketching the war's impact on borders, America's global role, women's rights, civil rights and immigration, she described the original "grassroots" campaign to build the memorial in the 1920s. The later addition of the names of locals lost in World War II, the Korean War, the Vietnam War and the Afghanistan and Iraq Wars provides evidence of "how Arlington changed with each war," she said.

The new and coming plaques "contextualize in local and larger history" the forces such as those that led original planners to separate the two "colored" World War I casualties from the eleven White casualties. The fact that less is known about the two Black casualties is "part of the continuing legacy of segregation," Finklestein said.

The plaque focusing on the monument calls it "a reflection of the systemic racism pervasive in Virginia and across the nation." Delivering the finale for the county board in November 2018 was Christian Dorsey. He spoke to the modern era, calling for a "functional zero" goal for homeless veterans. He asked Arlingtonians to let veterans know "we've got their back."

A year later, county historians returned there to erect five more weather-proof placards honoring vets of World War II, the Korean War, the Vietnam War and the Global War on Terror.

REMEMBERING THE LUNCH COUNTER SIT-IN

The strains of "We Shall Overcome" rang out over Lee Highway on Saturday, June 9, 2018.

With a crowd of some ninety assembled across from the old Cherrydale firehouse, the good citizens of Cherrydale witnessed the fruits of their decision to combine their 125th anniversary celebration with an addition to Arlington's civil rights heritage.

Unveiled on the façade of the District Angling fishing supplies shop is now a bronze plaque marking the June 9, 1960 lunch counter sit-in at the old Drug Fair, then at 3815 Lee Highway.

Inspired by similar protests against segregation nationwide that were launched the previous February in Greensboro, North Carolina, six students from Howard and Duke Universities showed up in Cherrydale at 2:30 p.m. to break the local law by taking seats and vainly ordering food. As they waited peacefully, they were "encouraged by some onlookers but endured verbal abuse and physical from others," the plaque notes.

The six students had to listen to taunts from members of the American Nazi Party, led by Arlington resident George Lincoln Rockwell. (Most of the White men shown crowding around the seated protesters in the news photographs were later identified by the police as Nazis, according to Cherrydale historian Kathryn Holt Springston, one of the impresarios of the 125th anniversary.)

Before departing at closing time, 10:00 p.m., the racially mixed protesters were joined by a Georgetown University student and a Drug Fair employee. Similar protests hit the Peoples Drugstore and Howard Johnson's farther up on Lee Highway and at F.W. Woolworth's in Shirlington. Just two weeks later, the Arlington establishments abandoned their "Whites only" policies. As event organizer Greg Embree noted, the cumulative effect of such sit-ins in fifty-five cities later prodded President Kennedy, in consultation with Martin Luther King Jr., to propose what became the 1964 Civil Rights Act.

Introduced to the crowd in 2018 were three original participants: Ethelene Crockett Jones, Dion Diamond and Joan Trumpauer Mulholland. Jones,

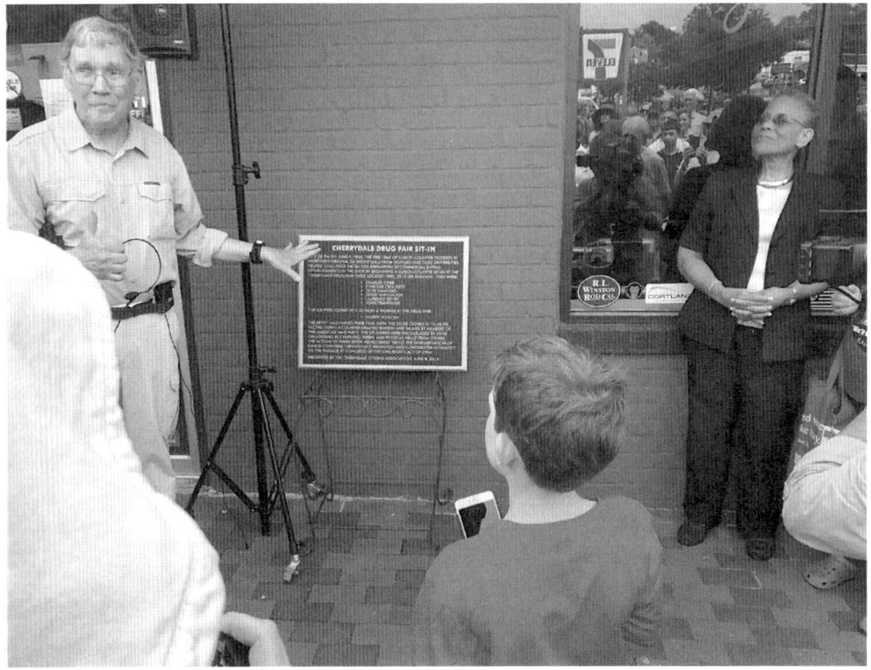

Greg Embree leads the commemoration of the Cherrydale lunch counter sit-in. *Author's image.*

who went on to become an OB-GYN, had traveled all the way from West Palm Beach, Florida, to witness the dedication. Diamond, a retired financial planner in Washington, D.C., who grew up in segregated Petersburg, Virginia, told this author he communicates with Mulholland regularly, as she, a White Arlingtonian woman, had become famous as the subject of a documentary on her broader civil rights work.

Mulholland spoke later at the Cherrydale Library, along with Springston, on other highlights of Cherrydale's history. It was all part of a festival that also included food, old-time music, a 1911 Stanley Steamer car and face painting for the children of residents who were sporting Cherrydale booster T-shirts.

As state senator Barbara Favola and Delegates Patrick Hope and Alfonzo Lopez looked on, host Embree praised the shopping strip landlord and the merchants who responded with an "immediate and emphatic 'yes'" to the planners' requests. That included the space to mount the $1,800 plaque (financed via crowdsourcing) and cordoning off the parking lot for an hour on a busy Saturday.

Mulholland, who brought her scrapbooks filled with clippings from that hot summer of 1960, told the gathered, "This was as big a crowd as we had when we left the sit-in, but much friendlier."

RETHINKING THE CIVIL WAR

The Civil War brought more action, danger and death to Arlington than is commonly believed.

So said historian and reenactor Peter Vaselopulos, speaking to Encore Learning enthusiasts at Arlington Central Library on January 27, 2020. His talk on "Arlington's Little War" brought context to Union and Confederate troop movements and skirmishes in neighborhoods where present-day suburbanites commute and shop.

Arlington contained strategic heights (Arlington House), a railroad and vulnerable Potomac bridges, explained Vaselopulos, a longtime Arlingtonian who, before his retirement, was an executive for the U.S. Agency for Global Media by day. The Federals' construction of two dozen forts by war's end made "Arlington the most fortified piece of land in the world," he said. Arlington also hosted breakthroughs in the telegraph and intelligence via hot air balloon.

There were also armed clashes. A key unit was the Union's New York Twenty-Third Volunteer Regiment (whose uniform Vaselopulos wore during his talk), based in the railroad hub of Elmira. They had come south to the District of Columbia in the spring of 1861, just after Arlingtonian Robert E. Lee was summoned downtown and made his fateful decision to fight for the South. "Lee knew he had to find a new place to live," the historian noted. Lincoln kept the Twenty-Third idle because Virginia itself had not yet voted for secession. That vote occurred on May 23, with most in the Arlington area voting no. The area's farmer's markets were in the district, not Richmond, and "they knew where their bread was buttered," Vaselopulos said. On May 24, Union troops occupied Arlington Heights.

"Lincoln needed seventy-five thousand volunteers" to defend against a siege of Washington, D.C., but he had raised an army only for the three months the war was expected to last, the historian said. Arlington became the scene of exhausting training for both calvary and infantry. The soldiers came "through Rosslyn and spent the first night near Clarendon," Vaselopulos said. Others camped near Carlin Springs and, later, what is now Bluemont

Park. On June 1, a skirmish erupted at Arlington Mill, near today's 7-Eleven at Columbia Pike and South Dinwiddie Street.

Troops also used Columbia Pike on their two-day march to the July 21, 1861 Battle of Bull Run. Following that surprising Confederate triumph, Rebel troops approached the Federal capital. "If they had taken Arlington Heights, Lincoln would have had to skedaddle," Vaselopulos said.

Of the twenty thousand Rebels in the region, commanded by P.G.T. Beauregard, J.E.B. Stuart and James Longstreet, some had penetrated to Hall's Hill and Upton Hill along Four Mile Run by the end of the summer. Vaselopulos focused on the unsung "Skirmish near Balls Cross Roads" of August 27, citing *New York Times* reporting and soldier diaries. Union cavalry were sent into thick woods, seeking stragglers from Bull Run. The four hundred Union troops confronting the six hundred Confederates had orders to make contact but not to try to win. For two hours, beginning at 2:00 p.m., the two engaged in small arms fire. The Rebels (near where Ashlawn School is now) held their ground. So, they could claim they won the skirmish, despite the eleven dead versus only "several" Union deaths.

In late September, the Confederates withdrew, and General George McClellan marched up Upton Hill. Arlington's legacy, Vaselopulos said, "is the building of the Army of the Potomac."

MODERNIZING CIVIL WAR SIGNAGE

This author's visits to the neighborhood off Wilson Boulevard caused him to take up another history dilemma. The metal historical marker at the entrance to Bluemont was bent in February 2017, apparently by an automobile. The text had always struck the author as similarly slanted.

"Confederate Outpost," said the headline written in 1969. The inscription:

> *In August 1861, while U.S. forces were constructing the Arlington line three miles to the east, the Confederates established a fortified outpost on the high ground about 200 yards west of here, to guard the bridge by which the Georgetown-Falls Church Road crossed Four Mile Run. In October, they withdrew to Fairfax Court House. The federals then established a signal station at the top of the hill and constructed Fort Ramsay just across the county Line.*

But the Rebels were there for just two months, while Union troops stayed from the fall of 1861 to 1865. The Fort Ramsay lookout at Upton Hill was where future president Colonel Rutherford B. Hayes was stationed with the Twenty-Third Ohio, and singing troops nearby inspired Juliet Ward Howe, while she was staying in Washington, D.C., at the Willard, to write "The Battle Hymn of the Republic." But the 1969 sign made no mention of that. How about a neutral headline, like "Civil War Outpost?"

The author consulted Civil War experts. Marymount University professor Mark Benbow, the director of the Arlington Historical Museum, agreed.

But Kathryn Holt Springston, who gives Smithsonian tours focused on Arlington during the war, didn't think the sign is pro-Confederate or pro-Union and cited space constraints. She would warm to a second sign, one that mentions the "Quaker guns," logs made to look like cannons, with which the Confederates successfully fooled the Yankees on nearby Munson's Hill. (She also says Howe's lyrics were inspired farther away on Columbia Pike.)

Cynthia Liccese-Torres, the coordinator of Arlington historic preservation, replaced the damaged sign in May 2018. The recast marker is titled: "Civil War Outpost."

Another change unfolded just steps away, where you could see a stone missing its plaque that stood for four decades. It read: "This red oak and stone were placed here as a bicentennial memorial to the men in gray who served on Upton Hill."

As part of its rethinking Civil War commemorations, the county, in January 2018, removed that plaque. County manager aide Benjamin Hampton said, "The county discovered that it had been placed on county land without county permission" by the United Daughters of the Confederacy. "The marker has since been returned to the Alexandria chapter of the UDC, as the Arlington chapter seems to no longer be active or in existence."

Chris Tighe, president of the Boulevard Manor Civic Association, which sought the removal, said the neighbors argued that the plaque was not historical in nature, was put there on private land before the county bought it and that no owners could be found, which leaves the decision to the county.

Similarly, in December 2020, the historically minded Caruthers family modernized the controversial sign near their compound on North Stafford Street, across from the Madison Center.

Back in 2016, neighbors were questioning the plaque that was erected decades earlier, referring to the property as a wildlife sanctuary at the "historical site of Civil War Fort Ethan Allen, which commanded all approaches south of Pimmit Run to Chain Bridge during the War of Northern Aggression (1861–65)."

Steve Caruthers said his family agreed late last year to spend $6,000 to remake a plaque for "those who didn't get the joke." The new plaque simply calls the conflict "The Civil War."

Historical Code Girls

Arlington's perennial part in larger national history was on display in March 2019.

This author was honored to attend a unique event at the Library of Congress: the first-ever reunion of the "code girls" who did so much to crack enemy communications and help win World War II.

The appellation "code girls" is the title of the groundbreaking 2017 book by Arlingtonian Liza Mundy. And as many know now but didn't for decades, much of the drama of that life-altering secret operation unfolded at Arlington Hall.

The author's mother, longtime Arlingtonian Cynthia Landry Clark (1922–2010), was a code girl. As was common, the subject seldom came up in the author's household and then only in the context of how his parents met.

So, the author was knocked silly when he learned that he would join dozens of other offspring (and actual code girls now in their nineties) in the backrooms of the world's largest library to march in a procession. They would hear testimonials and receive a (long overdue) certificate honoring those women's vital unheralded feats.

Broadcast live via YouTube, the March 22, 2019 ceremony during Women's History Month was ably coordinated (like an uncertain wartime adventure) by the library's Veterans History Project.

Guests descended from the heroines carried framed photographs of their loved ones.

Author Mundy—gratified at such proof of her book's impact—praised the code girls as the "hidden figures of the greatest generation." She recounted new stories that reached her after the release of her book. Most were variations on how the former code girls were so fearful of violating secrecy that there were miscommunications among families. Many men, Mundy said with a smile, had assumed the women worked as secretaries.

Human factor details were shared. The "government girls" recruited to Washington were "unchaperoned for the first time." All remembered at what time the Washington, D.C. liquor stores closed.

Speaking for the children of code girls was Bill Nye the Science Guy, the comedian and educator. Nye choked up at the memory of his late mother—who, the author judged from her photograph, resembled him. His wit returned in recalling his dad's experience as a prisoner of war. Nye counseled, "If you get a chance to be a POW, don't do it."

By prearrangement, family members presented library staff with envelopes containing donated letters.

The event prompted the author's sister Martha to dig out their mother's unpublished memoir. As a college senior and language major in New Orleans, their mother received a U.S. Army Signal Corps letter, inviting her to study cryptography. So, she took a correspondence course, and by September 1943, she was immersed in a "vague job" at Arlington Hall and living in a swampy barracks near Arlington Cemetery.

"My job involved learning Japanese so as to translate decoded cables—it was hard, boring, fascinating and romantic all at once," she wrote. "I was surrounded by men—my coworkers were signal corps inductees....Plenty of blind date invitations were extended," said this innocent. "We worked hard—five and a half day weeks, three shifts, but laughed and played a lot. We also drank a lot."

The author's giddy feelings at the ceremony gave a taste of the way it must have felt during World War II to be thrown in with strangers from all over the country for a shared slice of history. That afternoon, they all then returned, heartened, to present-day life.

The Greatest Arlington Historian?

Let us now praise Arlington historians—the few whose enduring works are frequently consulted (by fanboys such as this author).

The most popular books are those of C.B. Rose Jr., Eleanor Lee Templeman and Nan and Ross Netherton (all deceased).

Rose, a research assistant to the county manager, got her start in 1957 by penning a pamphlet on Native Americans in Arlington. Then, after getting many questions, she spent twenty-five years researching what became the most comprehensive history of Arlington, which was published for the

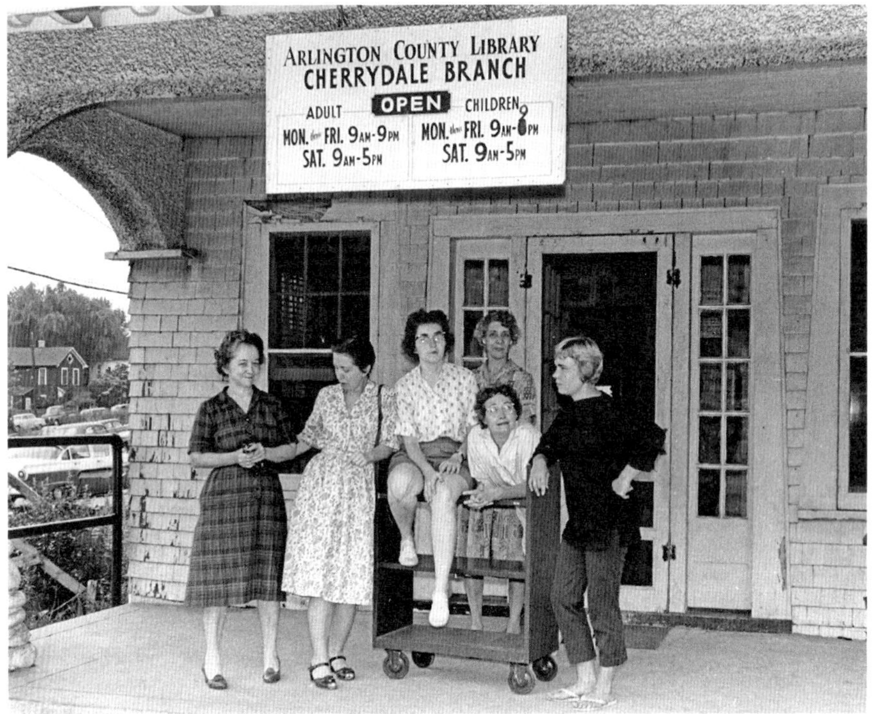

History is preserved by librarians, including these 1950s stalwarts at a beloved old branch. *Courtesy of the Center for Local History, Arlington Public Library.*

nation's bicentennial in 1976. The Arlington Historical Society gives an award named for her.

Eleanor Lee Templeman, a descendant of Richard Bland Lee (the first congressman from Northern Virginia), got her start in the 1950s, writing history columns for the *Northern Virginia Sun*. They were collected in a handsomely illustrated volume, *Arlington Heritage*, published in 1959. This author was the last journalist to interview Templeman, by phone, days before she died in 1990.

The Nethertons, who cooperated with Templeman for a 1966 volume titled *Northern Virginia Heritage*, produced their own illustrated opus in 1987 titled *Arlington County in Virginia: A Pictorial History*. It delivered a modern treatment of Arlington's government and politics. He was a law professor, and she was the executive director of the Northern Virginia Association of Historians.

We must also mention Kathryn Holt Springston (this author's schoolmate at Cherrydale Elementary), who has written the best history of Cherrydale and gives well-attended Smithsonian Associates historical tours of Arlington.

Author Garrett Peck discusses Arlington frequently, particularly in his volume *Capital Beer: A Heady History of Brewing in Washington, D.C.*

And this author appreciates the efforts of the late Sherman Pratt, a distinguished U.S. Army veteran and stalwart in the Arlington Historical Society. His self-published 1997 history of Arlington is most reliable for its military history, and he tossed in a bit more of the modern politics than the aforementioned volumes.

But the most influential works on the national level are two by the unsung Charles Stetson, who was our county's first historian. The late attorney from the Carlin Springs neighborhood published, in 1935, an authoritative volume with the deceptively narrow-sounding title *Four Mile Run Land Grants.* This detailed history (reprinted in 2013) is surprisingly engaging because, as with his more regional 1956 follow-up, *Washington and His Neighbors*, Stetson used painstaking research to nail down events in the life of George Washington that unfolded right by Stetson's Arlington home. The land grants include Washington's purchase in 1774 of 1,200 acres (at seven dollars per acre) along Four Mile Run and Long Branch, how Washington surveyed the area in 1785 with his enslaved valet William "Billy" Lee and enlisted cooperation from neighbor and Arlington citizen Moses Ball (1717–1792). "'The small branch which comes in on the No. Et. Side' now makes its way to Four Mile Run under a railroad culvert, and the depression of the old mill race can still be traced," Stetson wrote.

That survey referred to a white oak tree (a cutting is still displayed at Glencarlyn Library). In 1914, a stone marker was placed there by the Daughters of the American Revolution. Stetson himself honored Moses Ball with a plaque when the historian repaired the masonry spring walls of the original Carlin Springs. In 1946, he wrote the foreword to the first major Arlington history book by Dorothy Ellis Lee, who said Stetson "had done more research on county history, possibly, than anyone else in the county."

Present-day history buff Karl VanNewkirk cited Stetson's work in a 2021 Zoom talk on Arlington's first subdivision. He detailed the development of Ball-Sellers House (the county's oldest) and the original Carlin Springs. Stetson was also indispensable in recounting the life of William Carlin (1732–1820), one of George Washington's tailors. His cabin remains a private home on a hill on Carlin Springs Road, occupied for eight decades by his granddaughter Mary Carlin.

Stetson's home at 605 South Carlin Springs Road, shared with his wife and three children, was built in 1874 by Confederate veteran Howard Young. It was called Eastlawn. When it was threatened in the 1950s by plans to build

Northern Virginia Doctors Hospital, Stetson's son Francis (like his dad, a law professor) and daughter-in-law Margaret moved it one block. But in 1976, nearby medical buildings were expanding, prompting Margaret Stetson to truck the home yet again to its current site on South Kensington Street.

When Stetson died in 1958, the Arlington Historical Society, of which he was a founder, adopted a resolution of condolence. Four years later, the local DAR announced its plans to add a new plaque near the worn-down text of the old George Washington marker, which Stetson's history-minded wife had kept an eye on.

In 2021, this author hiked the woodsy path from the Long Branch Nature Center and revisited the stone marker enclosed in modern bricks. The elements have rendered its lettering illegible. It is time for the county to refurbish it. Charles Stetson would insist.

A Stickler for Facts

When the county board considered plans to rename Lee Highway, all could expect an appearance from naysayer Bernie Berne.

"It's political correctness and should not be done—it's blackwashing history," says the longtime Arlington history activist and tour guide. "They're taking away names that have been around for a long time. It's a culture war that's been going on since the Civil War."

A member of the Arlington Historical Society, Berne often shows up at public forums and speeches to correct statements he finds inaccurate (this author hears from him). But the retired federal agency medical professional with an MD and a PhD can boast meaty contributions to the preservation and telling of Arlington's story. And he does his homework.

Berne played a major role in planning the re-created ruins of the eighteenth-century Abingdon Plantation home off the parking lot at Reagan National Airport. Back in the early 1990s, "I was first to recognize what was happening," he recalls of the airport engineers' plans to tear the ruins down. He teamed up with the Arlington Civic Federation and the Arlington Heritage Alliance, wrote letters to the editor and helped Delegate Karen Darner get a preservation bill through the General Assembly.

He initiated the 1996 naming of Andrew Ellicott Park at the west cornerstone of the 1791 District of Columbia boundary stones (at the Falls Church–Arlington border), for which Ellicott was chief surveyor.

In the 1980s and 1990s, he worked on the Bluemont Junction Railroad display along the W&OD Trail near Wilson Boulevard. Visitable on summer weekends, it includes signage, a partially exposed section of an electrical substation, railroad artifacts and an actual caboose that houses historical materials Berne donated.

The passionate, detail-rattling Berne pushed for the historic trolley poster display at Marymount University's Ballston campus erected in 2017. And he helped lead an effort in 2014 to preserve part of the Benjamin Elliott Coal Trestle near I-66 in East Falls Church, now more visible after the construction of a new bicycle bridge over Lee Highway. (See page 48.)

Berne has cooperated with the Historical Affairs and Landmark Review Board and the county historic preservation program, which he believes is understaffed. In the case of the trestle, "they were slow to act," he said, which would never happen in the more historically minded Alexandria, according to him.

Like all who pursue history, Berne admits he is occasionally proved wrong. "Some of my efforts did not turn out as well as I had hoped, and many failed," he said. "That's part of the game."

The native New Yorker who came to Arlington in 1980 finds time to be president of the Buckingham Community Civic Association. He conducts historical walking and bike tours of Arlington for the Center Hiking Club (much cheaper than those run by Smithsonian Associates, he boasts). He is also an active writer of Wikipedia entries on Arlington.

"Bureaucracies don't really care much about history," Berne says. "Most people don't care about history. Only the Civil War, Vietnam—big things, not local history. It's too bad, because that's how people get lost."

Compiler of Arlingtoniana

If there were an award for unearthing the shiniest visual gems of Arlington's past, this author would bestow it on Andrew Ratliff.

When the author spoke to the fifty-five-year-old government contractor in July 2018, he'd been long familiar to denizens of the popular "I Grew Up in Arlington, VA" Facebook page (twenty-one thousand members) for his deep research and frequent postings.

"Metro construction next to the Pentagon," Ratliff noted in one photograph's caption. "Red Head gas station from the Yorktown [High

School] '81 yearbook." "A 1939 *Washington Post* photo feature for Arlington Forest homes."

"Why do all that digging?" this author asked him. "Obviously, there's no money in it, and it poses challenges to work-life balance and my relationships," he said. But his hours spent online in history and photograph archives "is just one of those things that sprung up over time." It may seem like a compulsion to some.

The son of a State Department official, Ratliff actually grew up in Japan and graduated from Annandale High School in 1981. "I went to an all-boys Catholic school in Japan and was fundamentally Asian in culture," he said. So, the one-time outsider had to get culturally acclimated when he returned to the United States.

But he worked in Rosslyn for nine years at a language school and lived at several addresses in Arlington, north and south, as well as Seven Corners. So, he comes by his Arlington fixation authentically.

Ratliff began by joining online nostalgia groups, including ones for Annandale and Fairfax, eventually becoming a site administrator and helping create groups for Seven Corners, Bailey's Crossroads and Alexandria.

"Sometimes, there's a specific thing I'm trying to find," he said, citing one specialty—photographs of the old Hot Shoppes restaurants (eateries are popular on these sites). He went through a university's digital collection (from the comfort of his home) and posted some that few had seen. "I got two hundred *likes*."

Almost everything is online, at public domain places like the Library of Congress, he said, but not everything is properly labeled. For example, a photograph of Arlington's old courthouse in 1918 was labeled as "Alexandria Courthouse." (Though Arlington then was part of Alexandria, there was another courthouse in Old Town.)

Old shots of Rosslyn and the Potomac became Ratliff's fixation. He has posted early photographs of the U.S. Army Air Corps in action there early in the twentieth century.

Photographs of the old orange-painted putt-putt mini golf course in Ballston have probably run their course, he thinks (*see back cover*). Many people have posted memories of the 1973 collapse of the Skyline Towers, then under construction at Bailey's Crossroads, which killed fourteen workers. Ratliff assembled nearly one hundred photographs into an online album.

Frequent posters can "run afoul of administrators," he said, for using items that have already appeared, for vague captions, for failing to credit sources. "The more active you are, you either get the kind of recognition for what you're giving, or people get annoyed because you're dominating the forum."

Like many online entertainment outlets, "I Grew Up in Arlington, VA" comes with "a little bit of competition," Ratliff said. "People get territorial."

His discoveries show up in "Back in the Day in Northern Virginia," Pinterest and the Fairfax Underground discussion group (not always attributed).

It's hard to predict what will be a hit. But Ratliff persists: "1950s Arlington Towers postcard on eBay"; "Cherrydale Baptist [church] in 1928"; "The newly built Cherrydale firehouse in 1919."

Bring on more gems.

AFTERWORD

By Eric Dobson

The nonprofit I help run, Preservation Arlington, sparks dialogue by keeping track of demolition of homes and commercial buildings, which we list monthly on our website under "Lost." This always prompts debate over the value of old houses, and that's a good thing. Our mission is both practical and philosophical.

An old house I lived in on North Roosevelt Street was a typical 1890s–1900s farmhouse that once stood amid many acres owned by the Crossman family. Until recently, it sat on two acres and had long defied the market. It provided income for the owners as a "group house" rental over several decades. After the owner died, it was sold in March 2017 to a developer. While I had not lived there in more than twenty-five years, I would often drive by to check whether the newest crop of college grads were respecting the old girl and taking care of her. The driveway for the house always had a multitude of not-so-new cars. It was the starting-off base for many young people.

While many saw it as quaint, neighbors probably saw it as an eyesore. But the house also hid many secrets—including one really important one. Once demolition began in October 2017, people were able to access the site in off-hours and look more closely at the house's bones. It emerged that this was most likely the long-lost location of the home of Civil War major William D. Nutt, a secessionist. He fled the property in 1861, and Union troops burned it to the ground. In 1863, the lot was taken by the Union army, and a contraband farm, Camp Rucker, was built there.

The 1890s structure I occupied had been mounted on the older foundation, which was at least a foot in width. The foundation could have told us stories of camping soldiers and things they left behind. It is all gone and plowed under, now in a cluster of "modernist houses whose owners probably wonder how a piece of land that big only just now got developed." We have lost that Arlington story.

This churning gets repeated at an accelerated pace these days. All around Arlington are locations that contain the history of several phases of our growth. Post–World War II, our booming population needed housing and needed it fast. Arlington had the answers—garden apartments, the innovative all-metal Lustron homes, poured concrete homes in South Arlington. Some of these styles represented an effort to get houses built quickly; others represented innovations in design and construction. They all tell a story of opportunity about Arlington as a burgeoning suburb of a city growing in importance.

The same goes for our commercial development. As each mid-century commercial building gets demolished, we lose the story about how Arlington became an economic driver in the region. In the 1950s and 1960s, our community was seen as an affordable and attractive alternative to the Washington, D.C. office market. Easy access, ample parking and our street-front retail locations of Clarendon and Columbia Pike provided a wide range of shopping. Some areas of 1950s street-level retail and then the 1960s and 1970s eras of tall buildings were leased out to the government and government contractors. And now, these buildings are old.

As each of these architectural landmarks is demolished, the community is losing something. A few decades from now, when we will want to tell the story of this Arlington, how will we explain that those period pieces really did exist? Are we to tell people if you want to know about the Arlington of the 1950s or 1970s, you will have to search the internet?

We should preserve at least a few of these buildings because they represent great design. And we are doing that with projects that are economically successful and architecturally attractive and that have been built with historic preservation components in Clarendon and Columbia Pike—it can happen, and it works. But they also tell our story of how this community was built and were it is going—and still going.

One of our greatest assets is also a great challenge. So many people here in Arlington today are from elsewhere. Because of this, their notion of local history is different; they know Arlington only from, say, 1997 or 2010. This became apparent during our discussions in 2016 to have the Stratford

School Building designated as a local landmark. Several people in leadership positions had not heard the story of the integration of Stratford Junior High in 1959, a first in the state of Virginia. Others dismissed its historic nature by suggesting that "where they came from" (elsewhere in the United States) contained the truly historic stuff. We observers learn to understand that our friends among the recent residents didn't hear our stories growing up. They didn't know folks who were part of America's story of integration.

The challenge for my group and for Arlington as a whole is this: when people move here after college or for a new administration or for their first real job in their thirties and are ready to settle down, how do we get them invested in understanding Arlington's story and to be part of it? Charlie Clark's new compendium of writings on buildings, homes, stores, lifestyles and personal stories now lost—beginning centuries ago but portraying the scene today—is an inspiring read. *Lost Arlington County* is a doorway to keeping our Arlington special.

ACKNOWLEDGEMENTS

Among the county staff, I wish to thank historic preservation program coordinator Cynthia Liccese-Torres; communications staff members Bryna Helfer, Susan Kalish and Mary Curtius; and school system spokesman Frank Bellavia. At the Arlington Public Library's Center for Local History, I received invaluable help from Judith Knudsen, Heather Crocetto, Arabeth Balasko and John Stanton. Among my friendly media competitors, I wish to thank the reporters and editors at the *Sun-Gazette*, *ARLNow*, *Arlington Magazine*, the *Connection Newspapers* and the *Washington Post*. I must personalize my appreciation to *Falls Church News-Press* leaders Nick Benton, Matt Delaney and Jody Fellows. For visuals, I'm indebted to Mariner Media, Michael Horsley, John Cameron Peck, Lloyd Wolf and Tony Awad at Photoscope. I must thank history enthusiasts Eric Dobson, Tom Dickinson and Bernie Berne, who each read parts of the manuscript. I'm also in ongoing debt to Arlington Historical Society stalwarts Karl VanNewkirk, Cathy Hix, Gerry Laporte, Jessica Kaplan, Eleanor Pourron, Mark Benbow, Johnathan Thomas and John Richardson. I'm also appreciative of the fine Arlington neighborhood histories that are now all online.

INDEX

A

B

C

D

E

F

G

H

N

O

P

R

S

T

V

W

ABOUT THE AUTHOR

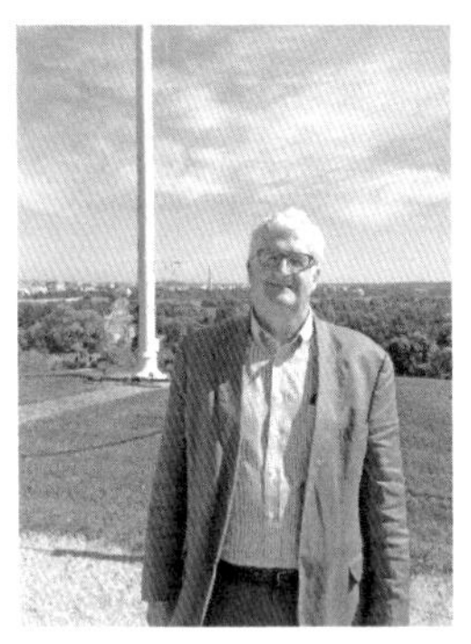

Charlie Clark is a longtime journalist in the Washington, D.C. area who writes the weekly "Our Man in Arlington" column for the *Falls Church News-Press*. He has written *Arlington County Chronicles and Hidden History of Arlington County*, both published by The History Press. His biography of George Washington Parke Custis is due to be released in 2021 from McFarland Books. In July 2019, he retired as senior correspondent from the Government Executive Media Group, then part of Atlantic Media. He has worked previously as an editor or writer for the *Washington Post*, Congressional Quarterly, *National Journal*, Time Life Books, Tax Analysts and the Association of Governing Boards of Universities and Colleges. He lives in the East Falls Church neighborhood with his wife, Ellen.